Soulful Courage

Embracing The Moments & Navigating Windstorms

including the play

TORCH

Bobbi H. Blok

*Living and giving with an open heart even when
faced with daunting challenges.*

Brilliant Books Literary
137 Forest Park Lane Thomasville
North Carolina 27360 USA

Because of the dynamic nature of the Internet, any web addresses or links contained in this book may have changed since publication and may no longer be valid. The views expressed in this work are solely those of the author and do not necessarily reflect the views of the publisher, and the publisher hereby disclaims any responsibility for them.

ISBN: 979-8-88945-433-5 (paperback)
ISBN: 979-8-88945-435-9 (hardback)
eISBN: 979-8-88945-434-2

Printed in the United States of America

Contents

Dedication 7

Preface... 9

Chapter 1: "F"Ing Relationships: Family, Friends & Foes 17

    The Age Of Wonder 19

    Near Death Experiences - The Life Force Reborn 20

    A Friendly Look At Science, Religion, Art & Humanity 22

    The Dark Shadow Of Denial 26

    Polarizing Family Affairs 28

    Children's Love & Wisdom 29

    The Death Of Innocence 31

    Embracing Blessings During Crisis 33

    Inspirations And Thoughts From Moments & Windstorms 38

Chapter 2: Faith 40

    Faith & Service: Consciousness Of Oneness With Wholyness ... 40

    Barbie: A Soul Sister Or Symbol Of Racism? 43

    High Yellow, Brick And Other Shades Of Passing 45

    Interfaith Vigil 48

    Teaching Hate & Fear... 50

    Witness To Miracles – The Power Of Love 56

    Toxic Righteousness & Politics 60

    Faith Beyond Religious & Political Rhethoric 62

Ah – Almost Heaven 70

Inspirations And Thoughts From Moments & Windstorms 72

Chapter 3: Forbearance 73

    Possibilities & Opportunities 74

    Discerning 75

    Motherhood & Women's Rights 80

    Follow Your Bliss 85

    Why Weight And/Or Wait? 87

    The Moment Is Now 90

    Improving The Possibilities 92

    Remembering "Nice" 95

    Inspirations And Thoughts From Moments & Windstorms 95

Chapter 4: Freedom 97

    Political Polarization & Paralysis 100

    Sexually Degrading Polarization 101

    Religious Freedom Threatened 102

    Challenging The Silo Mentality 104

    Acceptance & Denial 106

    Overcoming Moral & Political Wreckening –
    Haunted By Ghosts 109

    Media Messages – Manifesting The Word 113

    Technological Addiction 117

    Beyond The Chaos 118

    Taking A Stand For Children 119

    Promoting Disheartening Policies 122

    Compassion: The Key To Freedom &
    Antidote To Polarization 124

    Inspirations And Thoughts From Moments & Windstorms 127

Chapter 5: Flow Of Life 129

   Affirmation 130

   Continual Flow: Conscious Evolutionary Oneness (CEO) 136

   The Children Will Lead 138

   Parenting 140

   Divorce – A "Kids" Perspective 146

   Choose To Walk In Faith Not Fear 148

   Inner Child 149

   Unconditional Love 152

   Inspirations And Thoughts From Moments & Windstorms 155

Chapter 6: Fearlessness 156

   In The Beginning – "Let There Be Light" 156

   Respect – Rich In Spirit 158

   Unity – A Part & For Giving 164

   Disconnected - Disrespected 165

   Heart, Mind, Body & Soul 169

   Beyond Life & Death 170

   I Am Worthy / We Are All Worthy –
   "Peace" Of A Greater Whole 173

   Inspirations And Thoughts From Moments & Windstorms 176

Chapter 7: Forgiveness 178

   South African Truth And Reconciliation Commission 178

   Guilt & Fear 181

   Amish Grace 182

   Never Too Late – Reconciliation Almost 50 Years Later 183

   Forgiving Is An Act Of Self Preservation 184

   Challenge Of Forgiving Ourselves 186

   You Can't Take It With You.................................... 187

   Vision Quest.. 190

"Fear Not" Being Open To Unconditional Love 194

Inspirations And Thoughts From Moments & Windstorms 197

Chapter 8: Full Circle.. 198

Walking The Talk 199

David & Goliath.. 204

Solidarity 204

It's A Beautiful Day In The Neighborhood............................ 206

Inspirations And Thoughts From Moments & Windstorms 208

Acknowledgements 209

Appendix 212

Torch: A Glorious Celestial Light Show And
Dramatic Interactive Theatre 213

Dedication

This book is dedicated to: The Divine Loving Presence which is an Inspirational Source

My Godchildren – Rachel, Meryl. Thomas Glenn and Dylan plus their children as well as to my stepson Will, my step nephew and nieces: Sam, Jennifer and Becky; and my surrogate nieces and nephews including: Brock, Elizabeth, Julianna, Gregory, Lauren, Allison, Alex, Brianna, Charlotte, Sylvia, Emma, Dariel, Brandon, Randy, Gabriel, Maribel, Arvo, Benjamin, Emma, Asher, Sonia, Alexander, Alison, Sparkle, Jules, Zoe, Zev, Xavyer, Joseph, Carla, Bella, Kallan, Avis, Kate, Bobby, Victoria, Rose and Aiyanna along with ALL God's children.

Preface

"Only the body dies when death occurs. Consciousness lives on eternally. The meaning and purpose of life is to love one another."
Elisabeth Kübler-Ross, MD, author On Death and Dying

There are reasons for everything in the world. I always wanted to start a play or book with that sentence. Now I have The real "now" is eternal, here and hereafter. As soon as we take our first breath the only guarantee is that eventually we will take our last. Then the issue becomes how much love and compassion did we share and experience between those first and last breaths. I have become more aware of the key role and reason that I had the opportunity to work with Dr. Elisabeth Kubler-Ross. Her message, of love is even more important now than when we started working together.

Elisabeth passed away in 2004, yet in the silence, her wisdom, is still resonating with me; in both my personal life and the world arena. I have been an advocate for young children since 1973. A mutual friend thought it would prove advantageous for me to meet with Elisabeth. Even though Elisabeth is best known for her book *On Death & Dying,* her friend insisted that we were kindred spirits regarding the welfare of children. Most people are not aware that Elisabeth was trained as a child psychiatrist. We sat and talked for hours and I realized that we both were passionate about the future of the world's children. As a playwright I also realized that Elisabeth was a wonderful character. Our work together began in 1991 and continued for over ten years.

The play we began working on, a one woman show, was initially titled Living & Giving, which was based - on the lessons she shared. The play, now titled Torch, has been expanded with three characters and includes Elisabeth's home being burnt down as well as the challenging firestorms that occur in life. The spirit of the play is also captured by a quote from George Bernard Shaw "Life is no brief candle to me but a splendid torch that I have gotten hold of for the moment and I want to make it burn as brightly as possible before handing it over to future generations."

Elisabeth and I often spoke about politics, and I keep wondering what she would say about Donald Trump. One of her favorite expressions when she was dealing with difficult people was "what a phony baloney." I am willing to bet that she would definitely classify Donald Trump as a "phony baloney." She would probably use other words to describe him, however, while we were working together, I promised her that I would limit the four-letter words in our writing. The exception being LOVE.

Polarization and chaos in the world can feel overwhelming and Love is needed more than ever. SOULFUL COURAGE shares my multi-faceted experiences that reflect a tenacious uplifting approach to life's challenges. It's a personal journey. I have been an artist and community advocate in Washington, DC. From the streets of the inner city, to the White House, to the District Building, to the halls of Congress and law offices, early childhood programs and public schools along the way and then to the mountains of West Virginia. I am living proof of trials, tribulations, and triumphs. I am grateful for my faith providing me with a courageous compassionate voice. I am taking this opportunity to share my boots on the ground approach participating in nonviolent protests relating to the inequities we witness. Between life and death this book encourages us to laugh with insightful quotes and provocative stories. The stories reflect my mission to promote quality services for young children and persons of all ages who are dealing with injustices, grief, feeling isolated and marginalized. Highlighting the importance of evolving, that we're worthy is essential. Basically, being the presence of light from cradle to grave is fundamental. Life is filled with possibilities. While we're alive we can SMILE and experience blessings. It's simply a matter of perspective. The questions raised help us to be open and hopeful.

During these challenging times of Donald Trump's "fire and fury, witch hunt, border wall, twitter" mentality and the threat of impeachment we can become overwhelmed with the DTs, delirium tremors. This can be an opportunity for us to reflect. During our life and before death we have the choice of hopeless desperation which leads to depression or hopeful determination, which leads to revelation, an up-lifting awareness of empowering grace and compassion.

In her book Death & Dying; Elisabeth outlines in great detail the five stages of dying; denial, anger, depression, bargaining and acceptance. Working with Elisabeth was an opportunity and a privilege. In our discussions, I came to realize that there is more to living than focusing on the five stages of death. Life is not linear; it's more like a rollercoaster and we simply need to relax and enjoy the ride. In exploring my own life journey and dealing with several near death incidents, it became apparent that there was a book, Soulful Courage, that was to become the introduction to the play. I do believe that by simply being alive, for better or worse, we generate an energy that knowingly or unknowingly impacts the world the import of which cannot be overstated. As human beings we represent both nouns and verbs and as such we possess and exude energy. Love is also both a noun and a verb As we embody love we possess and exude a powerful energy. Einstein embraced the concept of the universal life force - speaking of an energy greater than the whole. I truly believe that Elisabeth would concur with Einstein. Sitting with people in hospice, it's an honor to experience the presence of the life force energy. Elisabeth continually stressed the importance of us ALL loving unconditionally.

Both the challenge and opportunity in this millennium is to harness our energy for the greater good, rather than the accumulation of "goods". It is no accident that individual spirit is deeply conflicted with overwhelming greed and the consequent loss of self-worth. We are at a point in time when we need to be willing to embrace our creative nature as we move forward. It is critical that we understand that there are reasons that things happen – good or bad, happy or sad all is here to help us to learn our own sense of wellbeing and self-worth.

In order to love our neighbors as ourselves it is essential that we love ourselves.

This book will explore the importance of highlighting Self worth – with a capital "S". Each of us needs to understand the power of our own individual SPIRIT and all that entails. The purpose of being alive is to be willing to have an open heart and share the love. At the end of life we experience a transition that is universal – the pure essence of the life force. We are ALL One and our purpose on earth is to simply embrace and share the loving energy.

The world has become divisive and there is a need for unity. To recognize that we are all inter-connected would hopefully help us evolve to higher ground and a greater understanding of the importance of Self-worth. Consequently, the quest for virtue and consciousness is not a task simply limited to the humanities but a never-ending necessity for those whom practice in the sciences and technologies, as well as society as a whole. By acknowledging that as human beings we represent heart, mind and soul it can help us to unite for the greater good of the whole

Elisabeth taught that at times of transition there are only two key things people remember: first the moments and second the windstorms. She describes moments as those times in our lives that we remember fondly, a feeling of peace, a sense of pure joy, a smile. Windstorms can include a variety of losses (death, divorce, fire, fore-closure, etc.) and violent upheaval personally and/or globally. In working with Elisabeth, being an advocate for young children and volunteering for hospice, I became a student of life as well as death. It is honoring the space of life's moments and windstorms before death that is truly humbling and inspiring. In our life there are both precious moments and turbulent windstorms. Whether we experi-ence windstorms or moments we are evolving and moving closer to a greater understanding of life as well as death. Getting past the fear of death as well as honoring the experience of being alive is inspirational.

We are witnessing both comedies and tragedies. There are end-less possibilities and we can choose to laugh or cry. Simply being open and trusting. There is still hope for humanity. Art is sensitive and reflective of the human condition. There is both an artist and scientist within us ALL. The key is the motivating factor. Love or greed? We are ALL a "PEACE" of the whole. When we march on blindly without regard to the welfare of our fellow human beings and creation we are blindly denying our own compassion and self worth.

The last time we got together it was extremely intense, it was almost like experiencing a Vulcan mind meld however this was a heart meld, "Focus on the children always remember and share Unconditional LOVE," Though Elisabeth stressed it was okay to cry I waited until I got to the car and the tears were flowing freely, I am glad I had brought her pizza and chocolates (Swiss of course) and she gave me a scarf she had knitted,

Elisabeth kept stressing that we needed to overcome the fear of aging and death. Her message is not new; in fact, PLATO believed that the Philosopher King became much more astute during the later years of life and with that maturity a person could reach the ultimate sense of Being one with the Divine. The reunion of the human and Divine is experiencing pure joy, peace, freedom and love. The human experience is beautiful when it's heart to heart.

Throughout her awe-inspiring work with hospice Elisabeth emphasized that life is a gift and that we need to live it to the fullest. Each breath we take, each smile we witness and experience are "presents" from the universal life force. We may choose to call it the Presence of Supreme Being, Higher Power, Our Father/Mother, Great Spirit, God, Goddess, Holy Spirit, Allah, Jehovah, Yahweh, Adonai, Abba, Divine, the Source, Lord, All Mighty, Christ, Krishna, Sai Baba, Shiva, Buddha, Baha'u'llah, Brahman, Creator, or whatever – Love and Light, Prince of Peace.

In looking at the past, thinking about the future and focusing on the present "now", I am humbled to share eight basic themes that have emerged from my interaction working with Elisabeth, as well as reflecting on my own experiences and witnessing the world challenges. We are in the process of evolving from what neuro-scientists refer to as the "old brain" which is also referred to as the primal reptilian brain which is located in the hypothalamus at the base of the brain. The focus of this neurological center is basically responsible for survival and is generally called the "Four Fs" –feeding, fighting, fleeing and fornicating (keeping promise to limit swearing). It reflects the Darwinian approach to evolution – survival of the fittest. As has been shared by numerous spiritual teachers throughout time "blessed are the peacemakers for they shall be known as the children of God": it really doesn't matter the name we use or if one is an agnostic or atheist. While sitting with persons who are in transition one begins to realize that there is more than simply surviving and the key is LOVE. Elisabeth would describe it as unconditional love. Once we accept that death is not the enemy; that it is the common denominator we all share as humans; we can begin to appreciate and love life and honor the life force within us all. William Penn, a well-known and respected Quaker, is quoted as stating in the 1600's "The truest end of life is to know; the Life that never ends…For though death be a dark passage, it leads to immortality. For death is no more than a Turning of us over from time to eternity. Death then, being the way and condition of life, we cannot love to live, if we cannot bear to die." In effect, life is more than survival - it is about living before we die, it's more than simply surviving, it's the joy of embracing the greater good and overcoming greed. This manuscript goes beyond the cliché "the one with the most toys wins" and focuses on everlasting LOVE.

In following the idea of "Fs" and incorporating our true nature of unconditional love as witnessed at times of transition, this book includes the following eight chapters: – "F"ing RELATIONSHIPS:: Family, Friends & Foes; FAITH; FORBEARANCE; FREEDOM; FLOW OF LIFE; FEARLESSNESS, FORGIVENESS and FULL CIRCLE. The purpose of this human journey is to embrace our true nature of unconditional love while we are alive and not necessarily wait until we're on our death beds. Basically, this is a life story with Elisabeth whispering in my ear. Each chapter begins with one or more quotes as well as having quotes throughout the text. The quotes include religious leaders, philosophers, artists, pundits, mystics and politicians as diverse as Emily Dickinson, Gandhi, Ronald Reagan, Rush Limbaugh, Miguel de Cervantes, Thomas Merton, John McCain, Chief Seattle and Dr. Martin Luther King, Jr. Finding quotes that resonate can be a way of opening up to a journey that focuses on soulful courage. Readers are encouraged to identify with any of the quotes listed or to consider other quotes that have touched their lives. This journey is not exclusive. The key is embracing the ALL both the loving moments and heartbreaking windstorms echoed in quotes. At the end of each chapter there are highlights and possible questions relating to the inspirations of both the moments and windstorms of our lives.

It is a challenge to love thy neighbor as thyself if you don't love yourself. The Golden Rule teaches us "Do unto Others as we would have them do unto us." Loving ourselves is the foundation of bringing peace to ourselves and the world. The beauty of the Golden Rule is that most religious scholars agree that it is the basis of the vast majority of the world's religious teachings and is the essence of our soulful being. There was an angry and embittered man who was in a quandary and he went to Hillel, a leading mystic scholar in the 1st century BC. The man asked Hillel "Can you teach me the Torah while I stand on one foot?" Rather than rebuke the man as being foolish and unworthy Hillel answered calmly and with an open heart "Very well, I shall share the powerful life force teachings of the Torah. What is hateful to you, do not do unto others." The man was touched by Hillel's respectful and compassionate answer, he then asked "Does that mean regardless of our religion that we all must be kind to one another like brothers?" Hillel then responded in the affirmative "Yes, that's the message of the Torah, all the rest is mere commentary."

The life force is neither Democrat nor Republican; fundamentalist or atheist; the energy is simply generated from the presence of spirit. Unfortunately, our leaders, be they political, religious or corporate, have continued to miss the mark on a number of issues including but unfortunately not limited to, environmental policies, education, gender inequity, economic inequality, social injustice, gun safety, the military and health care. Yet we can still be hopeful. The light within us can illuminate the darkness. by tapping into the life force. World leaders can be educated. We the people, ALL the people deserve LOVE. Educating those in leadership positions is crucial.

Neither Elisabeth nor I invented life, death or love. I am not pretending to have the answers. We all have the capacity to find our own answers. I am simply praying that the answers are found in the spirit of peace and love for the greater good.

Elisabeth taught me and the world not to fear death since it's simply a transition. Perhaps more importantly, she taught us to embrace life to the fullest. My approach in lightening the load and reaching out will hopefully provide solace and be a guide in empowering other people to find a prayerful inner strength, a playful perspective and an appreciation of forgiveness and peace. As a final testament to Elisabeth and a gift to readers, a copy of the play, TORCH, is included in the appendix of this book.

Chapter 1

"F"ing RELATIONSHIPS:
Family, Friends & Foes

"People are like stained-glass windows. They sparkle and shine when the sun is out, but when the darkness sets in, their beauty is revealed only if there is a light within." Elisabeth Kubler-Ross

"He ain't heavy he's my brother" Bobby Scott and Bob Russell

"F" ing relationships involve three key components in our journey through life, be it family, friends or foes. The title can change given different times, space and perspective. The role a person plays can vary depending on the moment. The loving newlyweds can become the bitter divorced couple. A friend can be someone who is simply an acquaintance or possibly a stranger, in effect the Good Samaritan, who is willing to be there when we really need a friend. At the same time someone whom you consider a friend can be missing in action or possibly be a negative presence. When people are in the process of dying, emotions can become very volatile; it's a time that allows families to bond or shatter. Unfortunately, family relations can be extremely tense and interactions can get ugly. Old baggage gets unpacked, issues of money get nasty. Feeling abandoned or betrayed is part of the human experience. Life is not easy yet it has the potential of being beautiful. Life is constantly changing. The only constant is having to accept that "f"ing relationships are a part of our lives and we have the choice to be angry or peaceful. The foe may be there for us and turn out to be a friend and at the same time we can witness friends who act as foes. Family relationships can be

17

extremely complicated. Healing sibling rivalries can also be intense learning interactions. The "f"ing aspects can teach us the importance of forgiveness with a capital "F" and helps us to open our hearts.

We can cause pain to ourselves as well as others when we cling to the scars of our "f"ing relationships which closes our hearts. Experiencing caring and loving relationships becomes much more challenging. Opening our hearts is the ultimate aspect of being alive. It involves embracing the capital "F", FORGIVENESS, for family, friends and foes including ourselves (which is discussed in greater detail in chapter 7). Finding the strength to forgive allows us to be free and overcome life's challenges.

Regarding family, friends and foes; one can simply read the New Testament and view Christ's relationship with his disciples. In regards to sibling relationships the Bible is ripe with stories from Caine and Abel to Joseph's jealous brothers and then there is the prodigal son. There is also the Bhagavad Gita an Indian epic that reflects "f"ing relationships that are as true today as they were thousands of years ago. If you're not into religious texts, Shakespeare wrote a wealth of dysfunctional family interactions both in his comedies and tragedies. George Bernard Shaw won the Nobel Prize for Literature in part for his play Heart Break House which exposes warring factions be it at a weekend retreat or on the world stage. Country Western songs are a treasure trove of tales of love and woe. Operas provide a spectacle of an array of musical dramatic upheaval. At the core of our relationships we have the opportunity to open our hearts and realize our fullest potential. We can learn to walk the talk and share the love in thought, word and deed. Are we open to share the love and show we care? Love in action can melt the venom buried in the tentacles of "F"ing relationships. The 21st century is giving us the opportunity to choose chaos or peace up close and personal.

Hopefully the "f" ing aspects of each of our lives will help us to experience liberating and wonderous moments. We need to get past the negative resentful storylines that sabotage our freedom and happiness. It is our birthright to feel love and tenderness toward all.

I believe that the Presence of the Divine is witnessed at every birth. I was born at Mount Sinai Hospital in New York City. I weighed less than four pounds and the doctors were afraid to speak to my mother - they didn't want to tell her I had less than a fifty/fifty chance of surviving. I was in the neo-natal unit for more than a month, I survived. However, there is more to life than physical survival – there is unconditional love once we open our hearts.

THE AGE OF WONDER

I have never been haunted by the age-old question "Why was I born?" I simply accepted the fact. The concept of birth is foreign to a new born or young child - they accept life as a given they approach the world in wonder. When I was two years old I somehow managed to lock myself in the bathroom. My mother was beside herself. She frantically tried to locate the maintenance man to help "save" her baby. They finally were able to open the door and to my mother's surprise and relief I was in total bliss unraveling an entire roll of toilet paper.

At the age of three, I remember looking at my parents' wedding album. At that age I was in awe of my mother being in a beautiful wedding gown and comparing her to a princess. I of course didn't notice that my father's top hat was too large. I was mesmerized by the pictures - I could locate all my favorite relatives. Then it dawned on me - I was nowhere to be found in the pictures. I was furious, how could "Mommy & Daddy" invite my cousins and not invite me?! I was closer to them then my cousins.

When I raised the issue with my mother she began to laugh and I can't say that I blame her! Trying to explain that I was not yet born and that I was just a gleam in my father's eye was of no interest to me. They had thrown this big party and everyone but me was invited. What I didn't understand then is that being born is simply being invited to a big party - some of us come a little later to the party; others a little earlier; while others don't have a clue. It's simply wonderful to LOVE ourselves and smile!

NEAR DEATH EXPERIENCES -
THE LIFE FORCE REBORN

To assume we are born or die only once - is a misnomer. While I am not addressing the issue of reincarnation, it is important to note that the vast majority of the world's population accepts the concept as a religious fact. While reincarnation is contrary to modern Judeo Christian doctrine, such disbelief was not always so. Catholic ecumenical meetings held in Constantinople in AD 533 where the teaching of physical re-embodiment (reincarnation) was struck from the New Testament on orders of Empress Theodora of Byzantium. Nevertheless, all major religions, including Judeo Christianity, accept that there is life after death; whether in the physical or ethereal realm.

When I speak of being reborn, I am simply focusing on reawaking the life force within us. It is an issue of the here and now and realizing that some NOWs are extremely powerful and labor intensive. Some of the most inspiring NOWs are those that take us completely by surprise. While they exhibit no rational explanation(s), they cannot be denied. They are as real as the sun rising and setting or the tides coming in and out. Those special NOW moments give the life force depth and breath. They can shake us to our core and we can be left with wondering: Now what?

We may experience the Divine as formless or as a breath inspiring sunrise or sunset. There might not be appropriate words that can totally describe the presence. The loving Presence is indescribable. The light is inspiring and humbling Numerous people, especially during near death experiences (NDEs), are embraced by the "light".

I remember at the age of four moving into our new house. It was during the late fifties. We lived in a split-level house with a one car garage. Every house was exactly the same except for the color or possible window trimming and the sedan or station wagon parked in the driveway. Having promised my mother, I would stay by the house, I was playing outside in the front yard. I didn't see any other children playing outside. There was a stillness that seemed mystical - a calm I shall always remember. I was playing with my doll and then I looked up. A man with a beard and the most loving eyes and aura appeared he didn't say a word. Suddenly, from nowhere there came a little boy riding a tricycle; falling right in front of our house, he began to cry.

I looked at the bearded man with those unbelievable eyes and he simply nodded a knowing smile. I ran to the little boy who was no older than I was. I told him everything would be okay. I ran inside the house to get Bactine (a disinfectant for those born later than the 60s) and a band aid because that's what "Mommy" did when I had a "boo-boo". I was only gone a few minutes, I running as fast as my little legs would go as if my life depended on it. Yet, when I returned the little boy was gone. I looked up and down the block knowing that it would have been physically impossible for him to have ridden his bike out of sight in such a short period. He had simply vanished! I then realized, the man was still there watching and he seemed to be glowing. I began to cry. I had wanted to help the little boy. The man comforted me - it was only then that I pictured him wearing a flowing white robe. He told me that everything would be okay. He seemed to know what I was thinking without saying a word. Once I stopped crying, he gave me a final hug and walked to the woods in the back of our house. At that point, I noticed he was actually wearing jeans.

Later, when I tried to explain my experience to my mother, as best I could, she assured me that the little boy was fine and the man was probably one of the workmen helping to build the rest of the homes in our new housing development. In hindsight, perhaps he was a carpenter. The NOW I experienced then is still with me today. His presence gave me the reassurance that an act of kindness is not random but deliberate and purposeful. It is a lesson I shall never forget; whether the experience was real or unreal is immaterial. The warmth and caring of that moment is beyond words - truly ethereal. I will always remember the loving glow of his blue eyes. In fact, the man looked like the portrait of the "Prince of Peace" painted by Akiane Kramarick, which appeared in the movie *Heaven is for Real* as witnessed by another four year old, Colton Burpo, during a near death (NDE) experience. The intensity of the blue eyes captured by the young artist brought me to tears remembering that moment.

Experiencing the presence of God is not unique to a four year old playing with a doll outside her house; however children are very open to the mystical. Numerous people have been aware and are embraced by the peaceful glow especially during times of innocence, uncertainty, humility trust and surrender. Many people have experienced similar "impossible" situations that are unexplainable defying rational explanation.

A friend of mine shared an unexplainable yet powerful event in his life. He was traveling in Europe and became deathly ill. He had very little money but had a rail pass and simply slept riding the train. He knew his fever was very high; he found a compartment completely empty and very dimly lighted. He thought such fortune was strange yet was grateful for the peace. He wasn't sure how long he had been sleeping when he woke to find a man in a black trench coat and wide brim hat looking down at him.

He was too sick to be frightened. He and the man were the only ones in the compartment.

He was not sure whether the man ever spoke but somehow he knew he was a healer. The stranger placed his hand on his head and the fire burning within seemed to subside. The man then gave him something to drink - it was soothing. My friend doesn't remember falling back asleep, but when he woke his fever had broken and he was feeling much stronger. Was he dreaming? Who is to say whether dreams are real or unreal?

A FRIENDLY LOOK AT SCIENCE, RELIGION, ART & HUMANITY

There is a very thin line between reality and imagination, and it is a nonexistent line in terms of the life force. Embracing or denying the presence of God has an impact on science, art and society as a whole. An example concerns the theory of evolution, the Scope Monkey Trials of 1925 and the play, Inherit the Wind which dramatically depicts defense attorney, Clarence Darrow against William Jennings Bryan prosecuting a science schoolteacher accused of presenting the theory of evolution in the classroom. The life force has the will to create its own reality. The word "God" has been hijacked spiritually and literally. Darwin's theory of "Survival of the Fittest" promotes competition as the prima facie arbiter, thus diminishing the importance of cooperation and compassion. God is... that's ALL. Sole ownership by one group or another is contrary to the "soul" purpose of the life force and being alive. There are more than 7 billion people on this planet and that's an unbelievable source of energy vibrating. Viewing God as love and light expands our universe. Love and light are both nouns and energy that go beyond our physical form and can help us align with our personal and universal purpose.

Society, experimenting with virtual reality, at this time in space, is simply a product generated by the life force. Does this form of technology pose a threat and is it an inherent obstacle to understanding our relationship with the world? Or can it bring us closer together? As with most human creation, depending on the intent of who is wielding the ax, it can be constructive or destructive. The form and function of technology is critical to any final conclusions. The intentionality is the determining factor. For example, is it for the greater good? Are the actions motivated by compassion, fear or greed? Russian computer hacking of social media is still under investigation and has undermined democracy. This will continue to have negative repercussions in years to come. History has demonstrated that a Machiavellian approach to technology can prove devastating. For example, technological radiation has both harmful and healing properties.

R.D. Laing, a Scottish psychiatrist questions the sanity of the individual as well as the sanity of society in his book *The Politics of Experience*. Laing highlights mass alienation and applauds the schizophrenic's ability to avoid being socially lobotomized - thus escaping the fate of being labeled normal. *One Flew Over the Cuckoo's Nest* (novel by Ken Kesey, 1975 Academy Award Winner for Best Picture, screenplay by Lawrence Hauben and Bo Goldman) makes one wonder who really is cuckoo. It is also interesting to note that there is a similar sentiment reflected in a quote attributed to Jiddu Krishnamurti, an influential 20th century philosopher, speaker and writer born in India:, "It is no measure of health to be well adjusted to a profoundly sick society." William Penn, a well-known Quaker was a religious and political activist who compared the madness of the world to the lunatic asylum, Bedlam, located in London. He believed that people in general were deeply disturbed and that there was a need for clarity and sanity

Modern society has witnessed a number of persons who have suffered from alienation and schizophrenia Ted Kaczynski, the "unabomber", had definite opinions on technology and the world environment. I do not condone violence though I must admit that in reading his Manifesto I could empathize with the points he raised relating to the increasing danger of the industrial-technological system. He spoke of the craziness of modern society, "feelings of inferiority" (e.g. low self-esteem, feelings of powerlessness, frustration, hostility and guilt), genetic experimentation and chemical warfare. The primal fear of technology is explosively embodied in the actions and writings of the unabomber. In his isolated and disillusioned state he simply reflects both society's and the individual's own power struggle - technology vs. nature and the elite vs. ordinary people. Kaczynski, a Harvard graduate, defied legal counsel and refused psychiatric evaluation. His refusal however did not preclude psychiatrists from across the country in presenting hypotheses and psycho-analyzing him. The most telling account comes from his family. Before he was even a year old, he had been taken to the hospital because of a mysterious illness that covered his entire body with hives. It was a terrifying ordeal for a small child and his mother noted that when he came home from the hospital be became unresponsive. As the years passed he became even less responsive and more detached; he even experienced what his family referred to as "shutdowns". It is the general consensus of a number of eminent psychiatrists that Ted demonstrated paranoid schizophrenic traits. It is obvious Kaczynski was driven by the need to share his beliefs and warn the general public of the impending doom. In his letter to the New York Times he stressed the importance of his Manifesto having mass distribution in minute detail. His hate for computers permeates his writings. It is therefore extremely ironic that he continues to gain global notoriety through the Worldwide Web. It cannot be over emphasized that the use of technology is a double edge sword, and Ted Kaczynski's warnings should not be dismissed as simply the rantings of a paranoid schizophrenic.

It is also sad that Kaczynski's concerns were clearly a foreshadowing on many of the challenges we are facing in the 21st century, including climate change and corporate pollution. Democracy is being threatened by the hate and fear generated through the use of technology and social media which in turn promotes polarization and acts of violence. However, at the same time it was collaboration and technology that helped to apprehend the alleged serial bomber, Cesar Sayoc, who targeted high ranking Democratic officials and liberal advocates in 2018. Unfortunately, it is easy to utilize cyberspace to build and access devices of destruction and espouse hateful rhetoric. The world witnessed on January 6, 2022 the culmination of the radicalization of individuals who attacked the US Capitol promoting an insurrection resulting in persons being killed and severely wounded including police officers. A scaffold was erected to hang Vice President Pence along with numerous threats "tweeted" and shouted to members of Congress; in an attempt to stop the counting of the electoral votes as mandated by the US Constitution. It is imperative that we be vigilant in protecting democracy and respecting freedom by encouraging community understanding and equality.

My Uncle Richie was diagnosed as being schizophrenic. My grandfather always questioned that diagnosis. I always thought of Uncle Richie as an adolescent who never went through puberty and was living in a grown-up body. He loved watching Laurel & Hardy movies. My father told me that my grandfather was convinced that the doctors were to blame for Richie's "condition". When he was around twelve years old Richie had a serious case of pneumonia and he was given an experimental drug, raw penicillin. When challenged, the physicians began to accuse my grandfather of being crazy because he continually argued that the drugs the doctors had given to his son had caused a chemical imbalance. My grandfather unfortunately died before the recent brain research confirmed his layman's theories that medications can cause chemical interactions that can adversely affect the brain.

When visiting friends in New York I've tried to visit Richie in Brooklyn, but I haven't spoken to him for years. He lived in Brighton Beach, in an apartment that looks like a kid's club house. On the wall there are home-made plaques with pictures of Richie, my father, my grandfather, Lincoln and Thomas Jefferson. While he generally is absent, there has never been any trouble getting into his apartment because he is afraid of locking doors. It became apparent that all his neighbors knew that his door was always open when he received a telephone bill totaling thousands of dollars of calls to Moscow when my uncle doesn't even speak Russian. Needless to say, his access to long distant telephone calls was disconnected.

One Thanksgiving I went up to visit Richie and brought a catered dinner from DC. The apartment kitchen was small and we needed to cobble together whatever dishes or silverware that he had; however we did the best we could. In the process of setting the table, I spilled the gravy and got up-set and began to apologize profusely – Richie's response "Don't worry about it we spill things all the time and then he laughed". It was vintage Richie.

The times I went to his apartment, everything seemed exactly the same except it was always a little messier than the previous times I visited. An array of clutter included: vitamin bottles, used books, broken televisions and phonographs. There was clutter everywhere indicating inhabitance, yet Richie was no where to be found. I've left him winter coats and groceries, and I trust he got them.

Once when I was visiting and actually connected with Richie, I took him shopping along Ocean Avenue. While we were walking he made an abrupt stop, he threw his arms up and spun around laughing hysterically - he announced to me and anyone else who would listen that most people are movie extras, they just don't know it. He then smiled at me and told me I was a leading lady. He obviously was very pleased I had come to visit and was thrilled I was going to buy him a roast chicken. He truly lives in his own world and I believe in his own way he is happy. In his own unique way Richie had quoted Shakespeare "All the world's a stage, And all the men and women merely players."

THE DARK SHADOW OF DENIAL

We are witnessing both comedies and tragedies. There are endless possibilities and we can choose to laugh or cry, to simply be open and trusting. There is still hope for humanity. Art is sensitive and reflective of the human condition. There is both an artist and scientist within us ALL. The key is the motivating factor. Love or greed? We are ALL a "PEACE" of the whole. When we march on blindly without regard to the welfare of our fellow human beings or the environment, we are blindly denying our own compassion and Self-worth.

It is a challenge to love thy neighbor as thyself if you don't love yourself. The Golden Rule teaches us to "Do unto Others as we would have them do unto us." Loving ourselves is the foundation of bringing peace to ourselves and the world. The beauty of the Golden Rule is that most religious scholars agree that it is the basis of the vast majority of the world's religious teachings and is the essence of our soulful being. There was an angry and embittered man who was in a quandary and he went to Hillel, a leading Jewish mystic scholar in the 1st century BCE. The man asked Hillel: "Can you teach me the Torah while I stand on one foot?" Rather than rebuke the man as being foolish and unworthy, Hillel answered calmly and with an open heart: "Very well, I shall share the powerful life force teachings of the Torah. What is hateful to you, do not do unto others." The man was touched by Hillel's respectful and compassionate answer; he then asked: "Does that mean regardless of our religion that we all must be kind to one another like brothers?" Hillel then responded in the affirmative: "Yes, that's the message of the Torah, all the rest is mere commentary."

The life force is neither Democrat nor Republican, fundamentalist or atheist, masculine or feminine. The energy is simply generated from the presence of spirit. Unfortunately, our leaders, be they political, religious or corporate, have continued to miss the mark on a number of issues including but unfortunately not limited to, environmental policies, education, economic inequality, social injustice, gun safety, the military, health care and peace. Yet we can still be hopeful. The light within us can illuminate the darkness. By tapping into the life force, world leaders can be educated. We the people, ALL the people deserve LOVE. Educating those in leadership positions is crucial.

Light can transcend denial. Many major religions speak of the light. In the beginning God said: "Let there be light." Jesus told his disciples: "I am the light", the Quran shares that Allah illuminated both heaven and earth; Buddhists believe that Buddha's last words were: "Be a lamp unto yourself, make of yourself a lamp." and Hindu writings refer to Brahman as the "light of lights". When we look at family polarization as well as the polarization of our world, one can understand our need to pray for light and for the healing of our families and the global challenges.

POLARIZING FAMILY AFFAIRS

The nuclear family has exploded. Families are becoming more disengaged. Parents and children are over scheduled; they seem to have the need to achieve rather than connect. Parents are overwhelmed with working - many parents having two or possibly more jobs in order to keep the household afloat. As a result children are left alone to their own devices. Literally devices, as IT gadgets have basically become an appendage for most children. The interaction between family members has become "texting". These forms of communication are quick however to consider "LOL"(Laugh out Loud) a real connection would probably be rated fairly low on the Abraham Maslow hierarchy of needs scale. Making a true heartfelt connection that includes a hug is a plus in human interaction. If only "LOL" was sharing "Lots of Love" (Technology Issues are discussed in Chapters 4 and 6)

Unfortunately, with more than 50% of marriages ending in divorce, the number of blended families has increased dramatically. The fall out of tensions in step-families is magnified during already tense situations such as family gatherings and funerals. Settling family estates can get very nasty, very quickly. Besides the money involved, old childhood scars reemerge fueling a financial and emotional battle. In such cases, the only ones at peace are those who have passed over. They have already realized that "you can't take it with you," and focusing on material wealth to the exclusion of human values is simply wasted energy. Being negative and bitter results in our own living hell before we pass. "Rest In Peace" often expressed as "RIP," is a familiar and well understood cultural icon. Acknowledging that peace is available in the here and now when we come together in the spirit of love and compassion is a blessing. Unfortunately, anger and resentment can create an unhealthy and polarized atmosphere resulting in a hellacious environment.

A divorce, even after one partner's death, can play out in a nasty and destructive fashion. According to a number of Hollywood tabloids, after an award winning actor, died, his seven year old daughter, was unable to attend her father's funeral. Both sides of the family provided their own spin, attempting to make the other look more selfish and vengeful. The actor's family requested his daughter be escorted to the ceremony by her nanny rather than by her mother. They found the comments made by his estranged wife offensive. The mother refused to have her daughter attend the funeral without her. Sadly, his daughter never had the opportunity to grieve and say goodbye to her father in a healthy and peaceful fashion because of bitter feelings that adults harbored regarding previous statements made. Some of the most painful family memories occur during the passing of a loved one. When bonding and support are most needed, old scars and greed take center stage.

CHILDREN'S LOVE & WISDOM

Children are wonderful teachers. They wiggle and giggle and vibrate life force energy. We are all born with the life force. We have the choice to activate the energy or allow atrophy to occur. I'll never forget when District of Columbia officials decided to cut 2,000 children from child care services. Parents were distraught and angry. I helped organize a group of parents to educate the Council of the District of Columbia.

One of the parents brought her three year old son Demian. By any measure, he was an absolute "cutie". During the meetings he was extremely well behaved, even when his mother began to cry. She was determined that she was not going back to a homeless shelter, she was finally making ends meet; without child care she would lose her job. I had a feeling it was not the first time Demian had seen his mother cry, and I am certain that his mother believed with all her heart that her son deserved the best possible care.

When the meeting was over and we were saying our good-byes and shaking hands, Demian smiled, his eyes were bright and shining, and he stuck out his hand to shake the city official's hand. We all began to laugh, Demian included. That simple gesture moved us all. I drove Demian and his mother back to the child care center. Music from *The Lion King* was playing on the radio and he began to sing along. After a couple of minutes the singing from the backseat had stopped. I looked in my rear view mirror, and the littlest advocate had fallen fast asleep. *Hakuna Matata* was still playing; "don't worry be happy" is indeed a wonderful phrase and it took on a whole new meaning; we had witnessed the life force at work. I am happy to report that the city restored the early childhood money, no child receiving government subsidy was denied care and I bought Demian a copy of *The Lion King* video. Leaders can be educated, even if our children are the providers of such education. The key is to approach the issue with love and have an open heart. Children are wonderful heart openers.

Adolescence can be a challenge. Peer pressure can be overwhelming. At the same time the need for me to be an individual was paramount. I was both popular and a loner. I seemed to be a square peg in a round hole. When I was a teenager I was blessed with experiencing the intervention of five little boys who were truly heart openers.

Even at the age of seventeen I had a passion to serve, and that tended to override personal relationships. I was elected to the Student Council, asked to serve as the Student Organizer to Support the Teachers' Strike, and founded and served as President of the Keyettes Club in my high school. I helped organize Christmas parties for orphans, coordinated book drives for local nursing homes and arranged field trips to the zoo for special needs children.

One project truly touched my soul. It involved a picnic for young children who were in foster care. I realized that some of my classmates were more interested in simply getting out of school than being with the children. In the early 70's they were called "Hoods" or "Greasers"; now they'd probably be considered gang members or Goths. That didn't matter to me. I simply wanted the children to have fun. I was playing touch football with some of the children. We were having a great time. Then several of the female "Greasers" came over and literally dragged me over to a mud puddle and dropped me into it. The children watched in horror. The whole thing seemed unreal to me. The girls left laughing hysterically; one of them was obviously high on drugs.

Once they were gone, the five little boys who were playing on the touch football team came running over to me; they were really upset. I told them I was okay and we gave each other a group hug. One of the boys got a stick and the others followed suit; they were going to teach those "mean" girls a lesson. They were going to protect me. At that point I was having a hard time holding back the tears. I hugged each and every one of them and told them I loved having them as my protectors. I also explained that hitting people with sticks was not a good idea.

I then told them about the Three Musketeers and how they used might for right and believed in "one for all and all for one." I am not sure they fully understood but they liked the idea of pretending their sticks were swords. I started calling them my "Five" Musketeers and then they began calling me "Snow White". Playing with them was pure joy. I hated to say goodbye, yet I will remember their hugs as long as I live.

THE DEATH OF INNOCENCE

The life force is a powerful vibration that moves in extraordinary, loving and challenging ways.

birth and death are both on a timeless continuum that is infinite. These transitions are identical, parallel and one in the same. This phenomena is becoming more apparent as we are in the new millennium and attempt to comprehend the expansive qualities of eternity. With each birth and death we all move closer to being a part of history.

The year was 1974, I was home for the summer, working full time and taking classes at a local university. I was rushing home to watch the Watergate Impeachment Hearings, when about a block away from my house I couldn't believe what I saw. On a neighbor's lawn there was a frightened full grown rabbit and a crow that kept tossing around a little bunny. I stopped the car. I felt I had to do something though I wasn't exactly sure what to do.

As soon as I got out of the car the "mother" rabbit hid in the bushes and the crow began to squawk. The "baby" bunny lay motionless on the grass. As I came closer the rabbit hid even deeper in the bush and the crow flew away. It was just me and the bunny. I didn't want to pick it up because I remembered from science class that the scent of a human could result in the bunny being rejected by the mother. I went back to my car hoping that there would be some positive movement.

The only thing that happened was that the crow continuously returned to terrorize the little furry creature while the other rabbit had disappeared. I noticed a paper bag in the car and decided to use it to pick-up the bunny. The crow was not pleased to see me return; it flung the bunny down and flew away. At that point I noticed that the bunny was wiggling its nose and trembling. I waited to see if the mother would return; unfortunately, it didn't.

The crow was perched in a tree across the street, squawking incessantly, just waiting for me to leave. I gently put the bunny in the grocery bag without touching it, drove home and took it to the back porch. I could tell it was alive because it was shaking. I called the Humane Society, they told me to simply put the bunny in a grassy area. I tore open the bag and placed the bunny in our backyard. I sat on the porch totally focused on the tiny animal.

When my father came home from work, he could tell I was upset. He joined in my vigil of watching the bunny. Every time it moved I prayed even harder for its recovery. It was starting to get dark. We turned on the backyard lights. I couldn't take my eyes off the bunny. I almost forgot that I had classes to attend that evening. My father promised he would keep checking on the bunny for me. I reluctantly went to my classes, I was there in body but not in spirit, I still worried about the bunny. I returned home praying for the best. My prayers were answered, my father reported that he had seen the bunny hopping around. I was elated and also began to hop around in solidarity with my furry friend.

Obsessed with the Impeachment Hearings, I remember that August as being gray and depressing. Barbara Jordan was my hero - her melodic voice was hypnotic and her brilliance awe - inspiring. My parents had gone out of town on vacation with my younger sister. I began cutting classes - I had two choices: I could sit in history class or watch history being made. While watching the Congressional hearings I began wondering about the little bunny. I suddenly heard a crow squawking in our backyard. I looked outside and saw a reenactment of the previous scene, this time there was blood. I watched helplessly as the crow devoured the baby bunny. The life force is everlasting even if the physical is temporal. The bunny continues to live in my heart to this day.

In psychology, class while studying dreams and Jungian archetypes, I was not surprised to learn that the rabbit symbolizes the Christ and the crow the High Priest in respect to the universal unconscious. Mother Nature had allowed me to witness a crucifixion within the animal kingdom. At the same time, the mass media was enabling the entire world to witness the impeachment proceedings, not only focusing on the downfall of one man but also trumpeting the death of idealism. The impeachment gave birth to a reign of cynicism and a legacy of "gate-isms" in the political arena creating the precursor to polarization.

Though I had actively campaigned for George McGovern in 1972; in the summer of 1974 I personally experienced Richard Nixon's suffering. I sat in my car listening to the radio between classes to hear his resignation speech. The apparent fact that the constitutional process was still intact was cold comfort. -The term 'poppycock" still resonates with me. Sitting alone in my car I felt no sense of relief when he finally resigned. I began to cry for our country as well as an innocent little bunny.

EMBRACING BLESSINGS DURING CRISIS

I am forever grateful for the angels in my life. This is a book about my life and as such it includes some major challenges and highlights some of the major windstorms as well as rainbows which I have experienced. I am currently in the process of dealing with a number of losses, enduring a prolonged divorce process as well as losing contact with my step-son, the death of my mother and step-father within less than a month of each other and the family fall-out from their passing, emergency surgery, a near death experience as well as other emotional, spiritual and financial challenges that have rocked my foundation.

This crack in my foundation has enabled me to be open to miracles. I could have chosen to focus on the emotional and financial tsunami that was the result of these life challenges. I could have chosen to rant and belittle circumstances. However, for purposes of healing and moving forward I am committed to a more constructive path, looking beyond circumstance to view the world from a higher vantage point. I am choosing to reach out, truly thankful that my faith and belief in a Higher Power has been strengthened.

Consequently, I have been able to see things in a much more positive light. There are dark times and we all experience some form of challenges. To wallow in our own personal pain simply keeps us focused on the pain and blinded by the darkness. To quote the American author, activist and lecturer Helen Keller who was deaf and blind: *"The best and most beautiful things in this world cannot be seen or ever heard, but must be felt with the heart."* In order to heal we need to have a broader perspective. As the fox shares with the Little Prince in the book by Antoine De Saint-Exupery's book, "It is only with the heart that one can see rightly, what is essential is invisible to the eye.."

Mine is a soulful journey in an attempt to overcome emotionally, politically, and socially turbulent times. I am hopeful that, in moving forward, given a spiritual perspective in approaching these difficult life experiences, and by practicing unconditional love and faith, I can help others as they face everyday challenges of living. Rather than burning bridges, we can work together to build bridges. Putting it another way that reflects these universal turbulent times - rather than building walls we can all work together to tear them down in the spirit of brotherhood and sisterhood.

November of 2008, was a watershed election event. It was a big moment for the country and the world. I worked hard to help get Barack Obama elected President. I helped coordinate the campaign in Jefferson County, WV. I am pleased to report that the county went Blue and we helped turn West Virginia purple. I was thrilled! However, my joy was tempered six weeks later when my husband told me he no longer wanted to be married, that he wanted a divorce. When I suggested we go to counseling, he refused. As Barack Obama was inaugurated in January, I lost my health insurance and my salary was cut by 48% as a result of the fact that the nonprofit organization I worked for was facing serious funding shortfalls.

The major funding for our agency came from Fannie Mae and Freddie Mac who were faltering as a consequence of the housing bubble and economic downturn. I began to feel that the turmoil in my life was a reflection of the bigger picture we were facing as a nation. The irony was that the last picture my husband took of me was one of me dressed up as Josephine the Plumber for Halloween, which was designed as a parody of Joe the Plumber who had become the poster boy for the political conservative far right. It was truly a cosmic Trick or Treat. A cosmic kick in the butt that a number of people experienced. The election of Donald Trump in 2016 simply exemplified the fears and polarization that were still being harbored by those in the country who felt marginalized.

One of the major treats in my life was to have had the opportunity to work with Dr. Elisabeth Kubler-Ross. Elisabeth was an internationally renowned author, doctor and humanitarian who wrote over fourteen books. Her bestselling book, On *Death and Dying*, broke new ground in identifying the five emotional stages of dying and getting beyond the fear of death. Elisabeth was a child psychiatrist, and I am an advocate for children as well as a playwright. Our work together focused on transitions and loss. She joked about people needing a psychic kick in the butt, and I am a recipient and witness to several butt-kickings. As individuals and as a nation, we are confronted by loss and transitions.

In economic times that have shaken America's financial institutions, when things most precious to us – including homes, careers, families, health –seem vulnerable to the instability of world conditions, it can be helpful to step back and consider the lessons we need to learn from such change. In stepping back and looking at the lessons I needed to learn, I was batting four for four since I was facing challenges concerning my house, my career, my family, and my health. Throughout it all, I refused to lose my faith in God - a loving Presence. Now more than ever before, I realized the importance of "the audacity of hope," the "course in miracles;" as well as finding solace in reading the Bible and other spiritual writings.

In 2008 and 2009, I had a full plate (more like a platter) that pushed me over the edge: my mother was diagnosed with Alzheimer's, issues related to my divorce were daunting, and I was losing my job after working in early childhood education for over thirty years. The loss of my income threatened my ownership of my house. The impact of greed and scams was rampant. I was grateful that whatever savings I had had not been invested with Bernie Madoff. While I was expecting locust, I ended up with stink bugs instead. Thank goodness I didn't lose my sense of humor - it became my rock in turbulent seas.

My personal and professional lives were in chaos. It was a perfect excuse to find comfort in my old standby – food, especially ice cream. When I went to the doctor my blood pressure was very high, no surprise, given all the stress. At that point, I chose life, and that required a number of life lines - and we're certainly not talking "Who wants to be a Millionaire." Dealing with my depression and fiscal malaise required a healthy outlook. The key to my healthy approach was spiritual.

I began to realize that feeling like I hit rock bottom was a blessing. Little did I realize then that there were more "windstorms" to come. I was experiencing the rollercoaster ride that Elisabeth had explained years ago and it kept getting bumpier and bumpier. An unwelcome contrast at a time when I was looking forward to improving times and being at peace. During this period, in all honesty, I had considered suicide. Thankfully, I kept hearing Elisabeth's voice echo in my head – "Suicide is a No No," she was emphasizing the fact "we need to embrace the silence within ourselves and know that everything in this life has a purpose," and that "Fear and guilt are literally the only enemies of man."

I thought I had hit rock bottom – but I was so wrong! While embracing the silence I prayed and embraced our Creator. This rollercoaster life kept taking me in directions that I never expected. A week prior to Thanksgiving 2009, I was in a car accident. While driving home on a mountain, I had severe abdominal pain and hit a tree. I could easily have careened down an embankment. So, it was not surprising that I was thankful that I had hit a tree that stopped the fall. It was a miracle that I was able to drive home. Arriving home, I collapsed into my bed, exhausted as a consequence of the pain and stress I was experiencing.

Later, I called a friend and asked if she'd take me to the doctor in the morning; I thought the pain was from a urinary tract infection and that all I needed was penicillin. However, upon examination the doctor requested that I go to the hospital for tests. I was in no mood to argue, as I was in such pain. The subsequent MRI showed that my small intestines had become necrotic (death of tissue) due to a blockage. The surgeon told me that if I had waited an additional twenty-four hours to seek medical help, I would have died of sepsis.

It was at this point that I realized you never can be sure whether you have hit rock bottom. However, the key is to always look up and pray. I admit to being devoutly disorganized religiously. It is not my intent to preach but to praise the miracles that happen all around us, often, especially during a personal crisis. My friends and support systems were truly God sent. Thank God! My friends range from New Age to fundamentalist, Jewish, Muslim, Christian, and Buddhist; as well as agnostic, atheist and everything else in between. Myself, I love and believe in the Christ and truly believe the love of the Christ extends to all people whether they acknowledge him as their savior or not. I believe that the Christ epitomizes unconditional love.

In 2013, my step-father and mother passed away within a month of each other. My grief was accompanied with the less than gracious approach to their passing by family members. I thank God that there were still some family and friends who rose to the occasion appropriately and acknowledged my losses and provided support. They helped me to recognize the strength that I can access within myself. This is a strength that is shared by ALL, once we are able to get past our personal circumstance and joyfully accept our pain.

Such pain makes our joy even sweeter. As Elisabeth taught: the "windstorms" are our blessings. My life has truly been blessed. These blessings create a strong foundation for recovery from depression and the expression of joy. The only way was up, which offered me this opportunity to share ways to overcome challenges in a creative and prayerful manner.

A friend shared that "Fear Not" appeared in the Bible 365 times; that "blessings" appeared 419 times in the Old Testament; and that in the New Testament "forgiveness" was offered at minimum of 70 x 7 times. During this time, the 23rd Psalm gave me a great deal of comfort. "The Lord is my Shepherd, I shall not want....Thou prepares a table before me ... my cup runneth over." (Note all Bible quotes are from the King James Bible) I realized the Christ told us to turn the other cheek and that sometimes it feels like we are running out of cheeks, nevertheless we must persevere and keep smiling.

The challenges of life we face, both as individuals and collectively in the world during these extremely polarizing times can also be a catalyst for growth. To move such polarization towards growth, we must recognize that our essence is eternal and we are one. While it is said that we can choose to see the glass half full or half empty, I am forever grateful that we all have the opportunity to take it further - witnessing, as did I, that our cup runneth over.

Inspirations And Thoughts From Moments & Windstorms

- A faith in a Divine Power (aka Presence of a Supreme Being or whatever you are most comfortable considering) opening ourselves up to embracing unconditional love will give us an experience beyond words. The Divine Power can manifest in whatever form or simply be a truly loving energy within, shining through us.
- Being aware that things change, and simply accepting the moment as best we can. That doesn't mean it will be easy - it simply means that it is a process and eventually all will be well. Accepting our lives are blessed can be uplifting as well as frustratingly laughable.

- As I have pulled together this book, the challenges the world faces are greater. Be it major climate change, droughts, medical emergencies such an Ebola outbreak, a worldwide COVID pandemic angry political tweets, mass shootings and unfortunately the list continues to grow.
- Do you believe in a Divine Power? What is the rationalization for your belief or disbelief? Would you like to believe? Why or why not?
- Have you or anyone you know experienced the presence of the Divine? What were some of the memorable aspects of the manifestation?
- Is there a life and death experience you would like to share? Have you or anyone you know ever experienced a Near Death Experience (NDE)? What were some of the memorable aspects?
- What comes to mind and heart when considering being accepting of ourselves in the spirit of unconditional love?
- What would be a creative way to overcome the stress and tension of "F"ing relationships? A letter writing campaign to family friends and/or foes (even possibly local or national politicians) We may not get the response we want but it's one way to let go! Letting go represents the fundamental "F" – FORGIVENESS which is discussed in greater detail in chapter 7.

Chapter 2

FAITH

"Now faith is the substance of things hoped for, the evidence of things not seen" Hebrews 11:1 KJV

"The greatest tragedy is not death, but life without purpose." Rick Warren

"Faith is harnessing the energy of love" Pierre Teilhard de Chardin,

"Unless you assume a God, the question of life's purpose is meaningless." Bertrand Russell

"The Future belongs to those who believe in the beauty of their dreams" Eleanor Roosevelt

"....a sense of possibility ...inspires us to envision a better life for ourselves. It is this glimmer of possibility that is the beginning of faith." Sharon Salzberg,

FAITH & SERVICE: Consciousness of Oneness with wHolyness

We were born to serve and be joyful. Sharing the joy and reaching out to serve gives us purpose. As discussed in the previous chapter, our ride between birth and death can resemble a roller-coaster. Faith is an action, it's more than simply a weekly rote exercise to a religious institution. Once we can embrace the concept that life is temporal – in effect we will all stop breathing at some point, and, hopefully, we will have a smile on our face in the process – we can simply let go and be open to the universal Presence that is void of negative energy. Allowing ourselves to be awash in positive energy and compassion opens us up to a multi-sense of being and purpose.

Again and again, I wish to highlight the Golden Rule, its importance, and the fundamental message of: "Do unto others as You Would Have Them Do Unto to You." Acknowledging and respecting one another from our core/soul eliminates fear, which in turn eliminates hate, greed and any lack of self-worth. The lack of self-worth causes self-destructive behaviors such as abusive addictions, racism, terrorism and many other ugly "isms". Without understanding the beauty of diversity and embracing the life force within everyone, we undermine our own personal potential and thus jeopardize society as a whole. Until we recognize the importance and joy of respecting one another, the tragedies facing our own lives, communities, nations and our world will continue to be a reality.

During my human journey, faith has become a life raft for me. I am not anchoring this life raft to any particular religion, I am simply christening it Love, Light and Peace. I strongly believe that the Creator (or whatever name one is comfortable choosing; one friend calls it "howard" based on a comical interpretation of biblical text – howart be thy name?) has a wonderful sense of humor - I have dyslexia and I love to read and I love to write. An editing note: I am inspired to create new spellings for words; in effect spelling wholeness as wHolyness at the beginning of this section; combining these words is reflecting that we are all one and service is faith in action.

During these challenging times, I've had the joy of being introduced to the writings of Thomas Merton, a mystic and Trappist monk at the Abbey of Our Lady of Gethsemane in Kentucky. He died of accidental electrocution when he was in Bangkok while actively protesting the Vietnam War. His own personal challenges included a pretty bumpy roller-coaster ride since during his early years he battled alcoholism and drug abuse, heightening his understanding of our human frailty. His faith is a testament to Divine Presence. In his book the *Conjectures of a Guilty Bystander*, Merton beautifully describes the oneness of our being which I describe as our "wHolyness." Merton writes the following:

"In Louisville, at the corner of Fourth and Walnut, in the center of the shopping district, I was suddenly overwhelmed with the realization that I loved all those people, that they were mine and I theirs, that we could not be alien to one another even though we were total strangers. It was like waking from a dream of separateness, of spurious self-isolation in a special world, the world of renunciation and supposed holiness. The whole illusion of a separate holy existence is a dream. . . . This sense of liberation from an illusory difference was such a relief and such a joy to me that I almost laughed out loud. . . . I have the immense joy of being human, a member of a race in which God . . . became incarnate. If only everybody could realize this! But it cannot be explained. There is no way of telling people that they are all walking around shining like the sun. . . . Then it was as if I suddenly saw the secret beauty of their hearts, the depths of their hearts where neither sin nor desire nor self-knowledge can reach, the core of their reality, the person that each one is in God's eyes. If only they could all see themselves as they really *are*. If only we could see each other that way all the time. There would be no more war, no more hatred, no more cruelty, no more greed.

At the center of our being is a point of nothingness which is untouched by sin and by illusion, a point of pure truth, a point or spark which belongs entirely to God, which is never at our disposal, from which God disposes of our lives, which is inaccessible to the fantasies of our own mind or the brutalities of our own will. This little point of nothingness and of *absolute poverty* is the pure glory of God in us. . . . It is like a pure diamond, blazing with the invisible light of heaven. It is in everybody, and if we could see these billions of points of light coming together in the face and blaze of a sun that would make all the darkness and cruelty of life vanish completely." (Doubleday: 1966)

Science has further expanded on Merton's points relating to humanity. Being human results in our simply acknowledging our oneness rather than focusing on our differences. In looking at life at this point, in the 21st century, there are more than 7 billion humans on earth and the population is increasing every year and recent scientific studies have shown there is approximately.0.1% DNA differ-

42

ences between us. We're more alike than different and death is the great equalizing denominator.

Faith transcends all boundaries be it religion, politics, economics, education, race, social or whatever. Many people embrace faith as a way to grapple with death. The beauty of faith is that it has the ability in death to be an equal opportunity endeavor. For example, in 1845, as Andrew Jackson the 7th President of the United States was on his death bed surrounded by his family, his final words were "Be good children and we'll meet in heaven black and white."

In the 150 plus years since that time there has been a Civil War and a Civil Rights Movement. Barack Obama is the first African American elected as the President of the United States and yet we find ourselves seemingly still struggling with discrimination and prejudice. Subtle and blatant segregation continues to exist. When Donald Trump was elected President in 2016, there was a shedding of the pretense of tolerance and justice for all. Sadly, hate and love became too easily interchangeable simply by the ranting and raving on twitter Trump did not invent racism; he simply exploited it for his own advantage.

Such negativity involves more than race; religion, age, gender, and seemingly any discernible individual or group propensity have unfortunately become parts of the equation. In a world of "haves" and "have nots" transcending mere economics in having the biggest car, the biggest house, etc. and moves toward every other realm such as, having the best religion, the prettiest hair and skin, etc. With such a pernicious progression, we will all suffer the consequences of our bigotry. We need to heed the words of Dr. Martin Luther King, Jr.: "We must learn to live together as brothers (and sisters), or we will perish like fools."

BARBIE: A SOUL SISTER OR SYMBOL OF RACISM?

In the early sixties there were riots in Harlem, and cities around the country were engulfed by a firestorm of frustration and vandalism. My neighbor who lived across the street was a manager in a grocery store on the upper eastside of Manhattan. As a favor to one of his

workers, he agreed to have her daughter Carol come live in the suburbs with his family and be a mother's helper during the summer
break. I was eleven years old while Carol was almost twelve. That
summer we became best friends. I helped her with babysitting. She
was very thin, tall and dark; I was round, short and white. We were
a salt and pepper, Mutt & Jeff. We had a great time playing together,
especially since we both had Barbies.

In those days, Barbie's manufacturer Mattel basically manufac-
tured anatomically erroneous white dolls. She insisted her Barbie was
Black, yet her doll was no darker than mine. Carol suggested we
become "blood brothers." I wasn't too anxious to intentionally cut
myself, so I refused. Then one day, while we were playing on the
swings, I hurt myself and my finger began to bleed. Carol again suggested we become "bloodsisters," and I agreed. It was painful for me
to watch Carol intentionally cut herself. She then held her arm out
and our blood mingled.

It is only in hindsight that I truly came to understand the complexity of our relationship. I remember going into Carol's room
when she was putting this cream on her legs. The stench from the
bleach was overpowering. The one and only day Carol came to the
pool with me, none of my other friends would play with us. Carol
refused to come to the pool again, informing me that she didn't like
swimming. Additionally, there was her "Black" Barbie that I swear
could pass for white. While Carol was an obvious victim of racism, as
a young white girl, without such experience or additional education,
I wasn't able to fully comprehend her pain.

Nonetheless, I knew something was amiss. I began wondering
when people stared at us walking down the street. I was angry that
my other friends wouldn't come over to my house to play. Carol used
to tease me saying that for a smart girl I could be stupid. It is only in
hindsight that I came to understand what she meant. Consciously or
subconsciously Carol wanted to be white, not because of any absolute or intrinsic value in being white, but rather because that's what
society said, and more perniciously indicated in every moment, was
best. Nevertheless, I have at least one drop of Black blood running
through my veins, of which I am both humble and proud.

While working with Elisabeth and reading her books I came to realize that she had an affinity with African Americans and Native Americans. Her sense of being a kindred spirit with both these groups is explored in much more detail in the play, "TORCH."

HIGH YELLOW, BRICK AND OTHER SHADES OF PASSING

Growing up in a substantially white suburb outside of New York City, known as a "lily white " suburb, I have to admit that I led a sheltered life. My personal contact with persons of color was limited by any measure. Consequently, it was a real learning experience for me to come to Washington, D.C. and live there for over thirty years. During that tenure, whenever I mentioned that I lived in the nation's capital, it was assumed that, as a white person, I lived in the suburbs. In the 70's and 80's the demographics of the city were overwhelmingly African American (approximately 80%).

Living and working in a predominantly Black city, in the shadow of Capitol Hill, controlled predominantly by white males, is a unique experience. It's interesting to note that, through the early 1900's, it was illegal for a person of color to use the restroom facilities in the Capitol. When I first came to Washington on a class trip, it reminded me more of a southern town than an international metropolis. This racist practice took place while on top of the Capitol dome the statue of Freedom stood upon a pedestal with the engraved quote "E pluribus Unum" which in Latin means "out of the many one."

As an adult resident, my career was focused on working with the child care community and arts organizations. I am pleased that working with such organizations gave me a much more grassroots and humanistic perspective. Looking through the eyes of children, early childhood professionals and creative artists, has been a rewarding experience. Children have the ability to view life through prisms and find the rainbows. People in the arts have the talent of getting past a "lemming" mentality and reaching far beyond for the spirit and the soul.

Merely acknowledge that we are one big melting pot denies the variety and diversity that we need to recognize and honor. We are not some homogenous mixture of grey. I believe comparing our society, both locally and globally, to one large tossed salad is far more accurate and appropriate. All the ingredients are fresh; they maintain their own identity and culture, in turn adding to the flavor of the society as a whole.

At this point, many of you may be wondering, "What is High Yellow, Brick and/or Red?" I also had no idea about this meaning until one of my African-American friends sat me down and explained that there was a form of racism that's present within the Black community itself. Buying into the white-power structure's axiom that lighter is better, it was believed that the lighter the skin color, the better chances you had to succeed. This belief has caused and continues to cause a great deal of tension and mistrust between darker skinned and lighter skinned African-Americans. High Yellow Blacks have light skin and straight "white" hair, also known as "good" hair. Brick and/or Red have light skin and hair that goes back to their African roots. This self demeaning sense of identity gave rise to the key message promoted by the Black Panthers starting in the 60's – "Black is Beautiful."

On a number of occasions, I have been asked whether I am "passing" – a white skinned person who is actually African-American. To the best of my knowledge, my ancestors herald from white European stock. Nonetheless, I have accepted the passing queries as a complement. I simply assume the questions are generated by my soulful presence shining through. "Heinz 57" is not just the name of a ketchup, it is also a term that relates to the fact that there were a great many mixed blood births that occurred both before and after the Emancipation Proclamation. The liberties that slave owners took with their female slaves is well documented. Many slaves escaped to Indian reservations to seek refuge, further creating blood mixtures during the birthing process. The rest is history. We need to face and address appropriately that racism is a part of our history and in our contemporary life.

President Bill Clinton's Initiative on Race was a step in the right direction. It was designed to engage the nation in moving toward a stronger, more just and united American community, offering opportunity and fairness for all Americans. The purpose of "One America in the 21st Century" is to raise awareness and to help us to understand our differences as we appreciate the values that unite us. This is a noble endeavor. Unfortunately, these noble endeavors over the last century have experienced a backlash from a variety of political, institutional and/or individual racially motivated actions or inactions. In May 1997, the President apologized for the experimental black syphilis research done at Tuskegee, subsidized by the U.S. government and which used hundreds of black men without their knowledge and consent. Yet, it will take more than an apology to eradicate the evils of racism, social justice travesties, and ensuing atrocities.

Equality in education is the cornerstone to overcoming racial injustice. Many spiritual leaders including the Dali Lama stress that education is the key to compassion and totally respecting each other. Janusz Korczak, who is discussed in greater detail in Chapter 5, had the following maxim: "If you want to reform the world you must reform education." Educational systems as well as health care services, not only in much of middle class America, but especially in our inner cities and rural areas are crumbling – academically, physically, socially and morally. Now living in West Virginia, I am sadly realizing that our educational systems are eroding even more dramatically in our rural areas.

During the Pandemic there were a group of volunteers that were painfully aware that when educators were encouraging children to read that there were thousands of children in WV who d[d not have access to books since libraries and schools were on lockdown and there were families that did not have reading materials in their homes. A statewide nonprofit organization, Read Aloud West Virginia (RAWV). got creative, A RAWV chapter in Berkeley County read to the children on zoom and another RAWV Chapter in Jefferson County distributed free books at the food distribution sites at the schools it became a fun food for thought approach, The persons volunteering truly understood the importance of education and the meaning of Love thy Neighbor. It was truly a thrill to see the children smile and their eyes sparkle when they received a book One little one when asked if she wanted a book proudly stated "I am Ready!

INTERFAITH VIGIL

The Friends Committee on National Legislation (FCNL) supported by the Society of Friends (Quakers) is an essential intnational faith organization helping to coordinate and encourage fellow Quakers to participate in the 23 hour Interfaith Vigil Supporting Health Care. The kick-off was Wednesday, June 28th.2017 at 4:00 Pm and the closing session was Thursday, June 29, 2017 at 3:00 PM. The Vigil was held on the east lawn of the Capitol (across the street from the Supreme Court). There were more than 250 people who attended throughout the event. As an advocate and a member of Quaker Meeting, I was inspired to participate. A number of faith groups actively participated, including the Religious Action Center of Reform Judaism, The African American Clergy Network, American Muslim Health Professionals, Tribal Leaders from the Lakota Sioux, United Church of Christ, Bread for the World, Sojourners, the Network Lobby of Catholic Social Justice and many others. There were approximately fifty stalwarts representing the different faith groups and reflecting a variety of ages and races who continued the vigil throughout the night and camped out on the Capitol lawn. The United Methodist were extremely gracious and opened its building (across the street from the Capitol) to allow those participating to use the facilities. At sunrise, the Franciscan Action Network held a Catholic Mass which Senator Tim Kaine (D-VA) attended. Several Congressional leaders came to participate throughout the event.

The reason for the vigil was to highlight the need to promote "Health Care for All" and oppose any cuts to Medicaid in the American Health Care Act. Unfortunately, there are aspects included in the Senate draft legislation that will have a seriously devastating impact on our country's citizens, especially children and the elderly. As I am writing this chapter, the US Congress has allowed the funding for the Children's Health Insurance Program to lapse. Children's education is undermined if they are unable to access health care services. My heart is aching. I am continuing to pray for the children and families as well as the elected officials who seem to have lost their moral compass and I am focusing on those in our country who are most vulnerable.

Throughout the vigil people stressed the importance of the Golden Rule and the Good Samaritan. FCNL's "LOVE THY NEIGHBOR" signs and buttons were prominent. Rev. William Barber, President of Repairers of the Breach and Coordinator for Moral Mondays in NC, shared that we need to stand together – all faiths, ages, races and genders, "Health Care is a civil right as well as a human right. That as brothers and sisters we need to unite and protect those most vulnerable. Our nation is sick and is in need of healing. This vigil is simply the beginning." During the vigil Pastor James Walker sang "Kum Ba Yah" and shared an inspiring and hand clapping prayer that focused on "WWJD – What would Jesus Do?" People erupted in song and began singing "We shall Overcome -TODAY" Sister Simone, from the Network, Advocates for Justice, inspired by Catholic Sisters stressed that "We won't be silent anymore."

I am grateful for all the efforts of all the organizers and participants at the Interfaith vigil. During those 23 hours I experienced many personally heartfelt interactions with both new and old friends. Riley Robinson, FCNL staff, who I've known for over thirty years from Friends Meeting of Washington, managed to take a picture of me while I was eating pizza which FCNL graciously provided. Vanessa Clayton representing the Women's Home and Overseas Missionary of the AME Zion Church came from Connecticut at the last minute to ensure that she shared her prayers and smile with the participants. It's hard to believe but it was cold Wednesday night and I attempted to sleep in a beach chair and sat next to Sister Marge and shared a blanket. I looked up at the Capitol dome and I thought I saw a swarm of lightning bugs dancing around the Capitol, the sparkle was amazing It looked like stars falling from the sky; Sister Marge assured me it was bats reflecting the light. Whether it was lightning bugs or bats the brilliance and sparkles were phenomenal. I laughed and said whatever is generating the light, hopefully it will shine in the hearts of the Senators. In the middle of the night there was a prayer circle where people shared their health care challenges. A mother, Gabrielle, a Quaker from NJ shared that if they had not had health care her little four year old son Isaac could have died from respiratory complications. It was a joy watching him running around and giggling, giving people the thumbs up. Emma, a young Quaker from Stoney Run gave me a blanket that someone had given her. Both her smile and offer of the blanket were comforting. Christen Ashley, FCNL Quaker Field Secretary made sure that everyone was well fed, the space was clean, garbage was removed and she still took the time to give participants hugs.

On a very personal note, I had the opportunity to talk with Senator Cory Booker (D-NJ). I grew up in NJ and was very aware of the riots, drugs and racism in Newark that plagued the city during the 1960's and 70's. In high school, I volunteered at Integrity House, a drug treatment program in Newark (more about Integrity House in Chapter 4). I asked Senator Booker if he knew about Integrity House and he absolutely beamed and said it was a great program and that in fact he lived across the street from the program. It was a special moment, we had come full circle – an African American Senator from NJ and an advocate stood holding hands on the Capitol lawn praying for families needing the support of health care and a comprehensive drug treatment program.

TEACHING HATE & FEAR

In the Rogers and Hammerstein's musical "South Pacific", there is a song "Carefully Taught". It is sung by a young sailor during WWII who has fallen in love with a Balinese girl; he is torn between his love for her and the prejudices his family instilled in him as a child. He sings the lines, "You've got to be taught before it's too late, before you are six or seven or eight, to hate all the people your relatives hate, you've got to be carefully taught..."

Referring to the dark power of fear, those words are as true today as they were over sixty years ago. In evening news broadcasts and papers across the country, our children are bombarded with stories that foster fear and anxiety. Hollywood is notorious for creating stereotypes – doing so fosters grand profits by having people pay to have their stereotypes reinforced, Hollywood cashes in on fear. How do we ensure that children are protected from fear and intolerance? At a more fundamental level, the real question concerns whether or not society wants to protect its children. The issue of Critical Race Theory (CRT) became a very hot political issue with a number of states including Virginia and Florida as well as local school boards throughout the country banning CRT curriculums based on the belief that it would make white children feel guilty if the cruelties of slavery, Jim Crow laws and racism were shared.

When I was in high school, the Marines held a forum at the local Kiwanis Club and I was invited to attend. During the presentation, the Sergeant kept referring to the Vietnamese as "Gooks". "Gooks" is a derivation from Korean meaning "foreigners." Hence, Americans in Vietnam calling the Vietnamese foreigners in a foreign language was sad and ironic as well as demeaning. When I questioned him about using that term, he accused me of being naïve. When I responded that he sounded bigoted, I was asked to leave. It was not the last time I created a "scene" because of intolerance.

During my high school I had gone down to Hampton, VA with my high school advisor to a national Keyettes Conference. Miss Demurest – the advisor, another student from my school named Joanne, and I were the only Northerners at the banquet table. I was seated next to a Kiwanian from the "Deep South." He looked at me and wondered out loud in his very heavy southern drawl if he should talk with me since I was a "Yankee". I smiled politely and informed him, "We won. You'll talk." My teacher gave me a look that would kill, but I could tell she was amused.

That Sunday, after the Conference, we went to Palm Sunday services in Hampton VA. During the Catholic service, the priest started preaching fire and brimstone by damning the Jews for crucifying Jesus. I was dumbstruck, but not for long. In the middle of his hateful tirade, I stood up and informed him that Jesus was a Jew. I then marched out of the church with my teacher and Joanne following close behind. We were visibly shaken by the vitriolic rhetoric we had witnessed at the church, and were glad when we finally crossed the Mason Dixon line.

Intolerance is certainly not restricted to the South. I remember when a senior class trip was planned at a lake in upstate New York. My friend's father wouldn't let her go because when he was a boy that same lake had a sign posted "NO JEWS, COLOREDS OR DOGS". Haines Point, a national park in our nation's capital, had similar signs posted before the passage of the Civil Rights Act.

When I was a teenager, I was a dancer. In fact, I auditioned for Tony Grant's Stars of tomorrow and appeared on the world famous Atlantic City Steele Pier. There were a number of dance troupes that performed. I became friendly with some of the other dancers. Once while we were walking down the Boardwalk, one of the girls told an anti-Semitic joke. I told her I didn't think it was funny since some of my family was Jewish. She apologized and said she thought I was a Guinea-Wop. I again felt moved to inform this rather ignorant person that some of my family was Italian, and I didn't appreciate her comments.

On the way back to the hotel she told me that her mother had set her straight and told her that all the Jews were hoarding all the money. It was of course a ludicrous theory, yet it was not the first nor last time I'd hear it. I asked her in a nice way to ask her mother if she knew where the Jews were hoarding the money, since I didn't have a clue. She thought I was a pretty funny, friendly, Guinea Jew. Unfortunately, I couldn't say the same about her.

When I was a senior in high school, I was involved in the Drug Abuse Committee which was designed to encourage students not to use drugs. As part of this effort, we invited some former drug addicts to visit from a drug treatment clinic in New York City. The fact that the school I attended was virtually all white made it easy to see that the speakers, who were Black, were guests. Unfortunately, the school administration was less than welcoming. I was sent down to the principal's office along with one of the drug counselors. I was speaking to the principal when he asked our guest to step into the waiting room.

The principal then closed the door and went ballistic. He told me that he noticed that when the Pledge of Allegiance was read over the loud speaker, one of the "Addicts" (I chimed in EX-Addict) didn't recite the pledge. I was stunned, not because the pledge wasn't recited, but because the principal was so angry. I didn't help to abate his anger when I expressed my personal concern that "liberty and justice for all" was not necessarily a reality. He threatened to have me suspended.

When he finally calmed down, I was able to convince him that there was critical information these young men had to share with the students. Our visitors were wonderful, and there was a standing room only crowd at the Drug Abuse Committee meeting. Since that morning, when the Pledge of Allegiance is recited, I remain silent as a protest and put my hand on my heart in hopes that someday there will be "liberty and justice for all." Even after President Obama was elected I still refrained from saying the pledge; however I still put my hand over my heart. When "Justice for All" rings true throughout America, I will humbly put my hand to my heart and say the pledge. Flags can convey a myriad of emotions. I admit that the presence of confederate flags flying in WV disturbs me. Now the 45th President has helped to encourage negative hate groups and deny the existence of racial intolerance in our country.

Condemning football players for kneeling during the national anthem – when in fact the message of racial inequality they are sharing is heartfelt and true. I also viewed their act of kneeling as respectful and prayerful. How do we overcome the hate?

I've had some soul searching conversations with close friends. Teaching tolerance in our present society isn't easy, yet young people today seem to be more open to differences than the older generation.

However, our society is still extremely polarized which will be discussed in greater detail in Chapter 4.

I remember in the early eighties going to see Steven Spielberg's movie "ET". It was a real treat for me to take the five year old daughter of a woman who I had worked with to the movie. Both she and I were excited about seeing the movie. While I was parking the car, I noticed she was staring at me, and she had a troubled look on her face. I asked her what was wrong. She informed me that her father had told her that she shouldn't trust white people and that white people hated Black people. I stopped the car, leaned over and hugged her, and told her I loved her. I also told her that there were people who didn't know any better and judged people based on the color of their skin. However, there were also people like ourselves who knew better.

We held hands while watching "ET," and we both cried tears of joy when ET was finally able to go home. On the drive back to her house she was very quiet. I asked if anything was bothering her. She said she was thinking. She then made the profound statement: "Elliot loved ET even though he was different." I agreed. She than proudly announced that she also loved ET and I confirmed my love for him as well. We were both smiling the rest of the way home. I have since learned that Dr. Elisabeth Kubler-Ross also loved ET.

The year 1983 was challenging. I got an on- the- job crash course on racism together with a bonus lesson in faith and love. Certain persons in the organization I worked with started treating staff as if they were less than human. In hindsight, given the racial tensions and injustices in this country, I should have seen it coming. It's clear to me in hindsight, having seen my childhood summer friend subjected to the humiliation of racism, that there are at least five specific developmental stages of interaction when attempting to understand race relations. These developmental stages involve a mandatory trek through a racist obstacle course:

First, is patronizing behavior. Racists tend to over compensate for their hate. They ooze friendliness, not as a matter of guilt, but rather as a seeming subconscious strategy of laying a trap of false security and friendship. Once falling into the trap and recognizing the duplicity and lack of sincerity, one feels used and violated. It wasn't until much later in my career that I realized that folks who feel discriminated against feel insecure and have little understanding of loyalty or friendship. Relating this to the Trump era, one merely needs to look at the White House tweets and heinous behavior.

Second, there are subliminal messages. Racists have their own code words and phrases such as "she can't communicate," and "he has an attitude problem." Paranoia seems to permeate the immediate atmosphere. The turnover in top White House staff can make a sane person wonder and the paranoia regarding "leaks" runs rampant.

Third, racists exhibit behaviors that seem fascist in nature. They need to control. They are adamantly committed to structure and process when it relates to their "subordinates" – a code phrase for inferior, yet when it comes to structuring their own activities and actions, structured process seems to evaporate. And in so being, racists establish two sets of standards: one for themselves and another for persons they view as being inferior; (the "Haves" and "Have Nots" relating to power and its "legitimate" possession). Trump threatening the national press and accusing them of "fake news" would be laughable if it wasn't a possible means of undermining the First Amendment rights and freedom of speech..

I also realized, that questioning standards established by the "self-anointed elite" was considered being insubordinate – regardless of the constructive intent or content of such criticism. One had to be kept in his or her "place." I became aware that trying to focus discussions using open dialogue, compassion and logic was akin to speaking a foreign language. Unfortunately, the present day political atmosphere is polluted with rants on twitter which has become the new mode of communication.

Fourth, is outright hostility. Racists no longer whisper their lies – their false accusations and temper tantrums are commonplace. Public as well as private tongue lashings are not only cruel and degrading; they are designed to intimidate and rule from an instilled sense of fear rather than logic or justice. Unfortunately, such inappropriate behavior has exploded on social media and in the streets. White House response being very negative and critical regarding Senators who don't agree with Trump's agenda or tactics are publicly ridiculed; even widows of gold star military personnel are not immune from the President's rude discourse. A number of community groups are promoting interfaith and inter racial dialogues and vigils; and God knows we need to be prayerful in terms of improving race relations and tolerance in our country.

Fifth, finally, and indeed the most important stage consists of a self-assured superiority and smugness. When people are willing to stand together and challenge the aforementioned racist/fascist behavior, racists become blinded by ambition coupled with a sense of entitlement and begin to exhibit an intimidating sense of superiority, righteousness and smugness. It was completely over the top when the White House suggested people boycott the NFL and then threaten the NFL with higher taxes if they didn't take action to stop the players from kneeling. The importance of First Amendment Rights seemed to be totally ignored. Unfortunately it was a fore shadowing of the intolerable behavior of the 45th President especially when he lost the 2020 election.

It was at just such a point that, in an act of protest, over thirty years ago, I submitted my resignation as the Executive Director of the Washington Child Development Council (WCDC). It became apparent to me that the less than equitable leadership, with which I was dealing with at that time, were deaf to any form of criticism – positive or negative. I quickly realized that it is when you are in the throes of racism, that you understand how important your family and friends are to your spiritual well-being and sense of self-worth. At the lowest point during my struggle, a friend who was extremely busy took the time to meet with me and told me that "there would be no growth without sacrifice." In other words:"no pain, no gain."

Being human may not be easy, but it is always worth the struggle. During the struggle, people rallied. There was a standing room only crowd in the conference room at the downtown law firm, and the narrow minded bigots were ousted from positions of authority. I joyfully rescinded the resignation that I had submitted in protest. It was a difficult year, but I learned an important lesson –when we stand united, bigotry and narrow-mindedness can be overcome! The bottom line to understanding race relations in constructive terms is that there is only one race—the human race.

WITNESS TO MIRACLES – the Power of Love

The movie about the miracle of the Lady of Lourdes called "The Song of Bernadette" begins with a preamble that states: "For those who believe in miracles no explanation is necessary. For those who don't believe no explanation is possible." For me this is somewhat reflective of Elisabeth's teaching that there is a reason for everything. In the mist of the miracle this can be difficult to understand and embrace, however, with faith and hindsight I am able to smile and give thanks.

I was attending a District of Columbia Council Budget Hearing. Major cuts were being proposed in social services. Mitch Snyder, a homeless advocate who found dramatic means of getting attention had basically stormed the hearing with hundreds of homeless people. Everyone in the hearing was basically trapped since he had people blocking the doors. It was pure chaos – the noise, screaming and chanting "don't cut the homeless budget" was disconcerting. I wasn't about to start chanting, I decided to keep calm. I suddenly witnessed a stillness and through the commotion I heard the sound of a baby crying. I looked around and saw a mother holding a very young infant. I walked over to the mother, kneeled and smiled at the beautiful baby in her arms. The mother smiled as I totally focused on the mother and child, shutting out the noise of the protest. Indeed, to be present was to witness the power of love. The baby was smiling and her eyes were sparkling; the mother had tears in her eyes as she embraced the peace and calm bundle in her arms, she whispered "To know ya is to love ya." The mother told me that she had been on drugs but that once she saw her little girl she was determined to get off drugs. I asked her if she was clean (i.e. not using drugs). She smiled at the baby and said "I sure am for her but I am homeless because it's hard finding a job being an ex-addict and having a baby." I acknowledged her struggle and asked if she wanted help. She couldn't say "Yes" fast enough. I gave her the phone number of my friend (pre-cell phone days or I would have given her the cellphone to call), who was a supervisor at an innovative program that helped women focus on job training, life management skills and provided child care. I am happy to report that the mother telephoned my friend, participated in the program, graduated became gainfully employed, found a place to live and received subsidies to ensure that her little girl was in a safe child care program while her mother was working. Hearing that baby cry was a miracle. The love for her child was an inspiration.

There was a time that I was on Capitol Hill hoping to stop cuts in child care funding. The US Congress has oversight of the entire DC Budget. Congressman Charlie Wilson from Texas was the Chairman of the DC Budget Committee. He had proposed the cuts because he felt that DC was spending too much money on social service programs. The meeting with him was outrageous. We had come to talk about the lives of young children and he kept talking about having met the new Miss Texas and was hoping that she would become the new Miss America. The meeting was surreal. He was determined to cut the DC budget, and if some of that money came from the child care budget, that was just too bad. When we left his office I began to cry to the point of shaking; I was literally and figuratively quaking in my soul. The child care mothers who came with me didn't know what to do to console me. I kept praying in my heart, I knew it would take a miracle. I turned around and there was an African American gentleman who asked if I was okay. I asked if he knew where I could find Congressman Mickey Leland. He smiled and said that he was Congressman Leland. I took a second and caught my breath and told him about the awful meeting we just had with Congressman Wilson. I explained that Head Start child advocates in Texas had told me that Congressman Leland was a stalwart for quality child care services and that they would contact him and they were pretty sure that he might be willing to help. He started to laugh "You must be Bobbi - the Texas child care advocates explained that DC needed help" my tears became laughter and I asked "How did you know?" He simply said he was told I would be coming and then added "Don't worry, I'll talk with Charlie." I am happy to report that the child care budget wasn't cut. Unfortunately, I can't say the same for the rest of the DC budget. Congressman Wilson was ruthless when it came to the city's budget (simply wondering since Charlie was a big supporter of the Taliban who at that time were fighting the Russians in Afghanistan, he was using that money to garner support to help the war).

When entering the US Capital I silently pray for miracles especially when having to testify before the Oversight Committee on the DC Budget since they were usually focused on taking an across the board cut to the budget - no exceptions, I remember one year Representative Julian Dixon, from California was Chairman of the Committee. He was holding budget hearings and I arranged to have an articulate young student testify that after school care was needed in the city and it should be increased not decreased. Usually, I do not edit the testimony written by the students because I want them to feel proud of what they are presenting. Adam (not actual name in order to protect identity) was dressed in a suite and tie, thrilled that he was going to be testifying. We went into the hearing room The Congressman told us to have a seat at the table; Adam gave him a big smile and began presenting his testimony. He explained that he enjoyed after school care because he got help with his homework and was able to play with his friends. When care wasn't available he had to be at home with his older sisters who picked on him The Congressman asked him what he did when he was home and Adam explained he would play with his chemistry set and put chemicals in a coke bottle. My jaw dropped as Adam kept explaining his after school activities which basically sounded like he had fun making Molotov cocktails Rep. Dixon thanked Adam for his honest presentation and well written testimony. Adam was beaming. Before we left Rep. Dixon told me he wanted to talk with me. He said "Bobbi, the after school budget will be increased however he didn't want me bringing anymore children who would be describing how to make bombs to the budget hearings" We laughed. I promised and thanked him. We shook hands and then he went over to Adam and they shook hands. To say the least it was both explosive and miraculous.

I have had the privilege of watching the miracle of children's innocence melt the hearts of elected officials. I had brought several hundred children to the US Capitol at the request of the Children's Defense Fund (CDF). Senator Orin Hatch, a Republican from Utah was one of the leaders in ensuring the passage of the ABC Bill (the Act for Better Child Care). The children were singing their ABC's and the Senator sang right along with them. Before we left the Senator took my hand and told me that as a Mormon he believed that all children deserved quality early childhood services including education, nutrition and health care. Times change, children's programs are in jeopardy not only in the District of Columbia but throughout the country and the world. I am seriously praying for more miracles.

TOXIC RIGHTEOUSNESS & POLITICS

The term "toxic righteousness" is not used lightly; the continual denial of climate change and environmental pollution in regards to the far right and fundamentalists is frightening and having a devastating effect on the world. The US withdrawing from the Paris Climate Accord was inexcusable the fact that we rejoined was a blessing. A staunch believer in democracy and freedom; I view politics as a necessary evil. However, there is no excuse to deny the devastating impact industrial pollution and politics can have on a community. West Virginia has had more than its share of toxic waste issues. In January 2014, there was an environmental state of emergency declared in Charleston, WV and nine other surrounding counties. There was a ban on drinking, bathing and cooking with tap water because up to 5,000 gallons of an industrial chemical used in coal processing seeped from a ruptured storage tank into the Elk River, just upstream of the intake pipes for the regional water company. Now in 2019 the officials in the WV state capital are battling with residents living in Jefferson County regarding the approval of an industrial plant being built across the road from a public school and there are six other schools in a three mile radius. Toxicologists have testified that the emissions from the European owned plant contains chemicals that would adversely affect children and persons already struggling with compromised respiratory health concerns. I am not a chemist but the fact that the emissions from the facility will include formaldehyde and arsenic doesn't sound good. To paraphrase a quote from the play Hamlet rings true "Something is rotten in a country in the EU." The factory being built in WV is banned in the company's headquarters in Europe due to toxic emissions and the utilization of fossil fuels. The Community activists are doing their best to protect the children. However, when corporate greed is involved it can be daunting. This issue is discussed in greater detail in chapter 4.

Campaigns and environmental issues can be bought and sold and, consequently, the "best" or most qualified man, woman or decision is not necessarily the victor. For better or worse the judgment of the electorate and government officials can be manipulated. From the 1970s to the 21st century we have witnessed the toxic effect money has played in politics, as well as the world arena. In 2004, West Virginia Senator Robert C. Byrd published the book, *Losing America: Confronting a Reckless and Arrogant Presidency*. The Senator was a staunch supporter of the US Constitution. He was making reference to the presidency of George W. Bush. Senator Byrd died in 2010. I am sure that he would have had some rather insightful comments regarding Donald Trump.

Ethics and integrity appear to be in short supply. Quite a number of politicians seemingly have egotistical tendencies and are losing touch with the universal life force. Unfortunately, fear tactics are used as well as computer hacking and social media which has had an expeditiously negative impact on the electorate. President Dwight Eisenhower, a former general, warned the world regarding the dangers of the US military-industrial complex prior to his leaving office in 1961.

The greed of which President Eisenhower warned has resulted in the systematized creation of an oligarchy of wealthy industrialists and rests solidly on the mindless practice of war throughout the whole world – any war, anywhere, all the time, whether warranted or not. Since 2001 the Cost of War Project at Brown University estimates that the US has spent $5.9 trillion on military force which will also result in approximately an additional $8.0 trillion in interest Unfortunately, the young men and women fighting, and the civilians killed are simply seen by the military complex as collateral damage to the act of making business profits. Therefore, it comes as no surprise that the turnout for elections continues to be a challenge and public cynicism continues to increase. Despite such trends, we must be vigilant in our quest to ensure democracy and a peaceful world. The 2022 election can give us hope given the fact a young (24 yr, old.) Latino community organizer for gun safety, Maxwell Frost, was elected to Congress from Florida,

At the same time, we are struggling with religious fundamentalists, regardless of which religion, that has taken the position that their God rules. Be it ISIS in Syria, Buddhists in Myanmar, or fundamental zealots spewing hate on "talk radio." To paraphrase an anti-war slogan "Hate is not healthy for children or any living thing." Freedom of Speech is a responsibility and does not necessarily condone mean- spirited rhetoric that causes harm. There is a need for tolerance on both sides of the aisle no matter what side of the aisle we may be standing or sitting. I again want to echo the importance of compassion and the Golden Rule.

FAITH BEYOND RELIGIOUS & POLITICAL RHETHORIC

George Bernard Shaw, a famous playwright and political activist in Britain during the 1900s, wrote "Life is no brief candle to me but a splendid torch I have gotten hold of for the moment and I want to make it burn as brightly as possible before handing it on to future generations." I believe that education promoting compassion and understanding is the key to ensuring a peaceful world for future generations.

In 1990, I ran for the D.C. Board of Education. While I focused on children, unfortunately, the opposition kept harping on politics. One of the candidates became very upset because my name was drawn to be the first on the ballot. Not attending the Board of Elections' lottery, I was oblivious to the listing sequence. Instead of focusing on substantive educational issues, that candidate focused on their perceived injustice about him not winning the lottery for top listing. While that candidate churned with indignant injustice, I favored revamping the city's schools–children were the priority, not the bureaucratic top-heavy administration.

I wrote a position paper on the educational system in D.C. Public Schools titled, "Why We Can't Wait," in honor of the book written by Dr. Martin Luther King. In that book, Dr. King quotes President John F. Kennedy: ... " all Americans are to be afforded equal rights and equal opportunities ... Those who do nothing are inviting shame as well as violence. Those who act boldly are recognizing right as well as reality."

The position paper outlined concepts that were innovative and sensitive to the needs of the children. It promoted quality education for ALL children. Campaigning was exciting. My campaign manager felt that we needed to tap into the gay vote since they come out in force on Election Day. She arranged to have us escorted by some of the top gay leaders in DC. This was a new experience for me since I had never been to gay clubs before. I admitted to being a heterosexual, and I was happy that they didn't hold my gender preference against me. While a number of patrons at the clubs didn't have children, I was touched by their belief that providing a quality education to children largely was an essential aspect to ensuring a successful future. I must admit my surprise to find that several of the clubs displayed pictures of Dr. Martin Luther King, Jr. and President Kennedy – prominently hanging on the wall. Nevertheless, when you think about it, it makes perfect sense since both men symbolize human rights and freedom of expression.

However, going to forums and dealing with rumors was the low point and most draining. People kept asking me if I were "passing"? I was furious to find out that a supporter of one of the other candidates had started a rumor by telling people that I was gay. It was outrageous and insulting on two levels. First, it wasn't true. Second, he presented the rumor as a smear tactic designed to undermine my character in a negative fashion implying that someone who is gay wouldn't be qualified to be on the School Board and degrading the gay community as a whole. Sadly, but not surprisingly, that person has yet to admit to using such an underhanded campaign strategy and has not apologized.

The most hurtful attack came during one of the school forums. In a rather sad display of the toxic logic of discrimination reversed, a supporter of one of the other candidates publicly asked me in an extremely accusatory and derogatory tone: "What business does a white woman have running for a school board position when 95% of the children are Black?" I explained my commitment to children. I shared my love for Dr. King and quoted from his book, "Why We Can't Wait". I told them how he spoke of the need for all Americans to act and that moral courage is our strongest weapon.

As I began to realize that children and morals were not the primary issues in campaigning for the School Board, I called my campaign manager and told her that I was going to stop running. I wasn't quitting; I would continue to distribute the position paper I wrote, but all the campaign money would be donated to something more substantive related to children. Rather than additional campaign mailings, brochures or posters. I also made it clear that I would not participate in those kangaroo court style political forums; the campaign funds were donated to the Collier-Wilson Fund; a fund established for two little girls who sadly witnessed their mother brutally murdered while they were coming home from school.

I had a premonition that this act of violence was simply a foreshadowing of the cruelty and bloodshed our children would be subject to in the years to come.

I am both happy and a bit remorseful to report that I lost the election. I came in last and was reminded of the scriptures from Matthew (20:16 KJV): "The last shall be first and the first last." Given the disgraceful and unprofessional behavior on the part of public school officials and members of the Board of Education, I thank God I didn't win; attempting to instill substantive positive change in this kind of organization gives a whole new perspective to the Greek Myth regarding Sisyphus.

Where do I begin in explaining my relationship with D.C. Mayor Marion Barry? As both Mayor and a friend, he took the time to meet with me when I was confronted with the indignities of racism. I met Marion in 1974 at a D.C. Democratic Steering Committee. I had made a presentation on a get-out-the-vote campaign. I could tell he was intrigued and seemed to be wondering what a white girl was doing talking about voting rights and demographics. After the meeting he came up to me and introduced himself. We've been friends ever since, although I am proud to say I was never one of his enablers.

We began to work very closely together on the newly elected District of Columbia Council. I was a budget analyst for the Council's Committee on Human Services. In the early days, Marion really cared about the people most in need. One hot July night, I went with Councilmember Polly Shackleton and Marion to Oak Hill, the youth detention center in Laurel, MD. Polly was nervous about giving the speech I had written for her. Marion had a great deal of respect for Polly and came along for the ride. I was awed by his ability to relate to the young men. He shared messages with them from their families. There were no cameras and no reporters. It was vintage Barry.

It's somewhat ironic that I developed the greatest respect for Marion while we were working on the city's substance abuse budget. In the early seventies, D.C. only had methadone clinics, and I was making a strong case encouraging the DC Council Committee on Human Services to recommend that the city allocate funds for other therapeutic programs. While Polly Shackleton the Chairperson of the Committee understood the financial and programming rationale, she was not known for articulate debate, let alone dealing with street politics. I went to Marion for support. We talked for hours about my volunteering at Integrity House, a drug treatment program in Newark, NJ. Marion shared his experiences working at Pride, Inc., and Marion's Executive Administrator, Ivanhoe Donaldson – a DC political character and power broker – joined the discussion. At that time, they were simply two bright men who cared deeply about the city. It wasn't about power. It was about doing the right thing. With Polly's commitment, and Marion's support, the first therapeutic drug programs received government funding and were established in the District of Columbia.

When Marion Barry decided to run for Mayor in 1978, I was one of his staunchest supporters. When it came to key programmatic decisions on human services, I was part of the "inner circle". When Polly supported Sterling Tucker an opposition candidate, I didn't waiver on my support for her. Yet, I didn't abandon Marion. I believe they both respected my personal loyalty and political integrity. I'll never forget the day after Marion won. He came into Polly's office, winked, and gave her one of his charismatic smiles. He then asked me to serve on his transition team. Nothing could have prepared me for the late eighties to early nineties.

In 1984 Ivanhoe took me to lunch at a fancy restaurant on K Street. He had left the District government and was working in the private sector. He had not yet been indicted. Ivanhoe was insisting that I take a lead position in the upcoming Mayoral race and stating that "MB needs you." Ivanhoe could be very persuasive. Yet I was less than enthusiastic, as working on campaigns is one of my least favorite exercises. He kept stressing he wanted someone on the inside he could trust. I finally agreed to be the Campaign Coordinator for Special Constituencies (Labor, Clergy, Gay, Children's rights and Senior Citizens–critical voting blocs). After Ivanhoe had pleaded guilty to embezzlement, I still did not renege on my commitment.

I had a unique relationship with Ivanhoe. To say he is an extremely complex man is an understatement. In the early eighties, when Ivanhoe was the Chairman of the D.C. Democratic State Committee, we went out for drinks or lunch to discuss political strategies. During one of those meetings, I mentioned that I wrote plays. He insisted that he wanted to read my work. I was hesitant, as I hadn't shared my writing with anyone. However, as stated before, Ivanhoe could be very persuasive. He not only read my work, but was enthusiastic. Certainly a point of flattery, he compared the character development and internal conflict to Dostoyevsky, one of his favorite writers. He kept after me to send my work to different theatre groups. To this day, I credit Ivanhoe for giving me that nudge, although he's amused when I acknowledge this publicly. Ivanhoe prefers to remain behind the scenes. Yet, without his encouragement, I might have kept my writing on the shelf and not won best production at Source Theatre Festival in Washington DC or received an Honorary Mention from the American Film Institute.

Working on the 1986 D.C. Mayoral campaign was absolutely insane. Marion was out of control. It was only then that I began to wonder whether the rumors about his drug use were true. In retrospect, I thank God that I only committed to working on the campaign during the primary. If I had to deal with one more campaign crisis caused by blind ambition, pure ignorance, and a total disregard for campaign laws, I was going to scream! Yet, throughout the whole ordeal, I was surprisingly calm and professional. One of my last tasks was to arrange for a post-election night rally; Jesse Jackson, who was the keynote speaker, arrived with his entourage. Before going into the church meeting hall, he bent over and gave me a kiss on the forehead as if he were Glinda the Good Witch of the North. At that point it was all surreal.

In 1988 I was elected by the DC Democratic State Committee to be a Jackson delegate. I took that vote of confidence as a sign and decided to take a stand for D.C. Statehood – pledging to fast during the entire convention. My fast began July 4, 1988; the Convention was at the end of July. I am fairly certain that I am the only delegate on record who fasted during the political debauchery we call Presidential Conventions. To give a better sense of contrast, keep in mind that while I fasted for a cause to promote freedom for DC, this was the same Convention where Rob Lowe was video tapping his underage protégé. His video got substantially more play than the issue of D.C. Statehood. My fast only gathered some attention when I collapsed at one of the events. Luckily, Jim Vance, the Anchor from WRC-TV, saw me starting to fall and he caught me. Given my experience, I don't personally recommend going on political fasts, especially if you are a woman. The media simply assumes it's a new fad diet. It took me an additional two years to listen to my own advice.

In 1989 I could no longer deny that Marion showed all the signs of using drugs. We arranged to meet to have lunch after his son's Christopher's basketball practice on a Saturday morning. It was a memorable lunch. I asked Christopher if he minded having pizza with the security guards and allowing me to speak to his dad alone. The idea of having pizza was an easy sell. Convincing his father that he needed to reassess what was happening with his life was not going to be as simple. I told Marion I thought he had a drug problem and that he needed to deal with it. He said he didn't have a problem. I begged him to be honest with me and more importantly with himself. I broke down and started to cry. He assured me he didn't have a problem. I left knowing that his definition of problem and mine were totally different. The fact that Marion's son Christopher was to have a drug overdose from K2 in 2016 is an unfortunate legacy.

In late 1989, the issue of drugs was much bigger than Marion. The war on drugs was growing larger and children were the big losers. Several youngsters had witnessed a drug killing at an unlicensed child care home. I again decided to go on a political fast. It was a symbolic cleansing intended to demonstrate the need to confront the issues of drugs more constructively. I planned on starting my fast on January 1, 1990 and end it on Valentine's Day, February 14th.

In late December, the contract for the organization I worked for was canceled. If I had agreed to help on his campaign, Marion would probably have allowed the funding for the child care contract to continue. I scheduled a meeting with him. I am pretty certain he assumed I would urge him to continue the contract. However, the contract seemed immaterial when compared to the other issues plaguing the city. Consequently, I never mentioned the contract being cut. Instead, when I met with Marion I brought him a copy of *Choose Once Again*, the pocket version of The Course in Miracles. I informed him regarding my decision to go on a fast to protest the lack of federal leadership on addressing the war on drugs. Tears welled up in his eyes as he hugged me. He thanked me for the book and asked me to take care. I found his request a bit ironic, for while I was fasting on behalf of young children in the city, the world watched as Mayor Barry was arrested for smoking crack cocaine at the Vista Hotel on January 18th. I spoke to Marion several times after the arrest and before he went for drug treatment. I sent him a copy of the following verse from Gandhi: *There is no one without faults, not even men of God. They are men of God, not because they are faultless but because they know their own faults, they strive against them, they do not hide them and are ever ready to correct themselves.*

In 1992, I again begged Marion not to run for Mayor to no avail. I believed he needed to continue to heal himself and to focus his energy on Christopher and his new wife, Cora. However, once he declared his candidacy, I agreed to support him. That he won came as no surprise, given the politics of the city. Marion promised to give voice to people who felt abandoned and helpless. Whether he kept those promises is debatable. Yet, the city as a whole is paying penance for his re-election. The US Congress put the city under a federal Control Board, which had total control of the city's budget. It's interesting to note and ironic that in 2016, Donald Trump was sworn in as the 45th President of the United States based on a campaign that promised to give voice to people who felt abandoned and marginalized as well as feeling undervalued by the "elite" electorate.

During all this political craziness, I began writing a play, *STATE OF DENIAL*. It focuses on the racism and sexism present within the political arena. While writing the play, I decided I'd try to choose an innocuous name, Bill Thomas, for the political protagonist. When the U.S. Senate held hearings on Clarence Thomas and sexual harassment charges were raised, I called my agent and asked if I should change the name. He told me not to worry, Thomas was a Supreme Court Justice not a Senator. Now in 2018 we again face a Supreme Court nominee being accused of inappropriate behavior. Because of the #METOO movement of survivors of these unacceptable behaviors, accusations are taken more seriously The #METOO movement is reflective of the backlash to sexually inappropriate behavior and is also discussed in Chapter 6.

When the Jennifer Flowers scandal came out regarding Bill Clinton, my agent called me and told me to change the name. I changed the name to Brad Philips assuming no one with that name would ever consider running for office. Then a friend called me and pointed out that "BP" were the initials for Bob Packwood, the lecherous Senator who was forced to resign because he wrote about his exploits in a diary that was subsequently reviewed by the Congressional Ethics Committee.

In 1991 *STATE OF DENIAL* was performed at the National Museum of Women in the Arts as a benefit for early childhood education. Bea Romer, the wife of Colorado Governor Roy Romer, was in the audience. After the performance, I asked her what she thought about the play as a political wife. She was very gracious and said it raised some intriguing points. Ironically, her husband who became Chairman of the Democratic National Committee, was later linked to extra-marital affairs when he publicly supported President Clinton during the heated "Monicagate" debate. Romer got caught up in this country's obsession with alleged sexual indiscretions. In the new millennium, media features sexual scandal prominently – sex has always sold and a burgeoning internet demographic renders a larger consumption base for such scandal. Contemporary sexual peccadilloes regarding elected officials range from Governors disappearing with their mistresses to Congressmen tweeting their private parts. I am not likely alone in preferring our elected leaders and the media focus on substantive issues such as child care, education, gun safety and health care rather than scandal. However, I am not excusing sexual harassment in any arena which is also discussed in Chapter 6.

Today, political and philosophical pundits are at a loss to describe the state of affairs in our nation's capital. It seems they prefer to throw mud at one another rather than seriously address their differences concerning pressing issues. To say that the dialogue has gotten ugly and fear based is an understatement. Nevertheless, for the sake of our children, we cannot afford to entertain losing faith. The word "play," in the literal, educational, theatrical and/or political sense, is the manifestation of the energy generated from the creative source. Whether life imitates art, or art imitates life is in constant flux. Regardless, the life force is always with us. President Franklin Roosevelt said "politics is the art of the possible." Within the realm of possibility, we must play the hand dealt, having faith, learning to move to higher ground and keeping the torch burning.

AH – ALMOST HEAVEN

It's time to celebrate. We are alive and we have the opportunity to experience life. The "AH" is us being open to Love Life. True joy is having gratitude simply breathing, being still, having the freedom to laugh and the awareness of our bliss. A bliss that embodies authenticity, compassion and our heavenly connection.

In the theatrical comedy "*AH – ALMOST HEAVEN*" the main character, PAW, a native West Virginian is in awe while watching the wind blow and the Potomac and Shenandoah Rivers converge and flow. He has this insight that we are ALL connected and states: "I experienced that there are no easy answers. The only certainty is death. Before death is life and we might as well enjoy it whatever. There's the alpha and the omega and in between is the whatever. It's kinda like a cosmic s'mores – we are simply the gooey marshmallow between the alpha and omega graham crackers and the chocolate adds an additional sweetness. It's our choice to savor the treat while we are here and now rather than waiting for the hereafter. I am not sure they serve s'mores in the hereafter." In *Siddhartha*, the book written by Herman Hesse about the Buddha, he describes a moment when Siddhartha is at peace when he becomes aware that: "The world was beautiful, the moon and the stars were beautiful, the brook, the shore, the forest and the rock ... the flower and the butterfly were beautiful." Perhaps Paw is a reflection of the Buddha in his own way – simply being alive is a spiritual path and being aware of the miracle of life. One of Paw's greatest joys was catching lightning bugs and watching them glow and he shared that joy with his granddaughters. After he passed when they saw the glow of a lightning bug they would smile.

When President Thomas Jefferson visited the area where the Shenandoah and Potomac Rivers converged he was awed by its majesty and brilliance. Though during the Civil War this beautiful divine natural celestrial landscape was drenched with the blood of both the sons and daughters of the North and South. The presence of peace and war is a constant challenge that confronts us. Hopefully we can embrace, protect and sustain a peaceful environment on earth as in heaven.

The presence of light, joy and peace can be witnessed in amazing places. There are historical reports that in No Man's Land during WWI on December 24, 1914, a spontaneous truce occurred. German, French and British troops had begun celebrating Christmas and rather than hearing gunfire and bombshells blasting the melodic sound of carols being sung could be heard resulting in an unofficial ceasefire. Peace overcame hostility.

In Mattie J. T. Stepanek's book *Journey through Heartsongs*, he describes himself as a poet and peacemaker. This talented, creative and insightful young man died at the age of fourteen years old from muscular dystrophy. In his book he writes: "I have a heartsong and only I can hear it. .. If I take time and listen very hard I can still hear my Heartsong. It makes me feel happy; happier than ever. Happier than everywhere and everything and everyone in the whole wide world. Happy like thinking about going to heaven when I die. My Heartsong sounds like this I love you! I love you! How happy you can be! How happy you can make this whole world be! All people have a special song inside their hearts! Everyone in the whole wide world has a special Heartsong. If you believe in magical musical hearts and if you believe you can be happy then you, too will hear your song." Mattie was a beautiful spirit loving life in his fourteen years of living. I am blessed to have the opportunity to have worked with Elisabeth and be a Hospice volunteer. Sharing Mattie's poetry with Hospice patients and holding their hands it makes them smile. It's on earth as it is in heaven, in effect, focusing on our gift of being loving and giving is truly, almost heaven.

Inspirations and Thoughts from Moments & Windstorms

- When we come from a space of love and service our hearts open and our purpose and passion flows naturally and we are experiencing a Divine union with ALL people. Fear and anger dissipate and the ability to soar becomes reality regardless of the circumstances. We can witness a political arena based on integrity and the greater good reflecting the hope that "We are free at last."
- Embracing our true sense of joy creates a positive energy that taps into the Divine Source. We can witness our true strength and courage regardless of our age, sex. religion or race.
- Have you ever felt the joy of service? What is it about the service that makes you joyful?
- Were there times in your life when you or someone you knew experienced discrimination?
- Were there times that your actions could have been viewed as discriminatory? Do you agree or disagree? Do you believe that in hindsight that you might have chosen to act differently? How would your actions be different? Is there a means of making amends?
- What do you believe is the greatest asset and obstacle in acknowledging and manifesting your faith? (Please remember there are no right or wrong answers)
- Are there other questions that need to be asked to help identify and clarify your purpose and passion?
- If you were to die tomorrow have you left something unsaid or undone?

Chapter 3

FORBEARANCE

"You do not need to know precisely what is happening, or exactly where it is all going. What you need is to recognize the possibilities and challenges offered by the present moment, and to embrace them with courage, faith and hope." Thomas Merton

"I dwell in possibilities" Emily Dickinson

"You see things as they are and ask — Why? But I dream of things that never where and ask — Why Not?" George Bernard Shaw

"The journey of a thousand leagues begins with a single step So we must never neglect any work of peace within our reach no matter how small" Adlai Stevenson

"It is not the critic who counts; not the man who points out how the strong man stumbles, or where the doer of deeds could have done them better. The credit belongs to the man who is actually in the arena ... who spends himself in a worthy cause; who at the best knows in the end the triumph of high achievement, and who at the worst, if he fails, at least fails while daring greatly..." Teddy Roosevelt

"Well might the enchanters rob me of my good fortune but never of my spirit or my will" Miguel de Cervantes

"Man often becomes what he believes himself to be. If I keep on saying to myself that I cannot do a certain thing, it is possible that I may end by really becoming incapable of doing it. On the contrary, if I have the belief that I can do it, I shall surely acquire the capacity to do it even if I may not have it at the beginning." Mahatma Ghandi

POSSIBILITIES & OPPORTUNITIES

Possibility can be seen as the capability of being. Opportunity is defined as a good chance. Therefore, when "opportunity knocks," open the door! Being fully conscious of the life force energy helps us to embrace good fortune and release our fears. It also gives us the courage to have the patience to raise above adversity. There have been many new age books written about the need to let go of fear. Yet the most telling treatise and the foundation for all these texts directly or indirectly, implicitly or explicitly, is the Bible as well as other spiritual texts. In reality, "New Age" merely expresses ancient wisdom. I remember reading the 23rd Psalm in school. I have dyslexia and had always been afraid to read in front of the class, yet when it was my turn to recite the Psalm, I had memorized it and felt a real sense of accomplishment and peace:

> The Lord is my shepherd I shall not want.
> He maketh me lie down in green pastures;
> He leadeth me beside the still waters.
> He restoreth my soul;
> He leadeth me in the path of righteousness for thy
> name's sake.
> Yea, though I walk through the valley of the shadow of death,
> I will fear no evil, for Thou art with me, thy rod and thy staff
> they comfort me.
> Thou preparest a table before me in the presence of mine enemies,
> Thou anointest my head with oil;
> my cup runneth over.
> Surely goodness and mercy shall follow me all the days of my life;
> and I will dwell in the house of the Lord forever.

While I do not consider myself a religious person, I strongly believe in respecting one's spirit and honoring the universal life force. Nevertheless, I consider my lack of religious background an opportunity rather than a challenge. I describe myself as devoutly disorganized religiously. My maternal grandmother, Nana, always joked that when she was little, she decided that she would never marry a man with a beard. As a child, her job was to ensure that the makeshift shrine in her home was spotless and that the pictures included men with beards: Moses, Jesus and Marx were glistening

My father's family was no less religiously ambiguous. My Dad was named after Karl Marx, an indication of sorts that his father was atheist. My mother shared her grandmother's belief that as long as you followed the Ten Commandments and the Golden Rule you'd be okay.

Although my family never joined a religious institution my mother allowed me to attend church and temple with friends and family members. I had the wonderful opportunity to witness a diverse range of religious practices. I have since learned that Confucius teachings include a massage very similar to the Golden Rule: "Do not do unto others that you would not wish them to do unto to you." The Golden Rule appears in three of the four Gospels in some form – quoting Jesus on the Mount stating "Love Thy Neighbor as thyself." The Quaker commitment to peace and social justice also resonates with me. As an advocate for children in DC, the Friends Meeting of Washington had reached out and offered me space at Quaker House. I joke that some people attend religious services on Sunday; however I attended 260 days a year for over twenty-five years.

DISCERNING

Forbearance requires self-control, discipline and tolerance. Simply because a neighbor knocks at the door does not guarantee it will be welcoming - discernment could be warranted I remember when some neighbors came to our house with a petition. My mother got very angry. They were collecting signatures to protest the possibility of a Chinese family living in the neighborhood. I am proud to state that she refused to sign, but, unfortunately, that was not the case with other neighbors. As a consequence, the Chinese family chose not to move into the house.

Dr. Martin Luther King, Jr. is quoted as stating: "We shall overcome because the moral arc of the universe is long but it bends toward justice." The interaction of people in times of intolerance and inequity can create tension and unrest. We can choose to be passively noncommittal, angry or to take constructive action. I tend to choose the latter. I am humbled and honored to be involved in the Quaker Prison Ministry. I have visited local prisons and have been in correspondence with several inmates. The draconian manner in which the prison system operates would take volumes upon volumes to explain. One of the men is an intelligent African American man I met who was actively involved in Quaker Meeting in the prison. He was transferred to another prison which was not open to encouraging religious meetings and he also found it frustrating that there was no access to a library in the prison and therefore getting inspiring reading material has been close to impossible. His patience and strength has been impressive; he simply keeps focusing on the day he will be free. We have been corresponding via mail and in his letters he writes: "We need to keep the faith and continue to live the light, be the light, spread the light and keep the light shining even in these dark days. Especially in these dark days."

I also had the opportunity to attended the National Association for the Advancement of Colored People (NAACP) celebration in Loudoun County, VA with Goose Creek Quakers. It was amazing. It was very powerful; a young man, Norris Good, spoke about being physically beaten nearly to death, after a day of fishing, (there was a switch blade that had broken off in his brain). It was a miracle that he was alive and articulate and embracing life. At the same time he shared the fact that the "justice" system had abused him and treated him as a nonbeing because when the "gentlemen" (his term) basically white supremacists (my term) came to trial, the Judge was dismissive and ignored the facts of his injuries. He felt more abused by the judicial process viewing him as a nonhuman. However, his faith radiated and he felt that his life and his life situation had a purpose to shed light on the inequality that was occurring in our country, He kept expressing the importance of family and his gratitude for their support. They were there for him, literally every step of the way. He was invited to the NAACP event because they were helping him to challenge the court system. The fact that he referred to the abusers as "gentlemen" was unbelievable. He kept emphasizing the necessity of having an open heart and that it was unconditional love that kept him alive and it's unconditional love which gives him the strength to share his story.

Needless to say, to witness his testimony of unconditional love resonated with me.

The next day Quakers from Shepherdstown WV invited me to come with them to DC to participate in the March for Racial Justice. I couldn't refuse – there is a reason for everything. I was grateful and thrilled not only because I had been privileged to help organize the 25th Anniversary March honoring Dr. King and promoting the law that made his birthday January 15th a national holiday. The march was going to start at Lincoln Park; a park where I had organized a number of children's festivals. It was an inspirational and deja vu moment. However, I was in for a rude awakening that would require forbearance and a sense of humor. My friend and I had hoped that perhaps Congressman John Lewis would be one of the speakers or perhaps Senator Corey Booker. The organizers clearly had more of a local focus. They had a local DC advocate as the MC - she kept things upbeat and flowing. There was a young woman handing out material about the organizers and speakers. I went up to her and asked for the material. She handed me a plastic bag with info on the MC which also included small foil packets I thanked her and asked: "What are these packets?" She gave me a meek smile "Condoms." I "LOLed." I have to admit that when I helped on previous marches and festivals we never considered distributing condoms. I don't know why they included them and I am sorry I didn't ask her however I did get a good laugh. There were probably about 15,000 people from around the country marching. It didn't get much news coverage. Unfortunately, racial justice is not considered popular unless there is confrontation. My favorite signs were – "Dismantle Racism" and "Embody Fierce Compassion." I found it interesting and appropriate that the march was held on Yum Kippur, the Jewish High Holiday, the Day of Atonement and Forgiveness. With each step I took I kept each of these men in my heart keeping the faith praying things will change. Sorry that hateful interaction was prevalent even prior to 2015 and even more concerned that in 2017 there were white supremacist riots in Charlottesville, VA resulting in innocent people being injured and killed including a young woman, Heather Heyer. Polarization is painful and a sad commentary on the lack of civility and morale interaction.

Discrimination is a means of denying possibilities and opportunities to a particular person or a specific population based on arbitrary factors such as race, age, religion, gender, or economic status. Education is a means of liberation from such narrow mindedness, yet (as discussed previously), the quality of education leaves a great deal to be desired, especially for those most in need. A tribal mentality limits all those involved if can create an authoritative and fascist mentality. Internally the tribe mentality can be supportive however without the presence of love it can be manipulative, exclusive and destructive. As a result fascist structures are flaunted and deocracy is threatened.

Sports as well as arts have enabled very talented African-Americans to break the color barrier. BB King was said to have made the statement that the entertainment world was in the forefront of the civil rights movement and had the means of changing society one gig at a time. Frank Sinatra gave the Sands Hotel in Las Vegas an ultimatum that, if they did not change their discriminatory policies and allow Sammy Davis, Jr. to have full access to the hotel amenities as well as performing there, he (Sinatra) would not perform there. "*The Color Purple*", written by Alice Walker, with respect to both the book and movie, brought together very special talents. Oprah Winfrey's impact on television, film and the literary community has been dramatic.

As the 21st millennium began, exciting sports firsts captured the public's attention. Two African American sisters, Venus and Serena Williams, competed against each other at Wimbledon. Indeed, they rooted for one another as family. They began playing tennis from the time they were in kindergarten in an economically disadvantaged city near Los Angeles; Compton, CA. Their father, Richard Williams, told reporters that his daughters were very special. Without economic means, they practiced at public tennis courts and at times had to dodge bullets. Despite such challenges, at no time did they lose sight of their dreams of winning Grand Slam tournaments. In 1999, Serena won the US Tennis Open, and in 2000, Venus won her dream tournament at Wimbledon.

Less than three weeks later, Tiger Woods' dream also came true in England when he won the 129th British Open, at St. Andrews, Scotland, the historic home of golf. With his victory in the British Open, Tiger Woods, at the age of 24, became the youngest player to win golf's modern Grand Slam, by winning the Masters in 1997, the 1999 PGA Championship, the 2000 US Open and 2000 British Open.

There is no question that Tiger Woods is a gifted golfer. Talent meant little – skin color predominated as an arbiter of fitness; while he was growing up he was denied access to "White Only" country clubs. Tiger is very proud of his ancestry, which includes African, Asian, Native American and European. When he is asked to define his race - he responds "Human." The obstacles these sports greats have had to overcome cannot be overstated. The love and support they received from their families who taught them to DREAM cannot be undermined. Sadly, despite their acknowledged talent and achievement, the scars of lack of self-worth remain. Many sports greats and actors have exhibited self-destructive behavior.

For all humans regardless of race, access to education and health care is critical for personal and professional stability and success. Despite that obvious fact, study after study clearly indicates that there is obvious disparity based on income, race and ethnicity. A 1996 study conducted by the Agency for Health Care and Policy Research estimated that approximately 25% of the children in the United States live in single parent families and this number has increased over the years.

The health care insurance debate has played out and continues to play out in the political arena, indicating clearly how polarizing the issue has become.(polarization will be discussed in chapter 4). In 2012, the Agency for Health Care Research and Quality reported that people of low socioeconomic status – often tied with discrimination – have serious challenges accessing health care. Overcoming barriers is becoming more and more overwhelming. If there is any good news on the horizon, it is that the Center for Disease control has estimated that the Affordable Care Act is expected to extend insurance coverage to an additional 27 million people by 2019. This is the same Act that so many politicians are seeking to rescind. This seems myopic given that the more disparity in adequate access to health care services, the less possibilities and opportunities for a healthy and productive society. The Pandemic clearly exposed the existence of medical deserts in this country and the huge chasms that exist in the world.

MOTHERHOOD & WOMEN'S RIGHTS

There is no question that motherhood takes a great deal of patience and unconditional love. I find it difficult to put into words my true feelings and deepest thoughts about motherhood. I am in awe of women who take the responsibility of motherhood seriously. I believe parenthood to be the most challenging and rewarding job. I was extremely upset at eighteen, when I was informed by my doctor that I would not be able to get pregnant because my womb was not fully developed. As with so many others stunned by an unexpected diagnosis, I didn't think to question him, and I didn't have the heart to tell my mother. I was young, devastated, and angry. Despite my emotions, I took that anger and channeled the energy by focusing all my maternal instincts on the world at large. I began viewing every child as my child. I wanted them to thrive. This wholistic perspective gave me the stamina and vision to become a child advocate.

Would I have become a child advocate had the doctor not diagnosed me as being infertile? Maybe, but perhaps it would not have been with such vigor. Do I feel less than a woman? No, I certainly feel I can identify and empathize with all women. I had considered adoption but never seriously explored the possibility, because I strongly believe that the optimum for children is to have a minimum of two parents. Additionally, I am not sure I would personally be capable of handling the stress, both emotionally and economically, of being a single parent.

In making this decision, I am not negatively judging single parents, indeed successful single parents are simply amazing people. I recognize that parenting is a complex tapestry of demanding tasks and given such a challenge single parents certainly need our help as well as deserve our admiration. From my vantage point, I definitely can identify with the African proverb that "it takes a village to raise a child.." I applaud single parents for their herculean task of mothering/fathering a child.

The efforts of the women's movement has been phenomenal, yet I believe the "founding mothers" were somewhat short-sighted. Early Feminists identified too much with the male identity by targeting men's jobs. There was a push for women getting nontraditional jobs (construction and public safety) in a drive to get higher pay and thus equalize economic status. In taking that approach, they undervalued jobs held traditionally by women by not insisting on equalizing the value of these jobs.

As a consequence, the salaries for women working in child care are at minimum wage levels in many parts of the country, and many workers do not have health benefits nor adequate educational credentials. With such a focus on women breaking through the glass ceiling, one can't help but wonder if the political and economic pundits consider the women stuck in the basement caring for the children.

From the mid 1970's through today, inflation set against salary growth has dictated that, in most two parent households, both parents need to work to cover household expenses. The economic boom of the nineties and the collapse of the economy since 2007 has only exacerbated this need. This leaves single parent families in dire straits. As previously discussed, single parent families are in a serious financial bind, now made doubly difficult by the state of the current economy.

The rise in our divorce rate shows that over 50% of marriages end in divorce. We are in denial or simply plain selfish in assuming that this does not result in a negative impact on children on a large scale. Yet, the wholesale issuance of "no fault" divorce is simply a legal exit doorway – set up as a convenient and quick escape. While such laws were designed to avoid domestic violence, couples, nonetheless, are encouraged by such laws to avoid taking positive steps to re-evaluate and recommit to their marriage vows – "for better or worse." The possibilities and opportunities for such reconciliation are endless. In Scott Peck's bestselling book, *The Road Less Traveled*, he stated that love is volitional. No one said marriage is easy, and having children certainly doesn't make it any easier. I considered it a blessing to be the step-mother to Will (I discuss our relationship in greater detail in chapter 5) I learned first hand that parenting takes forbearance.

There is a crisis relating to our children's welfare, as well as the welfare of society as a whole. Educational systems are crumbling, our planet is being environmentally polluted, our economic institutions are unstable, and the bottom line is that there seems to be a lack of grace and respect. "I've got what I need; who cares what you need?" A selfish mode of operation seems to perpetuate a "Haves & Have Nots" mentality. I am not certain that anybody really cares to address this problem. Nevertheless, when looking at challenges we can always look for associated opportunities.

While we are living on earth, we need to begin to see what's important in keeping us all alive beyond limited personal and monetary gains. When we die, the one with the most toys doesn't necessarily win, especially if these toys came with a price tag of dooming our grandchildren and others. As I have stated before, "you can't take it with you." Teaching our children to respect themselves and the earth would be a radical and wonderful way of ensuring a healthier tomorrow, rather than fearing some Armageddon promoting pollution, war, terrorism and abuse – all stemming from unbecoming selfishness.

Recognizing that caring for our children certainly is not exclusively a women's issue, men are also encouraged to be responsible and loving. By allowing men to abdicate that responsibility, women become enablers, and the children become innocent victims of passive neglect. Additionally, our society benefits or suffers according to how committed it is to establishing strong educational systems providing equality which includes a safe and nurturing environment. Society also has vested interests and responsibilities in helping to ensure sufficient support for healthy child rearing and education is made available. If we viewed the needs of our children as a national security priority, the current paradigm would shift and there would be vastly increased peace and prosperity within our family, our communities, our nation, and the world.

This section would be incomplete without mentioning Hillary Clinton. The campaign of 2016 exposed sexism and inequality in more ways than one. Undoubtedly, history will reveal that the most qualified person did not win the 2016 Electoral College presidential election. .It instead reflected a society unconcerned about women's rights and with no real motivation to help women break glass ceilings. (Sexism is also discussed in Chapters 4 and 6) Unfortunately, a feeling of being marginalized creates more hostility especially among men and women. In West Virginia I witnessed people who had Hillary Clinton bumper stickers being harassed; bullying became acceptable in a mean spirited atmosphere. It's also really sad that there were also women who were willing to vote against their own best interests. The role of social media in the election has yet to be totally exposed and needs to be carefully monitored.

We need to value and honor the human spirit as priceless. No one questioned the cost of coping with potential Y2K computer shutdowns. Conversely, looking at childcare in our country if all of the child care programs in our country shutdown, Fifty percent or more of this country's working parents would surely call in sick. The associated economic and social impact would be phenomenal. Consequently, our economic and governmental entities are being much more than deceitful in pretending these are merely domestic issues; they are unbecomingly and antisocially GREEDY. The Pandemic open the eyes of the country to the demanding and under valuing of nurturing professions predominantly held by women be it in the child care or educational arena as well as the nursing or elder care fields.

By undermining the salaries and professionalism in the educational arena, society limits the possibilities and opportunities for talented women and men to seriously consider a career working with children. Nurturing our children should be viewed as an invaluable service. In spite of the obvious importance of such policy, America is the only industrialized country that doesn't have a comprehensive national child care policy. Foreign countries that experienced the ravages of two world wars on their soil, and the subsequent loss of a generation, understand the importance of protecting and nurturing their children. Doing so is fundamental if for no other reason than self-preservation and ensuring a financially stable social security funding stream. All Americans would benefit from a future generation that is productive, caring and economically viable. Artificial intelligence does not pay into the tax base and is forcing hard working humans out of jobs.

Discussing the Women's Movement would not be complete without addressing the sexual revolution. Personally, I believe we shot ourselves in the foot, and I am not sure who won. The Puritan approach to sexuality was clearly stifling, yet the concept of "free love" has proven to be extremely costly. The increase in sexually transmitted diseases (STDs), teen pregnancy and divorce has skyrocketed. The expense to society – morally, emotionally, socially and economically–is immeasurable. It is definitely time to reassess where we find ourselves after decades of social experiment with regards to sexuality. The turn over of Roe vs. Wade had opened the scars of decades of sexual inequality. The 2022 election demonstrated women's commitment to ensuring their freedom.

In 1970, I "crashed" a Key Club Convention in Atlantic City. I was an official member of my high school Key Club, a program designed to involve students in social and community volunteer services. Yet the state and national charters did not overtly recognize the participation of females in the organization. Since my name on the registration form had been misspelled the organizers assumed I was a male. When I arrived I am happy to report that it quickly became obvious there had been an error on the registration form. I was the only girl among 200 male delegates.

The Kiwanians supervising the event were furious. They wanted to ban me from participating in all forum discussions and voting. It was rather intimidating and at the same time awesome. Every time I walked into the convention dining hall, all the delegates were told to stand until I was seated. Even though I was treated like a lady, they wanted a letter from my mother stating that if I became pregnant they would not be held responsible. My mother simply laughed. She trusted me and she was amused that these men in charge, whom I described as old geezers, thought that women were only good for one thing. My school advisor, Mr. Clifford, was appalled that they made such a request. He was very protective, ensuring that I had my own private room next to the Sergeant of Arms. I left the convention with my virginity intact.

By focusing on the physical union of the sexes, many people have lost sight of the spiritual rewards of sexual abstinence. While I've been there and done that, I am not suggesting we become celibate. What I am suggesting is that we focus on the expression of humanity involved in embracing a soul-mate. While such an undertaking might require a life time or two or three to experience the harmony and bliss of the yin (feminine) and the yang (masculine), its rewards, both personally and socially, would be quite enormous. The bond between the Christ and the Magdalene can be described as mystical.

Many religious writings address the union of men and women; one such document is the ancient mystical Jewish text called the Qabalah. In the Hidden Treasures of the Ancient Qabalah, Elias Gewurz, describes the heavenly aspects of loving relationships. He explains that desire for the sake of desire creates havoc and imbalance. In order to reach a higher plane we need a spiritual understanding of devotion and honoring the Divine – life force – within us all. Quaker Pastor, Philip Gulley in his book *If the Church were Christian* focuses on a number of key points relating to spirituality one of which is his belief that "we should care more about love and less about sex."

Respect is the cornerstone of a fulfilling companionship between two consenting adults. While the union of two lovers strengthens the dominion of their wills, it is not a power play. Rather, it is a Divine gift of sharing wisdom and a true sense of purity. Given a "battle of the sexes," we both lose. Liberation is actualized when we recognize that men and women can both grow in spiritual worth, while enjoying each other's pleasures without guilt.

FOLLOW YOUR BLISS

I worked with the Washington Child Development Council (WCDC) for over thirty years. I took the job in 1978 knowing they only had $300 in the bank. Rather than focusing on risk and deficit,, I chose to focus on the possibilities and the opportunities. It took a great deal of forbearance. WCDC was incorporated in 1973 to promote quality child care services in our nation's capital. Joining it allowed me to tap into my need to serve children and families. Before I left WCDC, it had more than $1,000,000 in assets, a 333,333% increase. If it were a for profit organization, it would have been deemed successful on that basis alone – we helped to improve child care service in DC and the nation. The District budget for early childhood education increased by 1000% and the number of families served went from less than 6,000 to over 20,000; we also helped with the passage of the Act for Better Child Care which has been discussed earlier in the book.

The people involved with WCDC are very pleased that they have played a key role in the improvement and delivery of District child care services. Such accomplishments have been recognized by many publications, including:: Lady's Home Journal and Working Mother's Magazine as one of the top ten cities providing quality early childhood programs. During my tenure, I have met a number of wonderful people in providing early childhood services. Unfortunately, the numbers of such providers are dwindling.

Joseph Campbell, a renowned writer, and the author of *The Hero With A Thousand Faces*, stressed the importance of following one's bliss. Simply existing without experiencing such a bliss eats away at your spirit. If you enjoy fishing, then you need to go fishing. If you're a waitress, you need to be the best waitress you can be. In following your bliss, you must also be willing to bear any associated consequences. Many are oblivious of such consequences, and their bliss is simply the latest fad until a new fad comes along.

Following our bliss requires us to be warriors as well as peacemakers. We must be willing to defend our blissful state, while at the same time, educating those who doubt our capabilities by demonstrating our willingness to share this opportune experience. Negotiating such terrain requires a great deal of diplomacy, as well as give and take. No one can dictate what our bliss will be; it's a very personal journey that will enable us to tap into the life force.

What makes you happy? If you don't know, you need to take the time to find out. You may not die wealthy, but you'll live rich in spirit. Dr. Elisabeth Kubler-Ross sat by the death beds of thousands of dying patients. She explains that many of the patients expressed deep regrets: "I wanted to become a fireman, but my family insisted that I become a lawyer"; "I wanted to spend more time with my son, but I was too busy at work"; "I wanted to marry for love, but my mother made me marry for money". And the regrets continue: "If only ..." just fill in the blanks.

In the adventure book, The Swiss Family Robinson, by Johann David Wyss, a family is marooned on a deserted island. The young boy is obviously wanting and complains, "if only we had butter." The father is less than impressed and states that "if" will get you nowhere, noting that it's the longest and most cumbersome word in the dictionary. There is no end to "ifs". Elisabeth stresses that we may not always get what we want, but we will get what we need. What do you need? I realize answering that question may not be easy, yet once we honestly answer that question we may begin to understand what will really make us happy. Such an endeavor may even take a life time.

In *The Hero With A Thousand Faces*, Joseph Campbell asks similar and poignant questions such as, "What is the core of us?" and "What is the basic character of our being?" In contemplating these queries, we can explore our bliss and examine the true Self in the individual, and in turn, identify the Self in all beings. This exploration simply reflects the essence of Ecclesiastes: "To everything there is a season, and a time to every purpose under heaven." (Ecclesiastes 3 KJV)

WHY WEIGHT AND/OR WAIT?

We keep waiting and waiting. We're waiting for the other person to say they're sorry; we're waiting for Prince Charming, and we're Waiting for Godot. In the process of waiting, we create our own obstacles. Not taking action is an action unto itself. "Weight" is the consequence of the body's inability to burn calories. Therefore, it follows that the greater the body's energy, the less its "weight". Having struggled with weight all my life, I am very familiar with the dieter's dilemma postulating that we focus on losing weight when we need to focus on gaining energy. Does this sound familiar: "If I lose ten pounds, then I'll go to the gym"? Going to the gym, the movies, the beach, reading a book, and writing the great American novel need not fall victim to our "weight/wait." We need to realize as "beings," both as nouns and verbs, that we need to act and overcome the wait whether physical (weight) or energetically in terms of taking action.

The issue of weight loss is an issue that has plagued women for years. Obesity is plaguing our country as a whole for men, women and even our children. The obesity statistics keep increasing; it's estimated that approximately 40% of the adults in the US and that 17% of our children are considered obese.

I am sorry to share that my mother suffered from eating disorders and was obsessed with her weight, as well as her focusing on mine. Ironically, women who live in the USA, because of external social and commercial conditioning are born with weight problems. In effect, we tend to complain that our hips are too big or that we need to lose 25 lbs. to be attractive.

We can also use weight as a form of protective armor due to physical or emotional abuse. There are people who, because of either actual or imagined attacks, develop a callousing approach to life. This callousing results in people becoming unfulfilled and developing a lot of self-defeating behavior. Due to these insecurities and pain people develop hurtful activities that create even a thicker callousing mode of operation which can push those they love even further away and emotionally shutting down. In turn those they love may also develop a callousing approach or choose another form of protection, such as creating a "fat body suit of armor." When we are able to embrace the fact that we are attractive whatever our weight we will truly be attractive. It is truly inspiring when we are able to understand and rejoice that we are always protected and loved by the Divine. We can relax and find our perfect weight rather than worrying about losing weight.

While I was in high school, my mother was so totally focused on my weight that she went to counseling and insisted that I also go to counseling. It was amusing that, when we finally went to her therapist, he seemed somewhat uncomfortable about talking about weight since he was obviously overweight by at least 75 lbs. or more. At the time we had the counseling session I was a size 6, yet in my mother's eyes I was overweight and she was dealing with her own insecurities. In hindsight, she was focused on the physical which was challenging for me since my focus was more on the spiritual. At this point it really doesn't make any difference since that was many years ago. Now I am simply sharing it to emphasize the importance of loving ourselves. The key is changing the paradigm from losing weight to gaining a healthy perspective.

I have realized that the issue of weight is more a mental state than a physical challenge. It helped me to understand the importance of creating a peaceful state of being and taking the Lord's Prayer to heart: "…Give us this day our daily bread. And forgive us our debts as we forgive our debtors" was essential. It moved me closer to lightening my load and uplifting my spirits. Knowing that God provides a hedge of protection and mercy, I realized that the fat body suit of armor was unnecessary, ineffective and unhealthy. I also was glad to know that God allows carbs on a daily basis ☺

The Bible is food for thought. Verses which have given me solace are John 4:14 "…. whosoever drinketh of this [well] water shall thirst again but whosoever drinketh of the water that I shall give him shall never thirst; but the water that I shall give him shall be in him a well of water springing up into everlasting life." John 4:34 Jesus saith unto them. "My meat is to do the will of him who sent me and to finish his work." The key is that we are all "Beings" and that the body is an earthly illusion it's an energy that provides a sanctuary for the Holy Spirit. Simply focusing on the body is vanity. The Book of Ecclesiastes describes in detail vanities and the need for wisdom and patience; it states: "vanity of vanities; all is vanity,… there is no new thing under the sun … To everything there is a season, and a time to every purpose under the heaven." (Note: all the above Bible verses are from KJV) Being patient and gentle nourishes the soul. Be present and aware of spiritual nourishment – change is a gift from God.

Whatever we weigh, we are a light of the Divine and can overcome the obstacles that are holding us back. Now is the time to seize the day – Carpe diem. We are all masterpieces; it's a triple A approach: Awareness, Acceptance and Availability. It's possible to get past the dieter's obstacle course of the myriad of diets from A to Z and K in between, be it Atkins, KETO to the Zone. Once we avoid the yoke of dieting guilt and focus on the AAA approach which requires forbearance:

Awareness: that the "kingdom is within" We are Divine vessels Enjoy eating, food is a blessing to help maintain the Divine temple. Exercise can be invigorating and viewed as a joyful prayer.

Acceptance: Loving the body unconditionally no matter the size. In effect, would a skinnier Buddha be more enlightened? It's getting past the guilt and denial of dieting. It's more about kind and mindful discipline without beating ourselves up. There's a huge cake – do we enjoy one piece or gorge and eat the whole cake? The key is eating to live not living to eat.

Availability: Being open to healthy possibilities that allow us to maximize our physical capabilities and in turn align our emotional, intellectual and spiritual potentials -in making the time rather than excuses to exercise. It's much more loving to focus on the positive aspects and say that "we get to exercise" rather than "we have to exercise."

Life is short, we have the opportunity to live it to the fullest without carrying around excess weight and guilt. No specific diet is being recommended since one size does not fit all and it is critical that we each are open to our own personal AAA approach.

THE MOMENT IS NOW

The concept of "NOW" has become very popular as well as the concept of embracing the moment. In exploring these concepts, I realized that there is a need for us to be aware that the only obstacles to us experiencing the joy in our lives is ourselves. This is not a guilt trip. In fact, the most accessibly popular and draining journeys we take are "guilt trips", which are major detours to us reaching our fullest potential. Instead of moving forward or upward or inward, whatever the case may be we get lost in our insecurities. Focusing on fear of what's going to happen next, results in losing precious possibilities and opportunities. Caring and sharing is a wonderful way to be open to releasing the past and receiving the current miracle and in turn rejoicing. There is a flow and glow to us being alive and we can simply smile while on this trip called life.

Dealing with the physical challenges of collin dysfunction resulting in my weight dropping down to 80lbs. which, began almost a two year journey through the WV hospital system then an intensive rehab program. When my body reached 100lbs my GP and I began to dance, I learned we eat to live giving us the strength to move forward and embrace the loving possibilities.

My Nana had my great grandmother's good china and crystal; I only saw it after my Nana died. She had packed it away; she was keeping it safe. Safe from what? Finding those dishes and glasses gave me a great deal of joy. I share them with my family and friends when they come over to dinner. I have no intention of hiding my "treasures." I am not flaunting them. I am simply not waiting to enjoy the gifts that have been graciously given to me and in turn I am here to share and serve.

Joy is multiplied beyond our own understanding when it is shared. Peace becomes a reality when we experience it in the moment within ourselves and allow it to shine in our lives. The writings in Phillipians 4:7 explains that there is the peace of God which passeth all understanding, which shall keep our hearts and minds open. Seeing ourselves as a beacon of light can be both illuminating for ourselves and for others. And the moment when we see the light reflected, we shine with an even greater brilliance.

Life is precious and we never know when death will come. Many of us remember exactly where we were, and what we were doing, when President John F. Kennedy was shot in November, 1963. There is now a new generation who will never forget when it was reported that the plane John F. Kennedy, Jr. was flying had crashed and taken his life along with his wife, Carolyn and sister-in-law, Lauren Besset. They were so young. Yet there are people who exist until they are a hundred, not knowing why they are alive. Are we simply waiting to die or waiting to live?

We cannot afford to let the dream of Camelot perish. It is fortuitous that Jacqueline Kennedy chose an eternal flame to mark the grave of President Kennedy. We are the light of the world and together we can embrace the message of our present consciousness of being whole and complete right at this moment, continuing to shine forever. The inspirational quote President Kennedy shared during his inaugural address: "Ask not what your country can do for you – ask what you can do for your country" is as true now as it was then. The quest to serve continues in spirit, if not in body. George Bernard Shaw wrote: "You see things as they are and ask, Why? But I dream of things that never were and ask, Why not?" The possibilities and opportunities are endless. Why wait? Choosing life can prove exciting and challenging.

The challenges in 21st century keep unfolding and being "tweeted" on social media. There are people who are feeling threatened because of public policy. The environment is being ravaged and climate change is wreaking havoc with hurricanes, huge wild fires and floods. The wild fires devastating Hawaii in 2023 resulted in over 1,000 fatalities and billions of dollars in damage. Still each of us has the opportunity to take a stand for positive change. The fires in CA during 2018 have been devastating The small town of Paradise, CA was completely incinerated and was totally left with smoldering ashes. Governor Jerry Brown (D - CA) declared a state of emergency and noted that "Unfortunately, these fires have become the new abnormal." However even with these challenges California is attempting to be in the forefront of developing progressive environmental policies. At the same time the President continues to deny the existence of climate change and blaming California for poor management.

Why wait? The moment is now. Indeed, NOW is the only moment we will ever have actionable dominion over. We can make the dream a reality. It can either be a dream or a nightmare. As I stated previously, there is a generation that will remember where they were when John F. Kennedy was shot. The generation that was alive and remembers World War II is passing over, and now there is a generation that will always remember where they were on September 11th, 2001. Each generation has its memories–some good, some bad. The question is not "Why?," but "When?" and "How can we serve?"

IMPROVING THE POSSIBILITIES

As discussed earlier, possibilities and opportunities vary. The playing field definitely needs to be level. In the process, we ALL benefit. For example, in the early 1900's the powers that be realized that a number of America's enlisted men were suffering from scurvy – a vitamin deficiency due to malnutrition. Recognizing the need for healthy military recruits, laws were enacted that encouraged better nutrition, such as the Department of Agriculture's school lunch program, and distribution of surplus produce and commodities.

The military draft during the Vietnam War clearly demonstrated the inequities in society. Wealthy folks knew to register their sons with the London, UK Draft Board, from which no one was ever drafted. Of course, resource was required to send their sons overseas for such registration. Additionally, those with money could buy their way out of the draft by being perpetual students. Ironically the GI Bill helped many soldiers take advantage of a higher education; that is if they returned home from war in one piece. The Lottery for the Draft simply created a more equitable means of choosing recruits based on chance not on their date of birth rather than wealth. When the draft was abolished by President Nixon, I had mixed feelings. I realize there are a number of people during the 60's and 70's who would swear at the ROTC, yet at the same time, there were those who would swear by the ROTC. The biases broke down generally by race and economic status. Many in the African-American and low income communities saw the military as a way out – unfortunately it was via the Ho Chi Minh trail. Now the military arena is even broader with more uncertainties and challenges.

My father was in the service, Army, during WWII, yet the closest he ever got to combat was boot camp. He was not a proponent of the military; my mother often joked that when he got out of the army he burned his khakis and he would never again wear drab green. He was not big on authority and hierarchy, let alone killing. He once shared with me a very personal and telling experience. A guy in his platoon was from the South and had never met a Jew. He was shocked to find that my father didn't have horns or a tail. They became good friends. Based on his own experience, my father believed the real value for military service was that it was a great equalizer. When you're in a foxhole – black or white – you still bleed red. Additionally, the old adage that there are no atheists in foxholes may be true.

I am a strong believer that we were born to serve. Secretary of State Collin Powell is a star example of a military graduate. Unfortunately, there are no counterparts in terms of human services, except for the clergy. Non-bureaucratic secular options are limited, offer minimum benefits, and lack any overall structure. Nonmilitary government human services include Peacecorp, Americorp and Teachercorp with very limited budgets.

It could prove beneficial for both our country and individual growth to reinstate a mandatory draft for both men and women, permitting military or civilian service. It's fascinating that we now refer to our many military ventures abroad as peacekeeping efforts, while here at home, there are schools to be built and an aging population that requires as much if not more care and effort. A draft, so configured, could address shortages in both the educational and health care fields. A universal draft could bring us together for a common good and give people the opportunity to serve rather than simply get. Some people just don't "get it"; It's not about getting, it's about giving.

A life of giving does not necessarily require sacrifice and the benefits of giving can vary from moment to moment and person to person depending on the perspective. There are two parables, one reflecting altruistic behavior and the other demonstrating behaviors in different sacrificial modes of operation. The first, is a woman walking down the beach, there were thousands of starfish that had been washed ashore, and she kept picking up a starfish and throwing it back into the ocean. Another person saw her efforts and shock his head exclaiming that "You are wasting your time there are too many to save." The woman simply smiled, picked up another starfish. threw it back into the ocean and replied "As far as this starfish is concerned, I am not wasting my time." The second parable is a chicken and a three legged pig debating the meaning of true sacrifice. In order to provide the farmer's family breakfast – the chicken supplied eggs and the pig supplied bacon. Each made a sacrifice – the level and intensity varied reflecting on each animal's assets and the commitment and loss resulting from the sacrifice.

REMEMBERING "NICE"

It seems that the practice of civility and being nice has been devalued. Watching the evening news is like watching the World Wrestling Federation. As discussed throughout this book bullying is all too common in society. After graduating college, I remember that I read a short play I wrote, ABSENT PRESENCE to my parents. Sections of the play had been performed as a staged production in a local theatre in Washington, DC. After I finished reading the play, I asked them what they thought. My father responded "Nice" I exploded "What do you mean nice could you be more specific?!" He then explained " Adlai Stevenson was a brilliant man however he never became president. It would have been nice for the country if the progressive ideas of Stevenson became a reality." I then realized that "nice" was good my Dad was giving me a thumbs up however questioning society. Being compared to Adlai Stevenson is nice and humbling. In order to better understand Stevenson the following quotes reflect his prophetic nature and the tenor of politics both in the 20th and 21st centuries: "I believe if we really want human brotherhood to spread and increase until it makes life safe and sane we must also be certain that there be no one true faith or path by which it may spread"; "Making peace is harder than making war", "On this shrunken globe, men can no longer live as strangers"; "Those who corrupt the public mind are just as evil as those who rob the public purse"; "ignorance is stubborn and prejudice is hard" "He who slings mud usually loses ground." It's over a century and as a species we are still struggling with embracing the importance of civility and respect. It takes time and patience; that's one of the reasons Adlai Stevenson is quoted in this section as well as at the beginning of Chapter 3, Forbearance.

Inspirations and Thoughts from Moments & Windstorms

- Life is a gift, living requires that we get past the fear of death and focus on the present. Tapping into our souls and hearts is a blessing, where our talents and compassion abide and shine.

- Forbearance is essential to help us to overcome the challenges and focus on the opportunities Smiling and an open heart awakens the possibilities and opportunities
- What possibilities have you experienced? What opportunities have you created?
- Have you witnessed times when opportunities and possibilities had been denied?
- Have you been still and heard your heartsong? Are you able to share your heartsong?
- Have you experienced any personal starfish or chicken/pig challenges or possibilities?

Chapter 4

FREEDOM

"Oppressed people cannot remain oppressed forever. The urge for freedom will eventually come" Dr. Martin Luther King, Letter from Birmingham City Jail

"We are not enemies, but friends. We must not be enemies. Though passion may have strained, it must not break our bonds of affection. The mystic chords of memory will swell when again touched, as surely they will be, by the better angels of our nature." President Abraham Lincoln

"I have sworn upon the altar of God eternal hostility against every form of tyranny over the mind of man." President Thomas Jefferson

"Yes, the torch of Lady Liberty symbolizes our freedom and represents our heritage, the compact with our parents, our grandparents, and our ancestors .... we draw our people, our strength, from every country and every corner of the world." President Ronald Reagan

"The thought that so many people get their news from social media is scary" Rush Limbaugh

Freedom is indivisible.... For to be free is not merely to cast off one's chains, but to live in a way that respects and enhances the freedom of others." Nelson Mandela

"What about our future!?" Gretta Thunberg, Environmental Activist

Freedom is being threatened by polarization, a threat that must be overcome. Polarization seems to be increasing throughout the world – be it political, economic, religious or social. The 45th President does not seem to promote harmony and as a result there is a great deal of destabilization which causes polarization. Such polarization is reflected to our families on television and the internet in negative and counterproductive manners. Polarization is a toxic energy, literally tearing apart the web of humanity; regardless of orientation: right, left, liberal, or conservative. Simultaneously, these forces are creating inequity, fear and anger which devalues all those concerned, young or old; rich or poor, female or male; whatever the barriers. Being marginalized is painful. We are all left in a vacuum craving validation – be it angry females wearing pink "pussy" hats or angry males wearing "MAGA." hats. Lack of respect has led to violence and a drug epidemic regardless of the hat one is wearing. Obtaining validation by utilizing drugs or devaluing another is oppressive, destructive and counterproductive. As a result, we are degrading ourselves. The demonization of a population based on political affiliation, gender, age, race, religion, ethnicity, nationality or whatever group viewed derogatorily is classified as inferior undermines society as a whole Respectfully embracing our better angels can help to ensure freedom and promote the need for us ALL to come together.

Outside forces such as political propaganda, peer pressure or religious dogma are perpetuating an atmosphere of hate and intolerance. Unfortunately, many believe validation comes from outside forces resulting in either inflated self-worth or low self-esteem; depending on the psychological position of individuals as well as our own perspective. True validation and self-worth comes from within. When we close our eyes and are willing to embrace the silence, there is an entire cosmos within us – our souls. None of us is going to leave this planet alive in our physical body. So the question becomes: will we leave it in a polarized state or in a state of unity? It is in that state of peace and communion with the life force and humanity as a whole that we can recognize that we are all one (won) and in that state we are all winners. When we speak of humankind, we need to focus on being KIND in the most positive sense. For instance, the word kind can be utilized divisively by sorting humanity into a class system, i.e labeling and dividing. Then again, kind can be defined as a unifying factor focusing on a sympathetic nature and in being considerate, good, and benevolent. We can overcome competitive aspects of our nature by understanding the importance of diversity and the beauty of simply being. Compassion is the union of the mind and heart – in effect, wisdom and love. The long run ramifications of social and individual polarization can be viewed in terms of life and death.

Watching the polarization in the world be it in Ukraine, Gaza, Palestine, the UN or the US Capitol is heartbreaking. Witnessing the continual delays and backstabbing. In October 2023, was a sad reality that the US Congress had difficulty electing a Speaker in the House of Representatives. It reflects a dysfunctional state of affairs in turn jeopardizing freedom. The fact that elected officials are threatening one another is beyond bullying. Unconditional love is needed more than ever to help us all move forward and ensure peace.

Dr. Elisabeth Kubler-Ross was a trail blazer putting the world's spotlight on understanding life and death; in so doing she dared to stress the importance of unconditional love, which in effect is 180 degrees difference from polarization. Politicians, clerics and pundits throwing mud make poor role models for our children. The vitriol found on the internet perpetuates crude and violent cartoons as well as dialog; our children deserve better. You don't have to be a rocket scientist to conclude that bullying on the playground and on social media are unfortunately reflective of the polarized and fear-based culture we experience. The 21st century continues to witness increasing violence which is amplified by access to the internet. In January 2008 Congresswoman Gabby Giffords had an open forum in Tucson Arizona, inviting constituents to share their concerns which resulted in a highly volatile 22 year old man opening fire at the event seriously wounding the Congresswoman and injuring another twelve persons who were attending as well as killing six other people including a nine year old girl, Christina-Taylor Green. The tragedies at Sandy Hook elementary, the bombing at the Boston Marathon the shootings in Las Vegas, the killings at a church in Charleston, SC a shooting at a synagogue during Passover service near San Diego, CA and the numerous other shootings occurring in the country are sad commentaries regarding the opposition to the establishment of rational gun safety laws combined with a lack of respect for life. Since 2017 there have been 80 mass killings. Just in the first two months of 2018 there have been 18 mass killings in the US including 17 students at a high school in Parkland, FL. The list continues to grow. Unfortunately, it is worldwide with a mass killing at the Tree of Life Temple in Pittsburg, the Mosques in Christ Church, New Zealand and the bombings in Sri Lanka where over 250 people were killed and over 500 injured. How many more innocent people will be killed by hate and violence?

POLITICAL POLARIZATION & PARALYSIS

To reflect on the mean-spirited aspects of the 2016 campaigns would be simply rehashing a text book example of polarization both in the primaries and the general elections. As discussed in the previous chapter, even the electorate was involved in harassing each other's candidates. News organizations highlighted the negativity of the campaigns and people watching got caught up in the political hysteria. The Million Women march after the Trump inaugural is a perfect example of the backlash and frustration in the country.

The US Presidential Election of 2000 is a perfect example of the difficulties facing a political candidate without solid validation. Whether you are a Democrat or Republican, you would be naive to think that historians will not explore the validity of that election as well as the 2016 election. "Who really won?" will likely be debated throughout time The profiling of voters in Florida and denying citizens the right to vote is reprehensible as well as a direct threat to democracy. When President Johnson signed the Voting Rights Act of 1965, most Americans assumed "Jim Crow" was dead, - yet the presence of racist policies continues to haunt our country.

Sadly the 2020 election was simply a reflection of the manner in which the 45th President of the United States, Donald Trump operated. The anger occurring during that election campaign and after the actual inaugural is historical. Fear is unfortunately the predominant factor that is motivating people's response. There seems to be more and more chaos relating to state budgets police brutality, lack of civility, government harassment, employment discrimination, environmental regulations, access to health care, child nutrition, immigration policies, international relations and the list continues to grow. There are multimillion dollar defamation law suits, and derogatory rhetoric appears on television and the internet. It's indeed telling that in a public statement the 43rd President, George W. Bush, expressed his concern that "bigotry has become embolden in today's world."

That we have lived through this time seems so amazing to me, given that we are all one – that there is no right or wrong – that we are both part of the whole (hole). The English language offers a great number of words that possess different meanings as well as different spellings yet sound exactly the same. In the beginning of this chapter, alone, I've utilized two such examples – One/won and Whole/hole. Certainly, there are many more that can come to mind. The reason I am raising this issue is to illustrate that in prayer the whole is greater than the sum of all its parts.

Given the complexity of our lives and our universe, finding clarity and truth is not a simple task. Prayer and meditation allow us to view life in its totality and at the same time recognizes its limitations. Politics is very different than prayer, yet the Pledge of Allegiance states that we are "one nation, under God, indivisible with liberty and justice for all." Unfortunately, we have lost sight of the "ALL".

SEXUALLY DEGRADING POLARIZATION

We need to move forward together in a deliberate, positive fashion. Doing so in the context of respect renders that there are no losers. Given the manner in which we deal with losses is the test of a real winner. Both political and sexual validation is a moving target. In this day and age, little is left to the imagination. Derogatory comments about women and men as well as their sexual orientation has created a firestorm on the steps of the US Capitol, the US Supreme Court and local religious institutions, be they church, temple or mosque.

The pressure on young girls from pop "stars" with explicit and revealing rock videos is destructive. Similarly, some rap music degrades women and promotes violence. The pressure on men to "perform" or utilize drugs such as viagra can be both demeaning and dangerous. Neither see-through dresses, breast implants nor little blue pills make you a woman or a man. One's femininity or masculinity is simply based on understanding your sexuality, embracing it without guilt, and being thankful to the life force for sharing such a wonderful gift. Chapters 2 and 6 also address the importance of respect and overcoming sexually degrading polarization.

Using the mass media to confirm our sexual validation in turn results in creating another unhealthy polarization – puritanical rhetoric and gutter pornography. Each results in religious havoc and divisive behavior. Both freedom of religion and freedom of speech are protected by the United States Constitution. There has been a viral explosive increase in the pornography industry, the US exports 89% of the world's pornography and it is estimated that it also hosts 428 million porn websites. Exploitation of others undermines our own self worth. In validating ourselves we need to remember not only the importance of our individual rights but also of our responsibilities and the rights of others. Avoiding extremes can help us keep our balance as well as affirming our self-worth. The definition of such extremes will likely vary depending on each person and their experience.

RELIGIOUS FREEDOM THREATENED

September 11, 2001 is an infamous example regarding the state of polarization that has unfolded in recent history. There really are no words to describe the human, moral, and religious fall-out, nor could any words justify such heinous acts on the part of the terrorists. The world looked in horror as the planes flew into the World Trade Towers. The impact reached far beyond the towers themselves – the impact for generations to come is immeasurable.

DC Police had come to the child care center where staff from the agency that I had worked with were conducting a workshop. The center was about eight blocks from the US Capitol and the police told everyone to evacuate – that another plane was heading toward the Capitol (the United Flight 93 plane that crashed in Pennsylvania). The hijackers missed their intended target. The people on that plane were heroes and unwilling to proceed on the terrorist path. The next day I went to the Police Station to thank the policemen for their efforts in reaching out and protecting the staff and children at the child care center during that horrifying ordeal. My next stop was at a school in southeast DC, Ketchum Elementary, There were teachers and students from Ketchum who were attending a National Science Fair; their hopes and potential crashed into the Pentagon because of religious terrorism. Interacting with the little ones at that school was inspiring they drew pictures of hearts and wanted to share them with the teachers who were crying and to send a drawing to the family of Rodney, one of the young students killed on the plane.

The issue of immigration and the increasing refugee population due to war, environmental disasters and political/religious instability has created even more tension. The combination of religion and politics is a deadly, perhaps the deadliest of all combinations. Throughout human existence, people have lost their lives in battles arising from or with the supposition that "God" was on their side. God reflects no specific religion and to assume a monopoly regarding the Creator could be viewed by many religions as blasphemy. Nevertheless, few religions seemed deterred by such "blasphemy"; thus, such religions can be seen as tools used by powerful interests towards secular goals – often employing war in the attempted achievement of such goals. A "Holy" War, be it with weapons or words, is an oxymoron. Continuing to take a parochial view of religion and politics will likely result in unending wars and terrorism. Until we are able to embrace a paradigm of Peace on Earth that includes ALL religions, those who benefit from war and a fear based mentality will continue to use their power to perpetuate religious and political havoc and destruction.

Intimidation and hate whether on a small or large scale can be viewed as forms of terrorism. The Westboro Baptist Church of Topeka, Kansas prey on the families of slain American soldiers. Their lack of sympathy and empathy for the grieving families is appalling. They attend funerals carrying signs stating "God hates homosexuals and that our war deaths are evidence of His judgement on America." Freedom of speech and religion are sacred and we need to overcome the modus operandi of groups that reflect religious dogma "preying" rather than "praying". Such dogma promotes polarization and hate mongering. On a personal note; a friend on the mountain encouraged me to attend her Bible Study class in January, 2008. At the first class, she giggled and told me everyone had to share something that was not necessarily known. I shared the fact that I was extremely grateful for our friendship and that there were certain topics we just didn't discuss, like politics. Then one of the women in the class made the comment "You must be very excited about the inaugural." I of course shared the fact that I was thrilled. In turn another woman in the class stated that "most of us didn't vote for Obama but we are still praying for him." To be perfectly honest I didn't miss a beat and responded "that's great he needs all the prayers he can get." We all laughed.

Eight years later, on a similar note, Friends at Quaker Meeting ask for prayer and light for Donald Trump as well as sharing the message of peace and love for all those who are afraid of what will happen in the future regarding health insurance, education, the environment, employment, immigration, refugee status and the anti-Islamic rhetoric.

Religious freedom is a cornerstone of the United States Constitution and is guaranteed by the First Amendment. Thank goodness many have evolved beyond the negative rhetoric, ranting and behavior of fundamental extremists. I am pleased to share that, in November 1988 the United Nations approved a resolution to eliminate all forms of religious intolerance. It's still a struggle however it's a struggle that I am praying together we will overcome.

CHALLENGING THE SILO MENTALITY

It's a pleasure to share that in October 2017 in the mountains of West Virginia there was a special forum "Building Trust in an Age of Hate" sponsored by Covenant Church, Washington County Interfaith Coalition and Ezekiel's Place. There were over 100 people who attended. The pastor from Covenant Church (a fundamentalist evangelist congregation) and representatives from the Islamic Society of Western Maryland spoke. It was refreshing and enlightening to witness the friendly interaction and intelligent discourse. The Iman spoke of the loving message of the Quran and the Pastor spoke of key family concerns that united us all. The Iman joked that we are all cousins while the Pastor playfully offered to baptize him. The audience was strongly encouraged to "Love Thy Neighbor" and share a delicious Halal Dinner graciously offered by the hosts of the event. People engaged in one on one conversations focusing on the similarities and respecting the differences. It was indeed moving that persons of the Islamic faith were offered a special room to honor the fact that they had evening prayers. A Baptist church making space for Moslems to practice their evening prayers is a loving step in the right direction. It was heartening to participate with a group of people who were committed to get past the silo mentality that is perpetuating hate and threatens religious freedom.

Unfortunately, in Charleston WV in March 2019 Islamophobia was blatantly displayed at the WV Capitol. There was a poster connecting a Muslim congresswoman, Rep. Illhan Omar (D-Minn.) to the 9/11 terrorist attacks. The poster was at a table in the Capitol's rotunda, at an event sponsored by the WVGOP. It featured Rep. Omar under one of the New York Twin Towers burning with the caption "Never Forget" and then embolden under the picture of the representative's face "I am the proof you have forgotten". Chaos broke out which led to the resignation of the Sargent of Arms of the West Virginia House of Delegates who had been accused of using anti-Muslim slurs. In July 2019 in North Carolina at a political Trump rally reference was made regarding Congresswoman Omar and the crowd was encouraged to chant "SEND HER BACK! SEND HER BACK!" In response Omar truly rose to the occasion and quoted Maya Angelou "you may shoot me with your words, you may cut me with your eyes, you may kill me with your hatefulness, but still like air I'll rise."

The bottom line is that we need to reach the understanding that we are ALL One – one under heaven; inhabiting planet earth until we return to dust – we are ALL simply a "peace" of the whole. In the interim we can choose to love one another as we love ourselves. Polarization undermines everyone's self-worth and devalues the worth of peace within as well as any possibility of PEACE ON EARTH.

ACCEPTANCE & DENIAL

The racial tensions experienced in our country are exacerbated by the media which intensifies the polarizing atmosphere. In turn, young black men or a young white woman are killed; be it in Ferguson, MO or Sandford, FL or at a riot in Charlottesville, VA between White Supremacists and persons opposed to hate. Police killings of black men have triggered protests and riots throughout the country including Martinsburg, WV and Baltimore, MD. These tragic incidents are unfortunate. Perhaps Rodney King, victim of a police beating resulting in the subsequent 1992 riots in LA, summed up the issue most succinctly: "People, I just want to say, can we all get along? Can we get along? …." Issues concerning acceptance and denial have long been an ongoing challenge throughout the United States and the world, be it related to race, religion, ethnicity or gender. Probably the most intense police killing captured in real time was the murder of George Flloyd in Minnesota, in 2020; a police officer had pinned Mr. Flloyd to the ground digging his knee into his neck. his gasps for breathe still sends shivers down my spine as Mr. Flloyd cries "I can't breathe I can't breathe" while two other officers simply watch as he is dying. That brutal police killing triggered a number of protested "Black Lives Matter" banners and marches occurred throughout the country and the world.

During High School, I had the opportunity to volunteer at a drug program in Newark, NJ called Integrity House. During the 1970s, Newark experienced a number of riots coupled with an ever growing drug war – neither of these events had bode well for the city's economic viability nor sense of unity. While driving to Integrity House near Lincoln Park, I was stopped by a police car; the officer was concerned that I might be lost since it was dangerous for a "clean cut white girl" to be driving in the inner city. I explained that I was volunteering at Integrity House a Drug Treatment Center that was only a couple blocks from where he stopped me. He was gracious and offered to have me follow him to the Center (this was prior to the era of GPS aided navigation) and I was grateful.

When I arrived at the program, they asked me to help in the office and file some of their newsletters. One of their clients was also working in the office and he kept staring at me. I asked if there was anything wrong? He got tears in his eyes and simply said that before he went through the program he would have raped me just because I was white. Now that he understood the importance of every living soul, including himself, he simply was glad that I had come to volunteer. When it was time to leave he insisted on walking me to my car because he wanted to make sure that I got there safely. Looking back I realized I was personally experiencing a socially significant period in history when we were overcoming difficult polarizing times. Regardless of race or socio-economic background, be it a white policeman, a black ex-addict or young white high school student; the catalyst is and was acceptance and getting past fear. Senator Cory Booker gave a positive update as to the status of integrity House (see Chapter 2).

Anyone living in our nation's capital is constantly confronted with both acceptance and denial – usually more denial than acceptance. My play "STATE OF DENIAL" won best production in the Source Theatre Festival in DC in 1992. Little did I know that not only was I a playwright, but that I was also prophetic since the main theme focused on a powerful political figure that was having an affair with an intern. Granted the characters were on Capitol Hill rather than the White House, yet it was an omen and reflective of Clinton's denial that "I did not have sex with that woman" – a quote that will continually dog his presidential legacy. On a more positive note, the play included a monologue urging understanding and the hope that one day we would see an African-American elected President of the United States Have you ever wondered what would happen if politicians accepted responsibility and overcame denial? Extending that concept; what if we accepted our own responsibility and stopped denying our own roles in society? What would happen if we decided to act out our dreams rather than deny them? There likely would not have been a Civil Rights Movement if these questions were not answered in the affirmative.

In January 2001, I had the unique opportunity to hear Gary Younge, a columnist and feature writer for the London Guardian, address a public forum. I was visiting friends in England and we went to a symposium honoring Dr. Martin Luther King, where Mr.

Younge was the keynote speaker. I had no idea that this event was planned yet I was thrilled when my friends suggested it - crossing the Atlantic to celebrate Dr. King's birthday turned out to be a real treat. I had worked on the 20th Anniversary march and the legislation to make Dr. King's birth date a federal holiday.

The message of the slain Civil Rights leader is clearly universal as was Gary's speech "lifting as you climb". I was so impressed with the discussion that I bought his book NO PLACE LIKE HOME: A BLACK BRITON'S JOURNEY THROUGH THE AMERICAN SOUTH, tracing the history of the Freedom Riders and their landmark journey in 1961 to challenge the practice of racial segregation in the south. It touched me on a historical basis as well as on a personal level. During my career, I had the privilege of working with a number of persons involved with the Student Nonviolent Coordinating Committee (SNCC). I was excited to learn that the Freedom Riders met to discuss their plans at Friendship House. Friendship House is a community center in Washington, DC, which coincidently has close ties with the organization I worked with – the Washington Child Development Council (WCDC). I have to admit I was somewhat awe struck the next time I attended a meeting there.

However, it was Gary's personal observations that really hit home. At the end of his book he spoke of his own frustrations with racial discrimination and dealing with Customs in the United Kingdom. The irony and reality is that during my flight to London I realized my passport expired only two months prior. To say that I panicked was an understatement. I spoke with the Stewardess and she reported my situation to the head Steward who in turn reported my quandary to the Captain. As we were over the middle of the Atlantic, I had visions of being given a parachute and life preserver and told to jump! I was informed they were wiring Heathrow that I was coming. The response received aloft was that officials would meet me at the gate. Was I going to be arrested? Deported? Needless to say, I couldn't sleep. I sat in my seat trying to think positive thoughts.

Once we landed, a woman who was extremely young met me at the front of the plane. She pulled me aside and said that the airline should never have let me on the plane; moreover, her only suggestion was to simply smile and be very polite to the Custom Officer. Dah! That was it. Before walking up to Customs I took a breath mint and two very deep breaths. In an epitome of anticlimax, I walked through Immigrations and Customs without any problems whatsoever. I never mentioned the expiration date of my passport and neither did the officials; they simply told me they hoped I enjoyed my visit. By the time I got on the double-decker bus I was ready to kiss the driver. I tried several times to call the American Embassy while I was in London to see about renewing my passport and all I kept getting was a recording. I decided to take my chances and keep smiling. The worst that could happen on the trip back was that I'd get deported – and that was the direction I was going. I wasn't stopped once either in the United Kingdom or in the United States. When I shared this story with WCDC's Program Administrator, who was from the Dominican Republic, she laughed yet she pointed out a very obvious fact, I was a well-dressed white woman (this was before 9/11 with the subsequent airline guidelines and federal screening). The inequities can't be denied though that doesn't mean we have to accept intolerance itself in silence.

The Program Administrator's assessment was insightful and captures the manner the world views people of color or people who are different. The polarization has become even more intense. The immigration ban regarding Muslim countries and the immigration policies are being applauded by some Americans and challenged by others. Through my travels through life, I have learned that intolerance comes in all shapes and sizes and fortunately love also has many faces. The freedom to question also requires respecting one another which is truly a blessing. Again, I am reminded of the importance of the Golden Rule.

OVERCOMING MORAL & POLITICAL WRECKENING – HAUNTED BY GHOSTS

As our world, nation, individual states and communities grapple with our ghosts finding balance becomes more and more difficult

The message of love and tolerance is critical, again a reflection of the importance of the Golden Rule.

In 2019 the Commonwealth of Virginia is embroiled in political turmoil that has been a cruel reminder that we are haunted by our past ghosts – both racist and sexual oppression. Virginia was the capital of the Confederacy and one of the last states in the country to desegregate its public schools and abolish miscegenation laws. Unfortunately, it's no surprise that top ranking politicians had appeared in "black face" during their college years in the late 20th century. Sexual abuse has also haunted the halls of power regardless of geographic location and the title of the perpetrator be it President, Senator, coach, clergy, doctor, producer or whatever authority figure and possibly even friend. Neither South nor North; Black nor White, Republican nor Democrat can afford to deny the ghosts.

We are naive to assume that we are not haunted by ghosts. At a meeting of prominent leaders in Washington, DC a facilitator instructed the people gathered to break-up into groups and put together a little talent show. It was rather amusing seeing CEOs of major companies and community activists deciding what they were going to perform. One group began to sing "ol' Virgini" and a number of African Americans voiced their discomfort at that song being sung. I was glad that we could have an open dialogue about the less than appropriate choice of song. At that same meeting a number of the black male executives explained the difficulty they had hailing a cab to get to the meeting. I truly believe that those singing the song meant no offense they just weren't aware of the negative connotations - they had never experienced racism first hand. Apologies were made and accepted - and a lesson was learned - the scars of slavery are deep regardless of how melodic the tone - it still stings and it will continue to sting until a black man can hail a cab without fear of discrimination.

The pain of such discrimination is both personal and institutional. In 2001 the state referendum in Mississippi proposing the continuation of flying the state flag including the Confederate flag in the design was approved by the voters by a landslide. Such a victory is hollow given the negative symbolism. Accepting the rebel flag is in effect ignoring the fact that it is used by the Klu Klux Klan to promote hate. Americans would never vote to change "Old Glory" to incorporate a swastika. Until we recognize the struggle of ALL Americans - state by state, city by city, block by block, home by home we will continue to confront symbols that reflect the injustices perpetuated by hate and racism. Once justice becomes a reality the symbolism becomes secondary - until that time the symbol can prove to be a divisive force depending on the message and the messenger.

It is truly symbolic and reflective of change that the Northern Virginia Urban League has located its office in a National Historic Landmark, located in Alexandria, Virginia since that property, from 1826 to 1836, was once one of the largest slave trading companies in the United States. It is estimated that 3,750 slaves had been purchased, traded and transported from that site to the Deep South. During the Civil War the building was used as a military prison and by the end of the war it was used as a hospital for black soldiers and as a barracks for contraband-slaves who fled Confederate states and sought refuge with Union troops. In 1988 the property which was previously known as the Franklin and Armfield Slave Market was dedicated in the name of Henry Bailey who had been held as a slave in the building and sold into slavery in Texas. When Bailey was given his freedom he traveled by foot to Washington and founded five churches and two schools still in operation today in the Washington metropolitan area. The building now owned by Northern Virginia Urban League will be known forever more as "Freedom House" where a variety of projects are sponsored to assist African Americans and others in need to achieve social and economic equity through advocacy, direct services and facilitating constructive dialogue and programs to encourage greater cooperation between the races. A site that was once a bastion for slavery is now designed to be a means of empowerment and hope.

It is indeed fitting that Ruth J. Simmons is the 18th President of Brown University. Dr. Simmons has an exemplary academic background and credentials - clearly demonstrating the stamina of this outstanding African American woman. Yet the fact she is now stewarding this prominent Ivy League school is a testament to change given the fact that Brown University was founded by Nicholas and

Joseph Brown, who had achieved their wealth by manufacturing and selling slave ships and investing in the slave trade. Dr. Simmons eloquence in rising above is addressed in the following speech she gave:

'How do we form, maintain and affirm the kind of rich social context in which we respectfully acknowledge rather than denigrate difference? How do we ensure that, using many different lenses, we come to see better the limitations of the socially constructed categories that divide us? How can we ensure that education itself is a resource to us in navigating these often perilous waters? Answering these queries is one of the most important dimensions of learning, for in seeking answers we have the opportunity both for agility and generosity of intellect and for a continuous expansion of methodologies and areas of learning." When asked whether she experiences racism given her new status she politely answered "Everyday."

Robert Peck in his book *The Road Less Traveled* stated that "love is volitional." I truly believe that racism and sexism are forms of hate and therefore we need to be volitional in acknowledging, challenging and changing both public and personal perspectives. Love is clearly a way of overcoming racism. Government can pass anti-discrimination laws but it is "We the People" who need to put it into practice. It takes time and patience. Slavery is not something that was just invented and abolished. We must recognize slavery as a dehumanizing venture for economic gain. Even in today's society, young African, Asian and Latin American children are being sold into slavery as was noted in the UNICEF report "The State of the World's Children 2001". Yet to date the political indignation of such abhorrent practices is less than heroic. Almost two decades later an estimated two million children are exploited annually, forced into slavery as prostitutes and militia in an effort to overcome object poverty.

Racism is definitely not a new phenomenon - it has existed throughout history in both secular and religious venues. Even in ancient Greek mythology there have been studies done that suggest that Athena was black. Martin Bernal the author of The Black Athena states that the political purpose of his book was to lessen European cultural arrogance. Archeologists are now reporting that the depiction of the Christ as "blue eyed and blond" is probably misleading and the fact is that given his Semitic roots he was dark skinned with dark eyes. Yet prejudice and bias is a tough taskmaster. While attending church there were a group of teenagers that were performing the fourteen stations of the cross; the young man playing Christ was Caucasian and had abs that were washboard tight; Pontius Pilate was played by a Hispanic - when in fact the young man playing Pilate probably looked more like the real Christ - yet racism, conscious or subconscious can project a reality that embraces its prejudices.

Whether believing the Christ to be the son of God, a prophet or simply a man his words from the cross, spoken over two thousand years ago, still echo today: "Father Forgive Them For They Know Not What They Do."

MEDIA MESSAGES – MANIFESTING THE WORD

During World War II, Hollywood played a key role in promoting the national spirit and support for the boys on the frontline. Utilizing "star" power was deemed crucial to the war effort. Times change and television media brought the Civil Rights movement and the Vietnam War into people's living rooms. These televised historical events brought "ordinary" people face to face with human realities – good and bad; and in the case of Vietnam and the Civil Rights movement – bloody evil. Despite much of the cruel footage, while I was in high school I learned a valuable lesson - media does screen the news.

A friend of mine was devastated that her father's pharmacy had been burned in the 1968 riots. I didn't understand since the riots were not being reported on the evening news. Who do I believe – my friend or the television newscasters? I of course took my friend's word and at that point acknowledged the power of television in shaping our view of the world – whether based on fact or reflecting the desired views of the power-elite. The use of the internet and its viral capabilities is tremendous and expeditiously can prove even more influential.

I have a number of friends in journalism and realize that the politics within the newsrooms impacts on the sound-bites we hear every night. The "spin" over the years has begun to focus on the entertainment aspects of presenting news stories. In all fairness, network news is competing with MTV and the internet for the same audience and therefore believes they need to be more on the edge and present "hip" lead stories. Magazine programs and exploitive "reality" series have proved to be commercially viable for the same reason. It also helped produce Trump. He didn't create the fear and intolerance we are experiencing, he simply is magnifying and manifesting it.

One questions the importance for those in the entertainment industry to understand the difficulty for very young children to distinguish reality from fantasy. I remember walking into a child care center and encountering a group of three year olds surrounding the copier machine. It was a digital system that had an audio feature that spoke – "remove original", "copies completed", "needs toner". The little ones wanted to say hello to the man living in the machine. Most preschoolers assume that the PBS purple dinosaur, Barney, and Sesame Street characters like Big Bird live in their television. Fred Rogers, an icon of children's television, tells a funny story about meeting a little girl who wanted to know how he got out of the box (i.e. the TV). He was patient and took the time to explain the manner in which television worked. He then asked her if she understood – she shook her head in the affirmative, smiled and then asked "How are you going to get back into the box?"

Given the impact that television including videos and video games, have on our children we need to be responsible. The V-Chip that allows parents to block certain viewing is indeed useful. Nevertheless, producing programs designed to meet both the educational and entertainment needs of children and families would be very beneficial. When television started, it was truly a family affair and viewing Ed Sullivan was a Sunday night event that was shared by all, young and old.

Television is not only a part of American culture – it is a means of dictating our culture and style – "Plop, Plop, Fizz, Fizz", "Where's the Beef", "They're GRRRRREAT!" and "Just Do It" are just examples of commercial pitches we've been subjected to over the years as manufacturers try to convince us that we can have brighter smiles. Advertising on the internet is even more intense – with just a click of a button you can buy and sell just about anything including twin baby girls. Establishing safeguards relating to cyberspace is a social as well as a moral imperative. Both sponsors and censors have been instrumental in the development of television as well as the internet and the messages that we hear over the airwaves and through our modems.

Television has always had censors, though broadcasting standards have become extremely lax. For whatever reason, the negative and positive aspects of life have invaded our homes . I have had my own personal experience dealing with television censors. When I was approximately ten years old I was thrilled that my friend and I were on the children's program WONDARAMA with Sonny Fox - one of the first game shows for kids. I was chosen to tell a funny story or joke about my family. I told Sonny the story about my Dad being told that my sister was a boy when she was born – it really was quite amusing. One of my mother's doctors was watching her C-section from the observation booth and he mistook the umbilical cord for a part of the male anatomy. He went out to the waiting room and informed my father that he had a son. Only a few minutes later, the surgeon came out to congratulate my father on the birth of his new baby daughter. Needless to say, my father was rather confused; the surgeon went back to check and returned confirming that in fact his baby was a girl. Eventually the other doctor came down to apologize and noted that he needed new glasses. Even though Sonny laughed when I told the story and although I never mentioned the word "penis" the segment was considered too sexually revealing and was cut. Given today's standards the conception as well as the birth could be shown on prime time television! There is something to be said for childish innocence having a more positive impact than in your face explicit sex.

In the same manner that polarization usually creates anger, aggressive action on television also results in some children acting out aggressively. While many might find this statement controversial, those working with children routinely witness such behavior first hand. Once, I was shocked to discover as I walked into a child care center that there were several children, between the ages of three and four, who had broken arms and legs. Answering my concern that there had been an accident, the teacher explained that the boys were pretending to be the Incredible Hulk and jumped off the bookcase together and the bookcase fell. Luckily bones can heal, unfortunately, some childhood games prove more deadly. In Florida a twelve year old boy killed a six year old girl when he was simply playing and practicing the wrestling stunts he had seen performed on the World Wrestling Federation.

Since the election of the 45th President, teachers across the country have witnessed an increase of violence and bullying. Teachers say they're being terrorized by unruly students as young as six; in a Pennsylvania school district, 45 teachers resigned since the start of the school year. Unfortunately, violence in the classroom is not new. In the play, TORCH, an actual scene that occurred in West Virginia is described when I was a substitute teacher. During that time, I witnessed children hitting each other with chairs, and the verbal abuse was even more shocking with a little boy telling a little girl that she was going to hell because she didn't go to his church.

To blame or absolve the media for the rash outbreaks of violence in schools would be overly simplistic. I had the opportunity of volunteering on the MILLION MOM MARCH and helped with coordinating speakers. The strength and commitment of the mothers who had lost their children to gun violence was awesome. The courage of the young people who had been shot and survived was unbelievable. It was truly amazing that they were all determined to turn their own personal tragedy into a national wake-up call. Unfortunately, it will take more than a march – it will take political resolve combined with spiritual solace. As the number of children who fall victim to gun violence continues to increase seemingly without abatement, especially in schools, my prayers go out to those shot as well as to those tormented to the point of pulling the trigger. Is it polarization and fear that has created an environment resulting in the situation we face as a nation, unable to pass "sane" gun regulations after the shooting of a US Congresswoman in Tucson, Arizona, and the killing of young children, teachers and staff at Sandy Hook Elementary School in Newtown, Connecticut? It is a sorry commentary that there are a number of people who believe the shooting at Sandy Hook never occurred – it brings polarization to a whole new level and denial to an all time high. If only the nay sayers were correct, the children killed in Newton would still be able to enjoy spending fun birthday parties with their families instead of having their lives cut short by bullets.

The young people who survived the Parkland shooting at Marjory Stoneman Douglas High School have taken to the streets and are organizing. They have not been intimidated by a gunman's bullet or the political muscle of the National Riffle Association (NRA). The unfortunate murders of their friends and teachers has motivated them to speak truth to power – that fear and inaction to establish sane gun safety laws is more devasting than guns and bullets. Their heartfelt actions are inspiring and a testament to those who have lost their lives to gun violence. I am praying they can overcome the political inertia as well as the mean spirited media generated by the NRA.

TECHNOLOGICAL ADDICTION

Pope Francis has made a plea to families to limit the use of cellphones. He also urged people while attending mass in Rome to put down their phones and lift up their hearts.

Communications have become minimized even to the point of rudeness. Dependence on artificial intelligence responses can be convenient be it via e-mail or voice mail however they can also be dehumanizing and frustrating. In fact, one can even question the "intelligence" when misinformation goes viral. Making a true heartfelt connection that includes an actual hug is a plus in human interaction.

The use of Facebook is one dimensional. The term "defriending" brings the concept of rejection and hateful dialogue to a virtual reality that can prove counterproductive and mean spirited. Even the term "friend" can be misleading on Facebook. A friend during a group discussion shared that she had heard that a person with numerous "friends" posted on his Facebook page was so pleased that he organized an actual party to celebrate having over 100 friends and only two people showed up. During that same group discussion another friend shared her concern that the term "friend" in cyberspace is at best an acquaintance. (the disrespect and disconnect via technology is discussed in Chapters 2 and 6).

Dealing with website prompts or attempting to reach a cos-tumer representative that has a pulse can result in high blood pressure. Jobs are being lost to IT and in the process humanity is losing the ability to interact with fellow homo sapiens. Some may consider that IT is giving people more freedom. However, freedom at what cost? Is this technological addiction creating a wider gap between the haves and have nots? Children are becoming glued to their IT devices and getting lost in virtual reality. Can this virtual reality desensitize the next generation? Is the line between reality and fantasy becoming more blurred and we are becoming more disconnected as a society?

A drone can cause collateral damage without any remorse. The fact that we are at a point in history when we are discussing drones and totally automated cars sounds more "Sci-Fi" than current events. Are we or Hal from *2001 Space Odyssey* in charge? An auto mechanic was complaining that with the new cars it takes hundreds of dollars in computer chips to open a broken door when in the past it might only take less than $5.00 for a new key or a coat hanger to jimmy the lock. A medical technician was bemoaning the fact that a patient's records were lost in cyber space and couldn't be downloaded; therefore the patient couldn't receive medical treatment. OUCH!

BEYOND THE CHAOS

Beyond the chaos there is spirit that is ever present and everlasting. To transcend the toxic pollutants, be they physical, emotional, social, environmental, political or cultural is the purpose of our being. Polarization pushes our buttons for better or worse and can help us transcend the chaos and free the spirit. Suffering is a way of evolving. This can be viewed as a rather painful way of experiencing freedom, however, once we understand the vital role acceptance plays in our being alive as well as compassionately de-taching, we begin to be aware of the joy of peace and sharing. We have the choice to curse the darkness or be a beacon of light and love. As a result, uncondi-tional love becomes a healing balm and our souls become one and the essence of the Golden Rule (or its equivalent in whatever belief system you follow) takes center stage. To get past the state of fear is crucial and results in overcoming past pain and greed. I learned from Elisabeth that many people fear death and in truth there is no need to fear it. As is discussed in a number of sections in this book, the Bible along with a number of enlightened writings have highlighted that there is no need to fear.

I have had the blessing of volunteering for hospice. Watching persons transition and being there for them is both a blessing for those transitioning and those of us witnessing. Simply being there is a beautiful experience. Unfortunately, the woman I had been visiting had a roommate who watched TV news 24/7 and as a result I have had to assure the Hospice patient I am visiting, that she need not fear; that no one will kidnap her or bomb the nursing home. To comfort her I held her hand, smiled and told her fun stories. I also put my hand on my heart and encouraged her to put her hand on her heart. By the time I left her bedside we were both smiling. Over time, I am extremely grateful that when I come to visit the TV is turned off. During one of the visits she told me she wanted a McD hamburger. I am a vegetarian. Obviously she was not a vegetarian, and at this stage of her life I wasn't about to tout the virtues of vegetarianism. I simply accepted her desire for meat and took joy in her joy of eating a hamburger, no pickle or onions, only ketchup. Opening our hearts is truly a gift for all concerned, both the giver as well as the receiver.

TAKING A STAND FOR CHILDREN

In 1996, I volunteered with the Children's Defense Fund's efforts to mobilize a rally in Washington, DC on the National Mall. The purpose of the Stand for Children Rally was to demonstrate the importance of providing quality education, preschool programs and comprehensive health care services to children throughout the country. Over 300,000 people attended the event. It was the catalyst for the US Congress to approve the Children's Health Insurance Program (CHIP). Over two decades later the children of West Virginia are still struggling to gain access to quality educational services and live safe healthy lives.

To highlight the challenges faced by children living in West Virginia, there is a European company that is proposing to build an industrial factory that will be emitting toxics including formaldehyde, sufhur dioxide and arsenic right across the road from an elementary school. Because of the negative environmental impact this company is prohibited from building this type of factory in their own country. I was awed by the community mobilization to fight this threat to their children's well being and the environment. On May 16, a coalition of community groups sponsored a Rally & Moral Action at the construction site in the eastern panhandle of West Virginia. The turn-out was amazing – over 500 people came including children and dogs.

Folks rode bikes and there were wonderfully colorful signs making it clear that an environmentally toxic factory was not welcome especially across the road from an elementary school. An hour prior to the close of the Rally 24 people including me and Sammi Brown, a WV state Delegate walked peacefully towards the construction site and sat on the road. A special note about Sammi, - I found her to be charismatic, enthusiastic, intelligent and compassionate. She is an African American who WV legislators found to be threatening and they harassed her as she defended issues she supported. Unfortunately, she is no longer in the WV House of Delegates.

The nonviolent march and sit-in lasted about an hour and then the Chief of Police informed us that if we didn't leave the site we would be arrested. When we refused to leave they asked us to stand and put our hands behind our backs and cuffed us. Some of the protesters were placed in a paddy wagon. I waited patiently while the police were trying to figure out the logistics of transporting us. They finally decided to utilize police cars and I was put in a police car with several other women. I was fortunate, rather than getting shoved in the back seat they had also seen me testifying before the Jefferson County Board of Education and cleared the passenger seat and I got to sit in the front seat of the car. As one of the police walked me to the holding cell he whispered that he appreciated what we were doing on behalf of the community. There were about six of us who had to stand in a small holding cell with our hands behind our backs. I was starting to feel a little dizzy. The cops were accommodating and took-off the cuffs got me a seat and a cup of water. We spent about four hours in the county jail and then spent another hour at the Court House where we were arraigned and given a $1000 bond. Extremely appreciated the fact that the organizers provided a lawyer and money for bail. Very grateful for all those who kept us in prayer - a volatile situation was dealt with peacefully and graciously. There are still a number of court cases filed against the foreign company to stop construction and folks traveled to West Virginia's state capital, Charleston, WV, and brought our concerns to the state regulatory agencies and the Governor. It's not a done deal however it is still an uphill battle – while on this journey I am reminded of the Bible story about David and Goliath. The polarization, of those with financial power casts a dark giant shadow over those most vulnerable and innocent. In good faith, I am continuing to pray for the safety and protection of our community, children and the environment. Also have been testifying before the Jefferson County Board of Education (BOE) encouraging folks to summit comments to the WV Department of Environmental Protection (DEP)urging them to rake action that would require the company to take responsible actions keeping our community especially our children safe. As discussed through out this book it's all about the Golden Rule we need to "Love thy Neighbor"

Many environmental experts publicly shared their concerns. Dr. Jerome A. Paulson, MD, FAAP, who is pediatric consultant to the Mid-Atlantic Center for Children's Health & the Environment, also known as MACCHE. MACCHE is the Pediatric Environmental Health Specialty Unit (PEHSU) that serves, West Virginia, Pennsylvania, Delaware, Maryland, Virginia and the District of Columbia. His review of the projected impact this factory will have on the surrounding environment blew my mind and broke my heart.

In an effort to help educate people Dr. Paulson welcomed the community groups to circulate his review. His study was based on the fact that the factory is expected to use 84-90 tons of coal per day and release 152,935 tons carbon dioxide equivalent per year, 238.96 tons nitrogen oxide per year, 147.45 tons sulfur dioxide per year, 67.7 tons of formaldehyde per year, several hundred tons of atmospheric particulate matter per year, as well as various volatile organic compounds. The plant will be built with two, 213 foot tall smoke stacks. In a letter sent to the community Dr. Paulson stated "Some of the local impact will be decreased by the tall smokestacks. While not preventing the production of the pollutants they will disperse some of them far downwind from the local community and compromise the health of the populations downwind. One of my colleagues at MACCHE has developed some maps of the local area which includes Maryland, Virginia as well as West Virginia. The first map indicates that there are several elementary, middle and high schools within 5 miles of the factory site. In addition, there are many churches and child care centers within 5 miles of the factory. The second map adds in potential farm land. We do not have information about what that land is actually used for; but we would be concerned about contamination of the land itself or contamination of crops grown for human or animal consumption." Dr. Paulson further concluded that "the increase in the pollutants in the local atmosphere will present health threats not only to the children in the elementary school, but to the community as a whole. That said, it is important to recognize that given the physiologic, anatomic and behavioral differences between children and adults, children are often at greater risk of adverse health impacts of pollutants than are adults…. It is well documented that children growing up in areas with greater amounts of air pollution are likely to show decreased lung function as young adults relative to children growing up in areas of less air pollution. Particulate pollution can certainly exacerbate asthma in both children and adults. There is increasing evidence that air pollution is neurotoxic to children in utero and to young children. I agree with the community that it is not prudent to build this plant so close to an elementary school."

PROMOTING DISHEARTENING POLICIES

Actions taken by the Trump administration – have brought out a firestorm of polarization. Actions relating to immigration have been hateful and generated fear. The issue of anti-Muslim polices was demonstrated when there was a targeted travel ban on several Muslim-majority countries. It saddens me that the discrimination we are witnessing spotlights a very dark-side of a populist agenda

SOULFUL COURAGE

that the administration is exploiting. Because of the hardline polices the Immigration & Customs Enforcement (ICE) officers are literally and physically sending shivers throughout immigrant communities.

Unfortunately, discriminatory policies also existed in the 20th century. A number of early childhood programs contacted me because they were very up-set over the fact that they received telephone calls from the US Department of Agriculture personnel that only Americans could participate in the child care food program therefore any child looking like an alien would have to be dropped from the program The request was outrageous and discriminatory. I quickly sent a letter to the child care centers informing them that if the child did not resemble a Martian they could remain on the food program. If the government official had a problem with that analysis we could have our lawyers contact them. Happy to report thar the centers were not questioned whether any of the children looked like "aliens" again.

The actions taken regarding immigrants seeking asylum at the Mexican border also highlights a mode of operation that creates unnecessary tension and pain. The fact that children were being sep-arated from their parents and placed in make-shift shelters is totally heart breaking. It is estimated that over 2,000 children have been taken from their parents. The Time Magazine cover featuring a two year old Honduran girl crying and the President simply staring down at her with his arms folded in indifference went viral. The picture unfortunately captures the nature and tenure of the immigration pol-icies – "zero tolerance". Yes, the picture was photoshopped and that particular little girl was not separated from her mother. However, her tears are reflective of a chaotic and unwelcoming atmosphere as well as the thousands of Central American children removed from the arms of their parents. You don't have to be a child advocate or "bleeding heart liberal" to understand that young children are empathetic to other children crying. When as adults did fear/hate replace empathy? When did exclusion trump inclusion (no pun intended)?. We're losing touch with our heart's moral compass. I can almost imagine that the Statue of Liberty is also crying along with the children. The welcom-ing message on the Statue of Liberty is discussed in chapter 6. The all inclusive message on the base of the Freedom Statue on top of the US

123

Capitol dome, with the engraved quote "E pluribus Unum" which in Latin means "out of the many one." is discussed on page 23. What will it take to help us realize that we need to be willing to open our hearts and be open to humanitarian and caring approaches to ALL people especially, children. In December 2018, a young 7 year old Guatemalan girl, Jakelin Caal, died in US Border Control custody. This tragedy is not an isolated cruel human loss; it's simply a reflection of the fact that the moral fabric of our country and the world is being shredded by fear, hate, greed and inequality. The chaos continues over immigration and the border wall in 2019 with the longest federal shutdown in American history being utilized as an ill advised political bargaining tool; resulting in people's lives being inequitably and unjustly jeopardized Unfortunately, this polarizing sentiment is not limited to the United States, though the former President's tweets and policies have made the US a leader in the horrific treatment of immigrants. The EU countries have shut their ports to refugees and as a result a number of refugees have died at sea. Unfortunately, Asia is not exempt from initiating dehumanizing practices including the refuges from Myanmar as well as human trafficking in Thailand (it is estimated that worldwide 2 million children are trapped in the sex trade annually) . It seems that the message shared over two thousand years ago, the Golden Rule, is now falling on deaf ears.

COMPASSION: THE KEY TO FREEDOM & ANTIDOTE TO POLARIZATION

We can get beyond polarization when we are able to focus on compassion. What is compassion? First and foremost it is compassion for ourselves and understanding that we are ALL worthy. Unfortunately, through time we often develop the belief that we are not worthy, becoming angry and resentful. Getting past the anger is critical. Only when we are able to truly love ourselves, are we able to love others with sincere compassion and respect. "Love thy neighbor as thyself" requires an unmeasurable love for one's self, with sincere compassion and respect. Since there has been a rise in anti-Islamic rhetoric and policies along with the overall anti-immigration threats of deportation and building a wall between the US and Mexico, the Friends

Committee on National Legislation has been promoting the slogan: "Love thy Neighbor - No Exceptions". The message that ALL are included is beautiful and helps us to overcome fear.

When we experience an unhealthy energy such as anger, hate, greed, and the like, we project that energy on others and it begins to perpetuate actions such as mud-slinging, road rage, bullying, violence, terrorism, and war. A 1960's slogan "War is not healthy for children or other living things" is as true today as it was then, whether it be in the halls of power, behind closed doors, playgrounds, family gatherings, on air waves or within ourselves. Conversely, compassion unites our minds and hearts in an open and sincere manner while surrendering to the greater good. There is no need for hesitation as this can happen in the "here and NOW" rather than waiting until the hereafter. "Love thy enemy" is more than a quote from the Bible; it is the key to PEACE ON EARTH. Such peace within each of us is the foundation which vibrates a light that shines acceptance. Surrendering is the ultimate acceptance to one's self, forgiving without worrying or judging who is right or wrong. The Divine Truth is the shining Light of compassion – it's overcoming the lies. Freedom embraces anything – everything in a spirit of unconditional love.

As we Pledge Allegiance to the flag of the United States of America, it would be wonderful if we took the words into our heart "one nation under God with liberty and justice for **ALL**." In so doing, there would be equity and compassion, no child would go hungry, peaceful resolution to conflict would be possible - whether it's political, environmental, economic, religious we could resolve it on a personal, local or global level. In the US, one of the financially wealthiest countries in the world there are over 14 million children suffering from hunger and malnutrition. The Annie E Casey Foundation estimates that the child poverty rate is three times higher for African American children.

The singing of the national anthem at NFL games has become a lightning rod reflecting the frustrations and concerns of African American football players who kneel and pray for equality. There are those who see those actions as disrespectful (this issue is discussed in greater detail in Chapter 2).

While the battle of tweets and threats continues; I am moved to focus on greater harmony. The song "Lift Every Voice and Sing" also referred to as the Black American National Anthem is resonating in my Being. It was composed by two brothers, James Weldon Johnson (words) and John Rosamond Johnson (music) in the early 1900's. Maya Angelou titled her book "I Know Why the Caged Bird Sings" based on the song. I thought it would be appropriate, given the challenges we are facing and the heartfelt cry for freedom that is echoing in the world to share some of the lyrics:

Lift Every Voice and Sing

Lift every voice and sing Till earth and heaven ring,
Ring with the harmonies of Liberty;
Let our rejoicing rise High as the listening skies,
Let it resound loud as the rolling sea.
Sing a song full of the faith that the dark past has taught us,
Sing a song full of the hope that the present has brought us,
Facing the rising sun of our new day begun
Let us march on til victory is won.

Accepting that compassion is an initial core component of the life force and that each one of us can be an advocate for, as well as a practitioner of compassion, brings us ALL closer to being one. Reaching that point of compassion while we are alive makes life worth living. Far too many have suffered because of their own lack of self-worth and loss. As with the Beatles song, "All You Need is Love," we begin to realize the importance of uniting our minds and our hearts to promote compassion; in effect all the other stuff is simply stuff especially when the time comes to pass over. And we are ALL going to pass over sooner or later; as Jim Morrison of The Doors often remarked: "Nobody gets out of here alive." Freedom gives us the opportunity to choose – I am writing these words hoping that we can choose love and sharing compassion for the over 8 billion fellow "travelers" on earth rather than fear that will result in polarization and both internal and external war. Given a choice between polarization and compassion – which choice makes sense – both in the long and short run?

During the Civil War a woman from West Virginia named Ann Reeves Jarvis would go onto the battlefield and care for both Union and Confederate soldiers as she explained that each soldier needed care and she embraced all sides because they each deserved a mother's love regardless of the uniform they were wearing, In honor of her mother's devoted selfless care, her daughter promoted the creation of Mother's Day and in 1914 President Woodrow Wilson signed into law that every second Sunday in May would be designated as Mother's Day.

Inspirations and Thoughts from Moments & Windstorms

- Polarization is a negative energy force that can create havoc both externally and internally. Neither is healthy for our growth personally or as a community. Overcoming polarization requires a great deal of understanding and the desire to get past judgment and hate. Unfortunately, the media plays a key role in promoting polarizing messages and images regardless of the venue. Censorship or lack of it sends either a negative or positive message depending on our perspective.

- When confronted with chaos and in prayer for safety there is a desire for compassion. We are witnessing environmental disasters and sacrifice zones. The song written by Woody Guthrie, This Land is your land and this land is my land is an environmental treatise as huge companies pillage the world in the name of profit. It is unfortunately a wholesale approach to robbing and killing all of nature's living beings of their health and breath. The song Almost Heaven which is song by John Denver is beautiful however the environment in West Virginia is being ravaged by chemical toxins and politicians. Jimmy Hendrix singing Freedom is a cry for HELP as well as a battle cry for change. Greta Thunberg a young Swedish girl has been instrumental and spoken out promoting environmental activism.

- We can be open minded as well as open hearted to truly overcome the negative aspects of polarization. The Freedom to choose compassion is the antidote to a polarizing atmosphere.
- Do you find the present politics and reporting of news polarizing?
- Do you have ideas or suggestions how we can overcome polarization?
- Do you believe there will be a time when we will ALL get along?
- What community activities have you witnessed or participated in that you would like to share regarding gun violence and environmental responsibility?
- Do you have any ideas or suggestions relating to gun violence and/or environmental sacrifice zones?

Chapter 5

FLOW OF LIFE

"God we have pushed so many of our children into the tumultuous sea of life in small and leaky boats without survival gear and a compass. Forgive us and help them to forgive us. Help us now to give all our children the anchors of faith and love, the rudders of purpose and hope..." Marian Wright Edelman, Founder Children's Defense Fund

"Real love is a cosmic force which goes through us. If we crystallize it, it becomes the greatest power in the world." George Gurdjieff

"Let justice roll down as waters and righteousness as an ever-flowing stream" Old Testament,(Amos 5:24) KJV

"If your own life is like a graveyard to you, leave children free to see it as a pasture ... destined to live through many inspired moments... Feelings that have no other outlets flow into dreams" Janusz Korczak

"But whosoever drinketh of this water shall thirst again; But whosoever drinketh of the water I shall give him shall never thirst; but the water that I shall give him shall be in him a well of water springing up into everlasting life" New Testament, Jesus (John 4:14) KJV

Given the dangers and inequities confronting our young children, I wanted to share excerpts from the prayer, We Pray for Children, written by Ina J. Hughs:

We pray for the children who sneak popsicles before supper,...
And we pray for those who stare at photographers from behind barbed wire, ...

who are born in places we wouldn't be caught dead, …
And we pray for those who watch their parents watch them die…
We pray for children who like ghost stories, who get visits from
the tooth fairy, …
And we pray for those whose nightmares come in the daytime,
who have never seen a dentist, …
We pray for children … we smother …
And for those who will grab the hand of anybody kind enough
to offer it.

I will never forget the time I went to one of our child care centers at the end of the day with one of my staff to pick up her daughter.
While she went to her daughter's classroom, I took the opportunity
to play with the children in the lobby. We were laughing and giggling
and then suddenly a little boy who couldn't be any older than three
grabbed my hands.

Even at such a young age, his grip was strong and unyielding –
looking into his eyes we connected – he was starved for attention – he
was clinging to me. I had to leave and he was unwilling to let go – I got
one of the teachers to hold him. That chance encounter allowed me to
experience the fear and isolation felt by a three year old child. I couldn't
help but wonder how this child would feel at the age of thirteen and
how he would interact with the world. We can pray for the best and
start taking responsibility. Understanding that both our actions and
our encounters have the potential of making a positive difference.

Simply attending school can endanger the lives of children and their
staff. Unfortunately violence can be witnessed throughout the country
from metropolitan to rural locations and every hamlet in between.

AFFIRMATION

Affirmative confirmation is truly volitional and requires a willingness
and honesty to look at ourselves in the mirror, search our souls, and
ignore stereotypes. Coming to terms with and valuing our own self-
worth is much more valuable than focusing on the diamonds some
actress may be wearing to a glitzy Hollywood gala. True beauty is

allowing our spirits within to sparkle throughout. Prayer is the most authentic way to get in touch with one's spirit. In the book, SEAT OF THE SOUL, Gary Zukav defines authentic power as the ability to release the soul's energy in a loving and trusting manner. The life force within is stable and capable of conscious acts that are focused, intentional and illuminating, generating amazingly positive results.

Unfortunately, our children can experience violence without turning on their television. As I related in Chapter 2, the violence precipitated by the drug war on the streets moved me to the point of going on a fast in 1989. There had been a shooting at an unlicensed family child care home – a person had been killed as a result of an argument over drugs. I went to visit a child care center only to find yellow police tape, an ambulance and television cameras in the parking lot. The bedlam was a media fury reporting a drug bust that had gone bad. Thank God none of the children were outside on the playground; they were all safe.

While I was talking with the staff, the unexpected sound of a pop gun echoed loudly. As I turned around to investigate, I saw that all the children had hit the ground. I was stunned beyond words; when I was a child a pop gun made all the children giggle; we never imagined our lives were in danger. At that moment, I came to the cruel realization that our children were now living in a war zone. Believe it or not, the center was only ten blocks from Capitol Hill – essentially our children were experiencing terror in the shadow of "world class" power.

For the next several weeks I did a great deal of soul searching. I kept reading and rereading Dr. King's book *Why We Can't Wait*. That children's lives were in jeopardy because of senseless shootings was mind boggling. I believed with all my heart and soul that something had to be done. I kept praying and then finally I decided to go on a fast – starting on January 1, 1990 and ending on Valentine's Day. While it was not a fast 'til the death; it was a life affirming fast in hopes of touching the hearts of those in power.

Right before Christmas I called Marian Wright Edelman, the founder and President of the Children's Defense Fund (CDF). She is a very special advocate for children, and I asked if I could come by her house to talk. She obviously could tell from the sound of my voice that it was important. We talked for hours. She was touched by my commitment, and I was moved by her wisdom and solace. I listened intently as she played awe inspiring gospel music on the piano. It is an evening I will always cherish. She made me promise that I would be under careful doctor supervision. I agreed. Marian and a number of staff at CDF were supportive throughout the process.

To this day, I cannot adequately put into words the experience of fasting. After several days I was no longer hungry, but I was incredibly thirsty. All of my senses were heightened; I could actually taste the water, regardless of whether it was bottled or tap. I became very sensitive to perfume and the smell of food. At the very least it was an enlightening experience. As was discussed in the previous chapter, the incident involving Mayor Barry being busted for smoking crack cocaine during my fast only intensified my resolve in continuing the fast. The media began to contact me and I met with a few reporters. Sorting through the media hype became draining. My spirit was nourished through the support and loving prayers of the child care community and of course the fantastic pictures the children drew.

During the last days of the fast my mind began to wander. I had a revelation: people need not fast to show they care, there are other ways to demonstrate one's commitment to children. Consequently, with the help of children's advocates in the city and Councilmember John Wilson, the District of Columbia Drug Prevention and Children At Risk Fund was established with people donating dollars annually when they submit their taxes. It is a voluntary tax check-off and in an era where politicians are proud about cutting taxes, it is indeed refreshing to know that there are citizens willing to pay more to help young children in need. Over three decades later the drug wars are exploding and mental health challenges have been increasing at epidemic proportions as hate rhetoric is becoming more prevalent. Cutting taxes for the wealthy has become the Holy Grail for national, state and local politicians focusing on greed as well as consumed by self serving interests.

Though the political value of Barry's re-election in 1996 could be debated, the spiritual merit is understandable. He was viewed as a warrior for those who have suffered the hardship of drug addiction and poverty. Redemption and healing is a powerful force in the African-American community.

After the 1990 fast, I began to focus on reaching out to Mayor Barry and his family. His son Christopher was around ten years old and I knew first hand that the media circus could be extremely intimidating. I wanted to send him a book but was frustrated that I couldn't find any children's book for a preteen boy with a young Black hero. I decided to send him the book ROOTS by Alex Haley. He sent me a very sweet thank you note saying that he was "reading it at night a lot." During my search to buy Christopher a book, I realized what little value publishers placed on addressing the academic interests and dreams of young African-Americans. This fact simply spotlighted the impact of Mayor Barry's high profile drug sting and made it even more disturbing since he had been a role model for so many young Black men in our city - including his son who became a victim of a drug overdose in 2017

All people need a positive self-image that in turn gives them the confidence to contribute to the world. Authentic power reflects an image that is soul based. In this context, it is interesting to note that the African-American culture is extremely soulful in its approach, whether consciously or subconsciously, creating a means of self-preservation and a powerful mechanism to overcome racism in a biased society. Valuing "being" human and our oneness with God is the bottom line.

Fast forward more than a quarter of a century and drug addiction has become an even greater epidemic in our country. Opiate deaths are increasing on a daily basis both in the inner city and in rural areas. Many professionals attribute the increase to the feeling of hopelessness, isolation and a lack of self-worth.

Marshall Stewart Ball is a brilliant young boy who was born with developmental challenges including the inability to speak or walk. Despite these severe physical limitations, he had the inspirational insight to write the book KISS OF GOD: The Wisdom of a Silent Child. Marshall's goal of sharing his writing illuminates the beauty of being alive and the importance of respecting all people.

Included in his book is the following acrostic poem he wrote as a school assignment:

Man of good thoughts
Angel to all
Real angel giving good
Sharing feelings that go to God
Happy giving to others
Answers that bring harmony
Loving, teaching and
Listening

His creative skills and talents inspired me to write the following:

Butterfly Soaring Free
Overcoming naysayers
Believing in Myself
Being Aware and Fully Conscious Involved and Caring

Heaven's Gentle Hand
Ever Present
Loving / Learning / Listening
Energy and Light
Nothing to Fear
Embraced by the Life Force

Beauty Surrounds Us
Like Lilies of the Field
One Soul Unites Us All
Kindred Spirits – Sharing Laughter and Tears

When one is willing to reach deep within, there is a holy connection that allows one to be centered and to be truly grateful for divine gifts. I found writing this an intriguing exercise that enabled me to explore my soul's purpose. How would you write an acrostic poem based on your name? When there are aspects of your being that affirm your soul and embrace the life force, the "Kiss of God" becomes a reality. Such is truly a win/win experience.

Throughout this learning process of exploring the soul, it is critically important to give thanks to God. Without the support of the life force one's journey is hollow and wanting. Understanding the power of creative cooperation and the oneness of the soul helps us all come a little closer to heaven on earth.

During a meditation a beautiful vision was shared. I was visiting Elisabeth in Arizona and was focusing on the marvelous picture her son, Kenneth, who is a photographer, had given her for Mother's Day. The picture was an infant floating in heaven. The vision expanded and I saw children smiling – children of all races, cultures, religions and nationalities glowing in the stars. I called Kenneth all excited, and shared the vision. He then sent me an initial photo based on the vision. It was wonderful - however there still needed to be more children. He called me and asked "Are we talking about a maternity ward?" I was elated and responded "Exactly! All Children are Stars, twinkling stars!" While writing this story, I am reminded when we had brought hundreds of children to the US Capitol and were waiting to meet several Congressional leaders in the Senate Caucus Room. As we waited, the children began singing "Twinkle, Twinkle Little Star" I am continuing to pray that all children will be healthy, safe and experience peace even in these turbulent times.

I am humbly committed to a Supreme Being and accepting divinity as our true nature. Prayer is a form of petition, and meditation is a form of being open to guidance. The key is understanding the difference and respecting the stillness. Watching the leaves blow in the wind is a blessing and a testament to peace. The peace anthem written by Bob Dylan during the civil rights' movement and the Vietnam War, "Blowin' In The Wind," seems more appropriate now than it did when I was younger.

The ramp up of war seems endemic. There are many more wars we are fighting in a sense of struggle amidst negativity; be it within our families, political tug-of-war, environmental disasters, the drug war, economic, racial and gender inequality, religious battles, bullying in school, on the internet – the list can go on and on. Be it in actual or virtual, we are still searching for answers. The scars remain and the lack of respect is a sad commentary on the human condition and our evolution both personally and globally. Nevertheless, praying for peace within can be a powerfully uplifting experience.

Acknowledging unconditional love for ourselves and others is a life affirming practice bringing us closer to compassion.

CONTINUAL FLOW: CONSCIOUS EVOLUTIONARY ONENESS (CEO)

As was discussed in previous chapters, life is a continuum. Elisabeth spoke about quadrants that reflect our life story. After attending a number of retreats and visiting various contemplative centers while meditating I was struck by the vision of a cross that is embraced by a glistening circle that is a sphere. Within the sphere there are four sections that represent certain qualities. The vertical armature of the cross figure represents the infinite (the Divine or Heaven/Cosmos), the horizontal armature represents the finite (the human or Earth/temporal). Continuing to meditate, an androgynous vision appears that resembles Leonardo Da Vinci's drawing, "Vitruvian Man" reflected in pure radiance. Please note the artist envisions the Vitruvian man as an innocent child which embraces both the male and female essence. There is balance and freedom where all the elements and qualities of the quadrants unite. There is a non-dual energy which becomes apparent, peacefully vibrating in a sparkling orb. Continuing to meditate, a more detailed image appears that elaborates on the picture and the quadrants. The NW Quadrant is the Emotional that involves the heart which reflects acceptance, compassion, joy and empathy; it is the keeper of the Fire Sign Moving clockwise, the NE Quadrant is the Spiritual that involves the spirit which reflects unconditional love, forgiveness, patience and peace; it is the keeper of the water sign. The SE Quadrant is the Intellectual that involves the mind which reflects judgement including anger, hate, anxiety, and fear; it is the keeper of the air sign. The SW Quadrant is the Physical that involves the body which reflects science, gross matter, shame/guilt, temporal and sensual; it is the keeper of the earth sign. These quadrants are designed to spin and converge creating the merging of both the negative and positive energies of all four quadrants – resulting in a oneness and "wHolyness" of being. There's a cosmic awakening. It's the realization of the Christ Mind, Buddha Nature, Allah Compassion, Moses Law YHWH Way, the Great Spirit Being, All is All. It is a glowing illustration of "Love Thy Neighbor" In effect, western and eastern belief systems merging into the brilliance of Mind, Body, Heart and Soul are awakened to join; and there is an overall unity. The sphere representing earth and the Buddhist Wheel of Life as well as the Native American Medicine Wheel converges into a colorful harmonic resonance. There are glowing Islamic and Jewish symbols, the crescent moon and six pointed Star of David (the inverted triangles represents heaven and earth uniting) floating above and within the sphere. The vision includes the crucifix as well as a resurrection manifesting into Divine Love. All of this imagery reflects that even during turbulent times we can witness and experience peace on earth

It would be beautiful when humans embrace the Easter/Passover and Ramadan season as a time of unity and Spring - death/rebirth, crucifixion/resurrection, finite/infinite, and temporal/eternal. Focusing on peace we can faithfully view this merging from a religious standpoint as well as a naturalist perspective which promotes unconditional love. Evolving in a circular flow the physical (science/earth) and spiritual (metaphysical/heaven) merge, while the emotional (heart) and intellectual (mind) become intertwined. The overall vibration of these energies reflects our openness to the union of the human and Divine which Martin Buber describes in *I and Thou*.

I described the vision of the Conscious Evolutionary Oneness (CEO) including the quadrants to a friend, Maria, and she drew the following draft design that included an androgynous child who sparkles (Note: design of CEO can only be used with permission, all rights reserved).

THE CHILDREN WILL LEAD

The United States is sadly in mourning once more for the loss of children's lives because of another school shooting. Students are marching in the streets, standing-up and speaking out for their lives. Their passion and commitment are indeed inspiring. It is reflective of the Civil Rights Movement when African American youth took to the streets. ALL our children deserve to be FREE and obtain an education without fear – being in a safe environment where they can reach their fullest potential. I am moved to tears and at the same time thrilled that there are young adults willing to shine a light on the lack of action on the part of elected officials who refuse to pass sane gun legislation. I am humble and prayerful that through the commitments of the students we will find the balance needed to pro-mote Love. How many more acts of hate have to occur?! Each child and parent who has suffered a loss is a witness to our need to evolve. (There are more discussions on violence in Chapters 4, 6 & 7)

The continuing increase of the number of mass shootings in the United States has created a sense of normalcy that it is unsettling. We need to embrace the Golden Rule. The fact that we are grappling with triple digit numbers of schools throughout the country that have fallen prey to such devastation is beyond words. Parents, teachers and especially students are traumatized. emotionally and physically. Schools hold active shooter drills as regularly as fire drills as a preventive measure, The drills themselves can cause a sense of fear. It's beyond horrific. The students and teachers at Uvalde needed to be safe instead 19 students and 2 teachers at Robb Elementary school were brutally massacred.

Less than one year later an AR15 fire arm, basically a weapon of war was used to kill 3 nine year olds and 3 school administrators at a parochial school in Knoxville Tennessee. Students and teachers took to the streets in a peaceful protest marching to the state Capitol to make their concerns known. Three Tennessee legislators joined the people to voice the need for sane gun legislation to keep the students and community safe. As a result of their act of solidarity with those marching the extremely conservative pro gun Legislator moved to expel the three elected officials committed to protect the children rather than vote to enact much needed laws to address the violent epidemic plaguing the state. The state and country were stunned at the disheartening vote taken to expel two of the three officials Justin Jones and Justin Pearson both young, articulate, compassionate men of color. Gloria Johnson a former school teacher a witness of a school shooting who is white also participated in the peaceful protest however was not expelled. The expulsion vote on her lost by one vote yet it was the horrific actions by the state that helped to galvanize the people to raise their voices even more. The county supervisors voted to return the expelled representatives to the state house as interim officials with the assurance they would support them to regain their seats in the special elections. It was truly beautiful; to watch Representative Jones march into the Capitol with his supporters singing "this Little Light of Mine I'm going to Let it Shine" while Representative Johnson held the door to the House chambers to welcome him back with a hug. Hoping that this is a demonstration of a brighter future for Tennessee and our country as a whole. As Representative Pearson stated you can't expel hope to expel persons on the grounds of decorum as Rep. Jones stated is weaponizing decorum and silencing freedom.

As a result authoritarianism becomes the rule of law. Truth becomes a victim of fascism. The flow of justice is thwarted.

PARENTING

Since this chapter began focusing on prayers for our children by Ina J. Hughs therefore the inclusion of message "Children Learn what they Live" by Dorothy Law also seems appropriate Today's families include both biological and step-families which can result in a great deal of juggling, challenges and rewards.

This is probably the most difficult section for me to write since, as a step-parent, I have no parental rights and it is as if I am grieving the death of a son. As a step-parent I cherished my stepson as if he was my own, yet at the same time I honored both his father and mother. While it is challenging, as adults we need to put our own childish egos aside, and focus on the needs of the children. Being a parent is a sacred task, one of the most important responsibilities we shall ever bear, and offering one of the greatest rewards. While it's not always easy, it is always a blessing. The key to enjoying the maximum fruit is to ensure that each child knows that they're loved and given a spiritual foundation.

In Randy Pausch's *Last Lecture* he talks about the important role his parents played concerning his outlook on life. He shared that their encouragement was essential to his positive attitude even while facing his own mortality. His story reflects the insights that are shared in Dorthy Law Nolte's poem "Children Learn What They Live:"

> If a child lives with criticism, he learns to condemn.
> If a child lives with hostility, he learns to fight.
> If a child lives with ridicule, he learns to be shy.
> If a child lives with shame, he learns to feel guilty.
> If a child lives with tolerance, he learns to be patient.
> If a child lives with encouragement, he learns confidence.
> If a child lives with praise, he learns to appreciate.
> If a child lives with fairness, he learns justice.

Unfortunately, in the case with my husband he experienced the negative lessons. Before we got married, he talked about how important being a parent was to him and how he wanted a positive relationship with his son; not the kind he had with his parents. I realize now he was feeding my ego and I naively accepted the voluminous positive feedback he gave me about being a wonderful and caring stepmother.

When we separated, I experienced a disconcerting state of affairs since I had spent the week before Christmas with my stepson, Will. I had no idea that my husband was going to insist on a divorce. I kept talking to Will that week about the future and how much I appreciated his help, not knowing that he was keenly aware that his future would not include me. Looking back, I feel terrible that he had been placed in that position.

Kids often get caught in the middle of a marital mess, especially when mental health issues are involved. When the commercial says "depression hurts," they are not kidding. I attended the Parent Before Prom reception with Will's mom since his dad refused to go. Will had fun joking that he had two moms, as if we were a gay couple. His father was less than anxious to participate in Will's extra curricula activities.

After the separation, at one point while Will and I were talking, he shared his concern regarding his Dad's state of mind, indicating that he didn't want to isolate himself like his father had done. I assured him that he was a great kid and very different than his father and that I still loved them both and would be there for him. I could see the pain in his eyes – I am quite certain that he could also see my pain. For more than six months prior to the separation, I could see Will pulling away from me. When I questioned my husband regarding this distancing, he told me it was my imagination. Looking back, I realize my stepson was not as good at hiding his feeling and faking it as his Dad.

Emotionally, the pending divorce clearly had an impact on my stepson since he flunked out of college his first year as well as the ensuing summer school. When I offered to talk with him and see if I could help, my estranged husband became vocally upset saying he could handle it. Simultaneously, he told me that Will had asked if he could speak with me. When I asked him about what Will wished to speak about, my ex became agitated saying that he told Will we were both adults and we could talk. That's not what Will nor I needed to hear. He just needed to know that it was okay and that sharing our love is natural and that I was someone who still loves him, would be willing to listen, and help him in any way that I could. A friend later speculated that they thought that my husband might be jealous of my relationship with Will, noting that Will was still financially dependent on his Dad and perhaps didn't want to jeopardize that relationship. Since his father's emotional state was very mercurial, I am quite certain Will didn't want to upset him. Even in the best of circumstances, teenagers tend to live in a world of their own. Bottom line, he knows I loved him and still do – I have sent him birthday presents for the last several years. On his 19th birthday I sent him the following letter:

HAPPY BIRTHDAY!

Birthdays are special and I didn't want to miss your special day. When I packed the stuff in your room I noticed that the red squeeze pillow no longer had a talking mechanism therefore thought I'd get you a new and improved version that still said "I LOVE YOU" to go with the yellow laughing pillow. I will always remember the waffle sherbet treat you made me for my birthday the first year your Dad and I were married. We all had a good laugh. Even though your Dad and I are separated, I pray you realize that I will always love you and greatly appreciate the time we were able to spend together. Take care. Love Always.

My memories helping Will with his homework are priceless. Sharing my passion for the theatre was also very special. I truly enjoyed the fun gifts that I gave him, as well as the fun gifts he gave me. However, being a parent is more than presents - it's about being present. While we were together my husband made a big deal about wanting Will to attend church. My approach was much more low key. I suggested that we talk with him. What ensued was a positive, open discussion, wherein I stressed the importance of realizing that there is a higher power. Furthermore, we needed to understand that it is important to be grateful and from that state of grace to be gracious to all God's people. We talked in my study where I pointed out to him the Norman Rockwell picture of the Golden Rule, "Do Onto Others As You Would Have Them Do Unto You." He seemed to get it without any preaching or proselytizing.

After the separation, one morning I awoke upset because I had a dream about Will having problems in school. I called up his father relaying my dream and telling him that I was concerned about Will. Basically, he said it was none of my business; I guess he's right but it hurts. I love Will dearly and wish him the best, praying that he moves forward knowing he is loved, that he can realize his dreams given the greatest good and overcoming the past traumas.

As I pray, I am constantly reminded that he is God's Will not mine. Will is a child of God whether he attends church or not. I simply was an instrument in helping to nurture him while we were together. That message truly touches my heart as I remember the morning Will's Mom called and told us that Will had been in a car accident on his way to school. His dad rushed to the scene of the accident, promising to call as soon as he knew what was happening. He called later telling me that the car was totaled and that Will was at the hospital. I rushed to the hospital as quickly as I could, not knowing what to expect. Seeing Will strapped to a backboard was frightening. I could also see the fear in his face. I tried to comfort him with a smile, telling him that I had missed him; however I wasn't expecting that I'd finally get to see him strapped to a board! He laughed and I knew then that everything was going to be all right. The only physical damage was a strained pinky finger. They also had to remove the stud from his ear to take the x-rays.

It was truly a miracle. My belief that it was a miracle was confirmed when I drove his mom back to the scene of the accident to pick up her car. Will's car had already been towed away. From what I came to understand, his car had swerved out of control and to avoid hitting oncoming traffic, Will tried to maneuver the car into a church parking lot. He avoided hitting any cars; however, in the process his Prius had flipped over forcing Will to crawl out of the crushed side window.

As we scanned the scene, the only tell-tale signs of the crash were the shattered glass in front of a cross in front of the church. Thank God, that this cross would not mark the death from a fatal car accident. It was truly a loving and gracious irony. I could tell that Will's mom was still shaken and before she got out of my car we hugged. The love for a son is truly a bonding experience.

I realize in retrospect from reviewing past birthdays, how my husband and my own philosophies reflected major differences. On Will's 17th birthday, I had joked telling him I was going to buy him a car – implying a "muscle" car. I bought him a scale model replica of a "muscle" car. We were dining at a Chinese restaurant and a man acknowledged that we were celebrating Will's birthday and noticed the car; he then smiled and winked saying: "I guess the same car outside is yours also." Our jaws dropped; Will and I got up to go outside to look, however his father insisted that we sit down and not make a scene. We'll never know whether there was a muscle car parked outside yet somehow I want to believe that it would have been a neat coincidence. The philosophical difference here is obvious: I would engage in any reasonable activity that promoted joy and happiness while Will's dad, was more concerned with position and appearance.

The last birthday I spent with my husband he was angry and spiteful. He just kept insisting that the idea of being born was painful and gross. He didn't like celebrating his birthday. I am summarizing his feelings and omitting his rather graphic and gross comments. In hindsight, I have come to the realization that you can't celebrate unless you get past the anger. He was angry at his parents and he was projecting that anger on me. As a consequence, Will has suffered the continual fall-out from the stresses and unhappiness's of his parents' environment. I pray that in the healing process we can all experience peace. Reading the *Last Lecture,* by Randy Pausch helped me to understand the perspective of a parent who truly loved his family unconditionally and took great joy in celebrating birthdays. For one of his birthdays I sent Will a four leaf clover paper weight. Each leaf has a message – hope, faith, love and luck..

In Fred Rogers' book *Let's Talk About It: Divorce* he states the obvious "Divorce is a very hard time for families ... a sad and painful time. But it can be managed, and both parents and children can grow by helping each other through it." It's natural to grieve; yet unlike death where there is a burial, a divorce is an open sore or scab at best. Children want a "normal happy" home yet the "normal happy" is relative (no pun intended) My stepson, Will, in his short 20 years of life has experienced divorce up close and personal three times. Will was fourteen years old when his father and I started dating and he was eighteen years old when we separated. For four short years I watched him grow during his formative teenage years. I was really proud of him when he became a lifeguard at the YMCA.

I had a harrowing experience in sharing a neighbor's grief when they lost their three year old son who drowned in their backyard pool. When I went to the wake and saw the toddler size coffin – my heart ached not only for the parents but I could picture my stepson Will in the white satin covered casket. I intellectually understood that Will is a young adult. Nevertheless, in our relationship bonding as a parent/child, I found myself imagining that it was my step son in that casket given the same level of grief that I would have felt had my step son indeed died.

I am thrilled that I shared my passion for theatre with Will and that he returned to school after his accident, enjoying being involved with the theatre department. He is presently employed as a stage manager.

It is important to understand that blaming one gender over the other as being a villain is much too simplistic and counterproductive. A popular book several years ago was "*Men who Hate Woman and the Woman Who Love Them.*" By Susan Forward and Joan Torres. A popular mental health trend consists of labelling the dysfunction as narcissistic or borderline personality disorder. Losing touch with your core spiritual being results in a tenuous and destabilizing situation. There are no winners in divorce. Unfortunately, the biggest losers are the children – moreover, they are the innocent bystanders.

DIVORCE – A "KIDS" PERSPECTIVE

The impact and challenging aspects of a divorce can last a life time. In assessing my mother's perspective, over seventy years after her own parents' divorce she still experienced abandonment issues. In the twilight of her years, she struggled with the challenges of dementia for over four years. It became obvious that her synapses were not necessarily operating correctly. Ironically, before her last hospitalization, she was insisting that she and my stepfather get married in a temple. My stepfather was there for her while she was in the Nursing Home and was supportive. They had been married in a civil ceremony over twenty years before.

When I try to understand my mother's desire to get married in a temple, I began to remember the trauma she experienced when she married my father in the temple in NY over 60 years ago. My mother's closest friend, Rhoda, shared the drama of my parents' wedding and how it related to my grandparent's divorce. My mother was hoping that her father would walk her down the aisle. Supposedly, it was all arranged. However, my grandmother had another agenda. As soon as my grandfather appeared at the temple, she would have him arrested for back payment for child support and alimony.

Rhoda's mother warned my grandfather and as a consequence he never showed up. Needless to say, theirs was a bitter divorce. There was still an ugly aftermath from unresolved anger. My grandfather died before I was born, although I did find a picture of him with my mom and great grandmother at the beach. My mother joked that that picture was probably the only picture my grandmother hadn't torn to shreds or burned.

The reality is that any divorce is no joking matter involving the self-images of each party as well as the "validity" of their opposing positions. My mother's father fostered a great deal of anger from his divorce which he projected onto her. In his Last Will and Testament, he left his money to "his children" omitting my mom – again his child and an innocent bystander. Guilt through association ruled the day as the only children he listed were from his second marriage. In his will he took the overt opportunity to nullify and deny his relationship with my grandmother and as a consequence my mother.

One cannot know whether the action was wantonly cruel or simply a passive aggressive "Bronx cheer." Whatever his motivation, it was very hurtful and painful for my mother.

There is no question that my grandmother harbored ill will towards my grandfather beyond the period of the actual divorce and made sure that his grandchildren knew that he was a philanderer and that he had contracted several STDs. Much more information than we needed to know. I am sorry for my Mother's suffering as a consequence of her Dad's divorce and pray that she can find peace. She passed over in January, 2013; twenty-two days after my stepfather died. I trust that she is at peace with her father, my father, stepfather and our universal mother/father.

Unfortunately, it's not difficult to find young people in our society that have experienced divorce. In fact, many have witnessed multiple divorces. Rather than individualizing each of their trials and tribulations I have synthesized the four common concerns that seem continually apparent for children experiencing parental disintegration. First, they wanted to fix the marriage: "if I am extra good they'll stay together."

Second, they experienced a distrust of the adults for causing the sense of instability in their life. Closely associated with this point was a feeling, whether conscious or subconscious, that the adults had brought "toxic" baggage into the marriage and that they probably should never have gotten married in the first place. This realization creates a terrible spiritual tension since their existence hinged on a marriage that never "should have taken place."

Third, children of divorced parents often display anger at any subsequent stepparent, especially if that person was, or is seen to possibly have been, the cause for the divorce. Also the step-family dynamic can be burdened with increased tensions and instabilities relating to siblings.

Fourth, children of divorce, as adults question their own ability in making the commitment required of marriage and also question the purpose of getting married. Lasting for years after the actual divorce takes place, more disheartening is the fear of loving relationships and their own sense of wellbeing.

One young man stressed the importance of respect and that the need for honest communication was essential. It is strongly recommended that therapy would be very helpful and that any children involved need to understand that the decision to divorce was out of their control and not their fault nor a consequence of any of their actions. Happy family times are stressful and slippery slopes. Staying together for the kids is not necessarily the best solution, however trying to stay as positive as possible in a difficult situation is paramount. In any event, anger and hostility are counterproductive, especially if children are used as weapons. You were blessed with children and though the marriage is disintegrating, the children are caught in the crossfire and deserve exceptional attention, understanding, and love.

CHOOSE TO WALK IN FAITH NOT FEAR

As I struggle with the loss of my own marriage and my stepson, I am coming to the conclusion that the greatest pain consists of not being able to share my love and watch Will grow into the wonderful man I know he has the potential to become. He is always in my prayers and I pray for his well being.

There are scars from bullying whether the attacks were wanton or not. Unfortunately, those who have caused immeasurable pain by mass shootings in schools are simply reflecting the pain they themselves are experiencing. It doesn't make it right, nor is it appropriate to cast a shadow of blame on anyone. We all have the ability to tap into our better angels. The critical questions are when, where and how? - the answers are now, here and unconditional love (forgiveness) We need to understand the continual flow and attempt to maintain balance between the physical, emotional, spiritual and intellectual. A sincere expression of Love overcomes fear and is the cornerstone of faith. When all four quadrants are flowing freely we experience a state of euphoria that is generated from within. Acceptance rather than judgement allows for the Life Force to flow unencumbered. When we are connected to the flow it is impossible to perpetuate harm. It is a choice that deters us from perpetuating havoc and chaos. There is an incredible lightness of being – an immeasurable joy beyond words experiencing "peace on earth"

I am learning that parenting involves both loving moments and challenging windstorms all wrapped into one. Children are truly a gift to be cherished and protected from the shortcomings of inappropriate decisions. The inner child within us all lives forever. There is no age limit to the need for having a loving presence. As a volunteer for Hospice, I have witnessed a number of people in Nursing Homes who feel abandoned and call for their mothers or fathers even though they are 90+ years old.

INNER CHILD

I remember going to a theatre workshop where the instructor was encouraging the participants to get in touch with their inner child. One of my friends simply joked and said "I just want to know how to get my inner child to take a nap so that I can write." To truly get into the flow of life, making friends with our inner child can prove extremely productive. However, getting lost in our inner child story can get us trapped in the past. It becomes difficult for relationships to heal because we are carrying the scars from the past. When we learn to love our inner child, we can then learn to love all the "F"ing relationships discussed in Chapter 1.

An 87 year old Cherokee woman whom I visited in hospice still was carrying the scars of feeling that she wasn't loved because her parents insisted that she deny her Native American heritage. The inner child in me held her hand and sang to the inner child in her a song that I made-up "I am proud to be a Cherokee, I am proud to be a Cherokee, I am proud to be a Cherokee -yes sir ree -yippee!" While singing the song we both smiled.

The process of getting in touch with our inner child may benefit from occasional humor, however, it takes courage. In reviewing my childhood as well as my adulthood trials and tribulations I realize that there have definitely been some incredible bumps I am reminded of Elisabeth's description of life being a bumpy rollercoaster ride. I also remember the quote from *All About Eve* "Fasten your seatbelt;

we're in for a bumpy night." Then there are the mystic writings of John of the Cross who focuses on "the dark night of the soul." Oh if it were only one night. If we're lucky, these nights will last only a night, though these bumps can also last days, weeks, months, years or possibly a lifetime depending on our stamina and perspective. Meditation can help along with a commitment to moving forward, being open to the possibilities within and a boat load of sincere forgiveness which takes us back into the flow (forgiveness is discussed in the last chapter of the book).

There are several childhood memories that have tagged along into my adulthood that might be helpful to share. Staying in the flow with a cranky inner child strapped to our backs can prove counterproductive and tedious if not impossible to be in the flow I am truly starting to appreciate my friend's comment about getting his inner child to take a nap. I've already shared the "skinny" inner child who is reflected in our modern culture regarding women's negative image of their bodies in Chapter 3. The inner child I am open to sharing is the inner child that wants to connect and to be of service. In this process I am aware that I have become committed to overcoming fear and bullies. I have also realized that there are people who feel unworthy of love and/or who have an inner child who lacks empathy and who wallows in insecurities and in turn is defensive and egotistical. Does this sound like any political or elected official that has been seen on the nightly news or who has tweeted lately? Could it be a family member or friend at a holiday reunion? Universally we all want to connect, The key is to be open to the most appropriate manner without creating collateral damage be it in the overall society, our place of worship, office, or our own dinner tables.

Someone at Quaker Meeting stood and shared that Mother's Day was created by a woman in WV for her mother who demonstrated unconditional love. Her mother provided medical care to both Union and Confederate soldiers. Her mother's efforts were selfless She made no judgements and believed Love was a healing balm.

Fast forward to the 21st century. People have shut down their hearts and it all seems selfish and chaotic. Be it on the world stage or family perspective (which is different with each person), we need to

Love ourselves and view each other with respect. True Love is essential to healing - a Love that is simply more than four letters on a card or just lip service. The true inspiration of Love is a reflection of forgiving, acceptance and encouragement. I admit that my inner child is clapping at this time and hoping that others will clap along. We must realize that we can't do it alone, primarily this is an inside job. Even though things are crumpling around us and we never know what's next, the sun is always shining even during the windstorms – we can even witness a rainbow. I am smiling while typing this section and remember seeing the rainbow when my close friend Helen, a fellow child advocate and mentor who passed away.

Rainbows were a special bond between Helen and me. I had never mentioned that bond to anyone. Then a couple of days after she passed a staff person came into the office with a picture her young daughter drew and that her daughter, Amber insisted that the rainbow was for me. The drawing of a rainbow by a young child touched my heart beyond words. I am also remembering the insights that Elisabeth shared and her message that the sun is always shining whether we see the actual sun or not; believing the light is within helps us to shine and sparkle (Quote from Chapter 1).

The inner child within is the shining light – awareness of our oneness with our wHolyness (discussed in detail in Chapter 2). There is a beautiful story about a little boy four years old, who runs into his new born baby sister's room then closes the door. His parents are listening over the baby monitor and can hear him whisper to her: "Please tell me where you came from and who loves us. I am beginning to forget!" We are all forgetting, feeling insecure and becoming distracted by all the noise – be it mass media, computers, twitter or simply being busy being busy.

The concept of tweeting is totally foreign to me as I've mentioned before, I have dyslexia – which in this day and time I consider a blessing. After experiencing numerous life challenges, my inner child is wondering "What's next?" I can't pretend to know. My inner child is hoping that all our inner children can RIP before we die.

Being witness to our dysfunctional health system yet at the same time experiencing the healing balm of faith and the sincere caring of some health professionals is a blessing, With the help of friends I am realizing it is important to be discerning when navigating the medical (both eastern and western) systems. As a friend and I laughed the student who barely passes his/her exams yet graduates medical school, is still referred to as "Dr." and the same is true of alternative practioners no matter how many candles and incents they have burning in their office they might still throw you under the bus. With the present day technological insurance, pharma, hospital loops there is a good chance we can experience high blood pressure, stomach problems and bankruptcy. Healing is a joint venture and an inside job. The key player is the Divine with a whole lot of Love and trusting our inner child. Resting one's wellbeing in heavenly intervention is peaceful and powerful. Our inner child will thank us. Several of the doctors who worked with me considered me a "miracle" Sitting at a hospital; in take lab the nurse noticed that I was wearing a "STOP ROCKWOOL" button and she knew a wonderful massage therapist who supported clean water, air and soil but she couldn't remember her name. I began to laugh and cry she is wonderful her name is Mary she just passed last month. We could both feel her presence and we knew the surgery would be successful correcting the previous challenges confronted. It's been over one year of experiencing medical rollercoasters and fun houses including a number of hospitals and I am still standing.

UNCONDITIONAL LOVE

Many people are uncomfortable with the term "unconditional Love", believing that it is simply theoretical. Unfortunately, there are people who are stuck in their heads and the idea of opening their hearts seems to frighten them to death. Again, we find our way back to the "D" word; and until we are able to be alive without fear of death, people will continue to question the possibility of unconditional love. Perhaps the term "unconditional life" or "universal love" would be more palatable and marketable. However, in respecting Elisabeth's teachings and believing there is a peaceful Presence I am comfortable with "unconditional love." The inner child that has been traumatized by hell and damnation is fearful. Unconditional love is the ultimate act of forgiveness and letting go of fear. Fear arises from our judgments and is simply our human mode of developing barriers in an effort to protect ourselves.

Dr. Elisabeth Kubler-Ross tells a powerful story about a young woman by the name of Golda who survived the concentration camp at Majdanek. While visiting Poland after WWII, Elisabeth had this remarkable "moment;" she noticed a beautiful young girl, with eyes full of sorrow, staring at her. The girl's name was Golda; She was German-born and Jewish. They sat on a patch of grass and shared memories. Golda told Elisabeth that her father had been taken away in the middle of the night by the Gestapo and was never heard from again. In 1944, her mother, older brother, and sister had been deported to Majdanek and herded into a gas chamber, but because she had been pushed to the end of the line by a Capo, there was no room for her to be pushed into the "shower" and the steel door was slammed in her face. In this manner, she became her family's sole survivor. Golda pointed to the crematorium chimney and whispered, "The ashes of my mother, brother and sister floated up there."

Elisabeth asked Golda what she was doing now. She hesitated as if Elisabeth wouldn't understand. But then she told Elisabeth that when she was first liberated from the concentration camp, all she wanted was revenge. In spite of her anger and in order to purge her bitterness, she deliberately chose to help German children who were victims of the war, many of whom were paraplegics. Golda had come to realize that if she focused on revenge, she would be no better than Hitler himself.

Golda explained that she had come back to Majdanek and that she intended to stay at Majdanek until she had completely forgiven Hitler. Elisabeth was amazed and sat there with Golda trying to fathom how within the human mind and heart there could be both the potential for such cruelty and hatred as a Majdanek, and at the same time such forgiveness and love as was epitomized by Golda. Elisabeth began to wonder, if she had grown up in Nazi Germany, could she have been tempted by Hitler's Aryan dream of grandiosity?

Moreover, if she had been mistreated like Hitler had been as a child, how would she have turned out?

Golda was committed to touch one human life and turn it from hate to love; in her mind and heart, this was the reason she was saved. And she touched Elisabeth's life more than anyone else in the world. Golda taught her the lesson of unconditional love – love with no expectations, no "ifs", no strings attached. Golda inspired Elisabeth to go back home to study medicine and human behavior.

Dr. Janusz Korczak who is quoted at the beginning of this chapter and who was a renowned Polish children's author his *book King Matt the First* is a very famous fairy tale in Poland. He was a psychiatrist who was the director of a children's orphanage in the Warsaw ghetto during WWII. When the Nazis came to "exterminate" the Warsaw ghetto of all the Jews – the children were not excluded, and they insisted that all the children be taken away to the "camps." Dr. Korczak did not want the children to be frightened so he told them they were going to march and sing while they went to the trains. While they were singing as they marched to the trains, a Nazi officer recognized Dr. Korczak and told him that he did not have to board the train, Dr. Korczaks reply was: "I will not leave the children, where they go, I will go." Now that's unconditional love! As humans we witnessed one of the world's greatest atrocities – however, unconditional love was present and alive even during a "death march."

It was a historical moment and thrilling event when the Bishop Michael Curry spoke of unconditional love at the royal wedding of Megan and Harry in May 2018. Millions heard him preach, an African American standing before the Queen of England, powerfully stating with compassion "Now someone once said that Jesus began the most revolutionary movement in all of human history, a movement grounded in the unconditional love of God for the world. A movement mandating people to live that love. And in so doing, to change not only their lives but the very life of the world itself. .... For God is love. There's power in love. There's power in love to help and heal when nothing else can. There's power in love to lift up and liberate when nothing else will. There's power in love to show us the way to live.... everything that God has been trying to tell the world -

Love God, love your neighbors, and while you're at it, love yourself. When love is the way, then no child will go to bed hungry in this world ever again. When love is the way, we will let justice roll down like a mighty stream and righteousness like an everflowing brook. When love is the way, poverty will become history. When love is the way, the earth will be a sanctuary. When love is the way, we will lay down our swords and shields down, down by the riverside to study war no more."

Inspirations and Thoughts from Moments & Windstorms

- We need to be open to receive and share unconditional love. We are all worthy and our children deserve to have a sense of worthiness and belonging regardless of the circumstance they need to be safe.
- Unconditional Love and the power of prayer, meditation and positive reinforcement cannot be overstated.
- The message of the Golden Rule teaches us "Do unto Others as we would have them do unto us." Loving ourselves is the foundation of bringing peace to ourselves and the world.
- Being open to miracles is a miracle.
- How would you describe the flow in your life?
- What's your relationship with your inner child?
- Have you experienced a miracle?
- How would you write an acrostic poem based on your name?
- What does unconditional love mean to you?

Chapter 6

FEARLESSNESS

"Fear is pain from the anticipation of evil" Aristotle

"Fearlessness is the first requisite to spirituality. Cowards can never be moral." Gandhi

"Out of a mountain of despair, a stone of hope" Dr. Martin Luther King, Jr.

"Fear is the opportunity for courage, not proof of cowardice. No one is born a coward. We were meant to love. And we were meant to have courage for it. So be brave." Sen. John McCain

"We have nothing to fear but fear itself" Franklin Delano Roosevelt

IN THE BEGINNING – "Let there be Light"

In starting this chapter I am both humbled and awed. The insights and commitment of the men quoted above are inspiring not only during their struggle for peace and love in their time but for all time. Another quote that comes to mind is from Eleanor Roosevelt: "Women are like teabags they don't know how strong they are until they find themselves in hot water." It takes strength and courage to be committed to the path of peaceful action and to shine a light, especially during cloudy times and windstorms.

That quote by Eleanor Roosevelt relates to very personal windstorms. My mother's very close friend, Rhoda had given me an artistic bowl which creatively painted that quote. When my mother went into the nursing home I gave her the bowl. After her death, I asked my step-family about it; they denied ever seeing it. At that point I was mourning both the passing of my stepfather and mother and decided not to argue about the whereabouts of the bowl. I simply kept the memory of the gift as well as the quote close to my heart. Whether a particular windstorm relates to ourselves, family, friends, the community or the world these are challenges we will face as well as opportunities. Will we choose to shine or to perpetuate the darkness?

How would Dr. King and Mahatma Gandhi respond to the challenges that we are facing in the 21ˢᵗ century – the racism, xenophobia, inequality, and homophobia resulting in violence? The blatant inequity and the vitriolic rhetoric is toxic. What can we do? "Love thy neighbor as thy self" is the key. The forging of that key is based on our loving ourselves. I am not suggesting a selfish, self-centered love. What we need is to embrace the selfless love that comes from the Divine Source; it's a true sense of "SELF-worth," love that is referred to as "agape" which the Greeks considered understanding and creative. It involves empathy, compassion and wisdom. To realize, accept and respect that we are ALL interconnected. It is not the type of love that we can buy from the store or the internet. It is a priceless gift we receive from opening ourselves up to the "Light" within us and the truth that the "Light" is within us all.

A friend shared, that in the Islamic tradition, the 3-stage path is described as: "I am in the Light, the Light is in me and I am the Light." In the Christian tradition: "I am the spirit, I am the son and I and my Father/Mother are one." Basically, we need to shine - whatever the religion, race, creed, gender, and nationality. We All come from the same source; we are one. In the Jewish Book of Exodus, the name of the Divine is stated as "I am that I am." On numerous occasions Jesus shared that "the Father and I are one." Basically, it is reflective of a non-dual perspective in a sole (soul) source even though there are different names and forms.

The bottom-line to heal is to be conscious of the "ONENESS" and getting past the separate tribal mentality understanding that we breathe the same air, drink the same water and that the sun shines on us ALL regardless of our religion, race, creed, gender, and nationality or political affiliation. There is a true sense of peace and freedom when we can smile at one another rather than attack. On the top of the US Capitol there is a statue called "Freedom" (Note: the statue of Freedom is discussed in greater detail in Chapters 2 and 4); she stands on a platform engraved with the following: "E pluribus Unum" which can be interpreted as out of the many one or simply stated ALL for One and One for ALL! Wouldn't it be a peaceful and loving state of affairs if we ALL followed that dictum?

It is fear of the "other" or those creating fear that truly in turn create a clarion call for those of good will to be fearless. To overcome xenophobia the best approach is to highlight the need for unity in the spirit of peace, love, and light. Overcoming fear is a pathway to unity, understanding and creativity.

RESPECT – RICH IN SPIRIT

When I testified before the District of Columbia Council and the US Congress on behalf of the children and families needing quality early childhood services; I intentionally avoided using the term "poor" because the families were truly "rich in spirit." The love and commitment they had for their children and the potential the children possessed was bountiful. A friend of mine is a teacher in WV, she shared an interaction she had with a couple of her students. They had asked her what it was like to be rich – she laughed, being a teacher she wasn't financially rich however she took their question seriously and began explaining that it was having a lot of money, a big house, nice clothes and new cars. She then realized her definition needed to be expanded and reframed the answer by stating that it can also include having family and friends whom you care about and who care about you and that it's when we love each other. The young girls were thrilled and started skipping down the hallway proclaiming they were rich. She then realized that on a teacher's salary she might not be economically rich, however, to share those young girl's joy in recognizing their wealth she in turn was "rich in spirit..."

In 2018 when the teachers in WV stood in solidarity to strike there were over 22,000 teachers who participated and the schools were shut-down for nine days. The teachers in all 55 counties were united and they were indeed "rich in spirit." They were committed to improve the quality of educational services in the state as well as ensure that school employees receive health insurance. The teachers' concerns were supported by the community as well as local and state officials. The commitment they demonstrated had a ripple effect and there were teacher strikes across the country including Arizona, Kentucky, Oklahoma, Colorado, and California.

In his book *STRENGTH TO LOVE*, Dr. Martin Luther King, Jr. describes a very special woman everyone fondly referred to as "Mother Pollard." She was one of the most dedicated participants in the Montgomery, Alabama bus strike and even though she was uneducated and poverty-stricken she proved to have a keen understanding of the protest movement. Mother Pollard was an inspiration, after several weeks boycotting the buses by walking she is quoted as saying: "My feets is tired, but my soul is rested." Dr. King credits her soulful energy in encouraging him during those difficult times. Her insight in sharing when he was in doubt was a radiant calm reassurance that "God's gonna take care of you." It was a spiritual balm for the Civil Rights leader during his most challenging times battling racism.

Mother Teresa believed that the result of feeling disconnected and disrespected can cause a sense of unworthiness and chaos. As she stated: "... *the person who is hurt, who is lonely, who feels rejected, unwanted, unloved I think that's the much greater poverty, much greater disease, much great painful situation of today...and I think a destroyer of peace and unity.*" It is a sad commentary that this poverty is still being experienced throughout the world and in our local communities; and as expressed by Mother Teresa can destroy unity and peace.

The proliferation of gangs is a reflection of young people viewing gangs as a way of creating community and respect. Gang wars are discussed in great detail and compassion in the book, *Tattoos on the Heart*, written by Gregory Boyle, a Jesuit Priest and founder of Homeboy Industries. Gang wars in the "hood" start because somebody "dissed" one of their "homies." Gangs have become a reality in society because of young people's craving for recognition and respect. Gangs are not only a socio-economic phenomenon in the inner-city ghetto, they exist in economically challenged, drug plagued rural areas as well as upper class suburban areas with troubled youth. Young people, as well as older people, are feeling the need to belong and be noticed. Tattoos have become our own personal billboards. expressing a variety of emotions including love and hate. Charles Manson, the cult leader who promoted and participated in horrific murderous crimes in California had a swastika tattoo on his forehead. Many gangs find solace in belonging as well as causing counter-culture violence. Unfortunately, violence has become less counter-culture and angry behavior is becoming more prevalent (as is discussed in Chapter 4 focusing on polarization). The "mega" movement follows the same pathology as gangs and the brown shirts in Nazi Germany.

Lack of respect can result in isolation and self-destructive behavior; in turn self-respect can result in a sense of well-being and the ability to be open to sharing and caring. If there is a core understanding that whatever is needed, there is already enough - be it food, land, water or love. One of my neighbors on the mountain explained that he needed his gun because if his son was hungry and needed bread he would use any means possible to ensure his son got bread. This is a fear mentality, fear of scarcity and perpetuates a survival warfare mode of operation. I told him that if his son was hungry I'd be more than willing to share whatever food he needed. He laughed and said that wasn't how most people operated. He basically said that "We live in a world of survival of the fittest." Rather than argue the Darwinian theory with him, I simply chose to practice the principle of "Love Thy Neighbor as Thyself" and let him know that as long as I had bread I was willing to share it; trusting that all would be well It's simply a matter of respect and understanding that we are inter-connected – another example of the Golden Rule as discussed throughout the book.

In the process of touching base with our true core nature, we can begin to understand the importance of respect. Marginalization is a form of bullying and disrespect that results in a lack of self-worth. Accepting that we are ALL worthy moves us closer to peace. The act of bullying whether on the playground, mountain or the global stage is unnecessary, because there is a mutual understanding that we are all rich in spirit. I believe that respecting ourselves results in us seeing ourselves in our neighbor; that in turn manifests into the Christ message: "Love thy neighbor as thyself." The Darwinian theory of evolution is thus turned around. We are able to overcome a "survival of the fittest" mode and truly begin to evolve and it becomes the empowerment of the peacemaker and we thrive.

Fear that we may not be good enough or that we are not lovable erodes our self-respect. Being fearless gives us the courage to embrace our worthiness and state that "I am that I am" be it a quote from the Bible or from the song "I am What I am" from the musical La Cage Aux Folle. Ensuring that we and our children possess a strong sense of well-being and trusting our own internal strength is fundamental to developing respect. Having faith in ourselves and faith in the greater good brings us ALL closer to Peace on Earth and peace within. When we feel "less than" we make those around us feel "less than" in order to make ourselves feel more important. Respect is about feeling good about ourselves and we in turn project that feeling outward. We shine and begin to see the glow in others.

The stories shared in *DEER HUNTING WITH JESUS* by Joe Bageant and the *HILLBILLY ELEGY* by J.D. Vance spotlight the fact that there are folks who feel undervalued and dismissed by elite politicians.

Living in WV, I have witnessed the experience of Appalachian apathy, which reflects feelings of being unworthy and marginalized. Alienation can then result in a hateful malignancy creating a dark shadow of fear Even in one of the "richest" countries there are people relegated to live in the shadows. The true brilliance of humanity is the reflection of the Milky Way the courage to overcome the shadowy void. Giving us ALL the opportunity to awaken in the light. How wonderful to allow everyone's potential to sparkle in turn being free of hate and fear.

Perhaps one of the pivotal points in the 2016 election was when Hillary Clinton described Trump supporters as being "Deplorables" – it was a major catalyst that sparked a gigantic backlash and created an overwhelming get-out-the-vote (GOTV) phenomena as well as commercializing the derogative term with t-shirts and websites. Without realizing it, persons who felt invisible had become empowered to be fearless and placed their trust (unfortunately) in Trump. He exploited their pain, gave voice to their lack of tolerance for the "other" and the worst tribal aspects were unleashed.

The ugly aspects of this tribal mentality were apparent in 2008; however, then it was not mobilized. The "birther" campaign that was waged by Donald Trump against - Barrack Obama was racist and a foreshadowing of the hateful; manner Trump world would operate. When I was helping with the Obama election in 2008, I saw first-hand the folks who would be classified as "deplorable" but witnessing them as hurting, scared and uneducated would have been more accurate and much more empathetic.

I'll never forget November 4, 2008 the day Obama was elected president. I had been the volunteer GOTV coordinator for the Jefferson County Democrats. Friends in DC were concerned about my safety. I guess I was being fearless or possibly clueless in terms of the racial tensions that existed in WV. I got to the campaign office at 6:00 AM election day and there was already an African-American gentleman waiting to help; I was glad to see him and told him we'd be going to the phone banks across the street to remind people to vote. When I showed him the list to call, he kind of cringed and said "this is a list of white folks who live in Harpers Ferry." I assured him "this is a list of folks who will vote for Obama and if you get negative responses from any of the calls we will try and get a new list." After making several calls, I asked about the responses. He gave me a big smile and told me "they're voting for Obama and they are also taking their friends to the polls to vote." He then asked if his teenage daughter could make calls later in the day. I realized that it would be a special experience for his daughter to be participating in this historical moment with the first African American man running in the general election for the US presidency. I told him that she would be welcome and that if there were any negative responses that she could definitely talk with me. His daughter came in and I am happy to say she didn't experience any negative calls. She took an Obama poster home with her as a memorial souvenir.

Not everything that day went that smoothly. While I was crossing the street from the phone bank to the main campaign headquarters, I noticed that there was another campaign volunteer being harassed. I went over to see if there was something I could do to help. There was a somewhat disheveled white man who was yelling at the white woman who had come to help on the campaign. He kept pointing at the Obama button and shouting "I am not voting for that N...." I used my best early childhood voice and calmly told him "there is no need to use the "N" word and that we live in a democracy and he can vote for whoever he wanted." At that point the woman he was with who was also disheveled and possibly drunk chimed in with a shrill voice "No one is taking away my gun. I was raped and no one is going to take away my gun." I told her I was sorry that she had been raped. I agreed that she needed protection and explained that Senator Biden had sponsored strong legislation to protect rape victims. She wasn't impressed but the interaction became less confrontational. The man then asked me "Do you know who my favorite president is, he's a Republican?" I shook my head no; I expected him to say Reagan. He then said with pride "My favorite president was John F. Kennedy." My response was immediate, authentic and enthusiastic "WOW! John F. Kennedy is my favorite president too and he was a Democrat and his daughter Caroline is supporting Obama." At that point he got angry and insisted that JFK was a Republican. The woman who had initially been confronted was beside herself and got indignant and told him "JFK was a Democrat, the library is right up the block – you can look it up for yourself..." I could tell at this point that she was getting really angry and I am glad she didn't call him stupid. I again tried to ratchet down the tension and shared "I am sure there are a lot of books on Kennedy at the library and the librarian would be happy to help you." It became clear that the woman he was with was angry and repeated "No one is taking away my gun." Then she patted her pocket, I then began to pray, I didn't know whether she had the gun in her pocket. The next thing I knew I was pointing to the library "they've got loads of books on Kennedy." Thank God, he simply nodded and took the woman's hand and they headed in the direction of the library.

The Trump supporters that were on the street corner in 2008 probably welcome Trump as their winner in 2020 and their retribution in 2024. In 2008 the man viewed JFK as his favorite president

163

because he took the time to make a campaign stop in WV. Even though JFK and Trump are polar opposites they both are charismatic and had the political talent of making voters feel seen and heard. Eleanor Roosevelt's compassion was a gift and her concern shared when she visited the workers in the coal mine was memorable and appreciated by West Virginians even one hundred years later.

UNITY – A PART & FOR GIVING

I am amazed at what a difference just a little space and perspective can give to our lives. We can view ourselves as a part of a community rather than being apart and alone. We can understand that to truly reconcile is for us to be willing to be for giving (gracious) and open to compassion without judgement or expectations. There is a unity in being aware of our vulnerability of being human. Sharing that vulnerability is probably the bravest thing we can do in moving forward to becoming completely a part and being in unity with the greater whole. It is a gift for us to be alive and for giving ourselves love and compassion. Sharing the love and compassion simply multiplies that energy within and throughout the universe.

Studies done by Masaru Emoto have demonstrated that messages shared are reflected in the crystals of water. For example, when loving messages of gratitude and melodic music are played the water crystals that are formed are beautiful, clear and elegant. He also found that when water is exposed to negative words or heavy metal music the water crystals are deformed or barely formed. When we realize that approximately 70% of our bodies consist of water, the research done becomes even more relevant. In his book, *The Hidden Messages in Water*, he explains in detail the power of words and that the vibrations of good words, such as "love" and "gratitude" have a positive effect whereas the vibrations of negative words such as "stupid" and "hate" had the power to destroy.

We are all inter-connected, i.e. as stated before we are ALL One. Science further illustrates the fact that our life energy has a vibration that has an impact on all creation. There is another scientific study known as the "butterfly effect." Edward Norton Lorenz, an American meteorologist and mathematician, entered a figure for wind velocity into a computer to predict weather conditions. In order to simplify the process, he entered .506 instead of .506127. What he found was amazing - by simply eliminating the .000127 the ensuing weather predictions were drastically altered. The fact that something that seemed numerically insignificant could affect wind velocity and radically modified the forecasting of the weather was significant. He concluded that even a tiny variation, such as the velocity of the flapping of the wings of a butterfly, could result in a significantly different momentum that in turn could cause a chain effect of meteorological events that could change a sunny day into a tornado. There is an impact and shift even in the smallest variation and the reaction can create dramatically different results - peaceful or chaotic.

How we view ourselves and the world can also have a dramatic impact. Do we see one another as "apart" or "a part"? Being separate or united? Are we willing to be forgiving as well as for giving? Fear is a means of keeping us apart and love has the power of uniting us. Faith and respect are useful tools in helping us ALL to be "rich in spirit". Forgiving can be viewed as a top down personal judgemental pardon rather than for giving which can be viewed as a mutual acceptance resulting in reconciliation (discussed in greater detail in chapter 7). Recognizing the significance of our presence and the importance of our words can help us to evolve as a more for giving species of compassion and wisdom.

DISCONNECTED - DISRESPECTED

The more ways we have to connect, it seems the more ways there are to miscommunicate. People have become very busy and distracted, be it by voice-mail, by e-mails, Facebook, blog, skype, twitter, etc. We are in the age of "butt calls" amusing as well as disconcerting. At a meeting in Jefferson County, WV it was explained that one of the major reasons for the increase in drug and alcohol abuse was due to the fact that many people are feeling disconnected and are turning to drugs to self-medicate. During the presentation the facilitator was busy working on her iPhone; I have to admit my interest in the presentation thus began to wane. Granted she might have been utilizing her iPhone to enhance the presentation but I began to identify with people who feel disconnected. Watching families at restaurants on their iPhones busy texting away and not verbally talking with each other really baffles me. I have to admit it used to annoy me however now I smile when the message on a voice-mail says "You've reached me ...." No I've reached your voice mail "You are not your iPhone" It may be semantics but we really are more than our phones and our IT gadgets. As I mentioned previously, I have dyslexia, it is therefore difficult for me to text, and the streaming messages and pop-ups on Facebook can be extremely distracting.

It is unbelievable that the addiction to IT gadgets has created a lack of civility. The manner i n which people are hired "or not" is left to artificial intelligence. And as one friend stated she questions the intelligence. .Applications are done via computer screens, receipt of applications are auto-response and there is no response regarding review. Applicants are left in cyberspace limbo. We've lost that human connection simply regarding a friendly personal interaction. Simple common courtesy is no longer simple. The concept of "defriending" is simply a reflection of society's disconnect and the impact of social media. Friends have shared that they know of people who got divorced via Facebook and texting. On the other hand, there are internet dating sites which advertise that a number of those utilizing those sites have found the love of their life and have gotten married, yet there are also people on those sites ready to scam. In fact, I have a friend who has been scammed on one of those sites. We need to become much more discerning in a world with technology. There is a technological divide of the "have" and "have nots." Simply utilizing the computer is a challenge, however I admit having access to word processing and the internet is a plus. Technology issues are also discussed in Chapters 2 and 4.

The challenges between the yin (female) and yang (male) energies can create both positive and negative effects. The latter is blatantly apparent in the media be it television, given the scandals at FOX News; or the movies on screen or behind the scenes, given the scandals regarding Harvey Weinstein and other people in the entertainment industry; including Bill Cosby. These high-profile cases were a catalyst in creating a #METOO movement which heralds the fact that survivors of sexual assault are not alone and encourages survivors to voice their concerns and promote healing.

When attending a charity dinner in 2016, the people at the table began to express concern about the vitriolic rhetoric that was occurring in the 2016 political debates. I simply listened as they discussed the Access Hollywood excerpt that was released focusing on Trump's derogatory comments relating to women. What is interesting is that people were complaining that they didn't know who they could trust and that the media had somewhat of a strangle hold on the information that was being shared or not shared. It sounds kind of like social media meets George Orwell's *1984*, Big Brother.

The sexual harassment allegations made concerning Donald Trump prior to the 2016 election were disgraceful and unacceptable behavior. A misogynistic mode of operation is disrespectful and a major disconnect. It devalues both parties and is unacceptable whether it happens in a backlot of a studio, school playground, college campus, church or our own house, the White House, the house of Congress. Issues relating to sexual harassment and sexism are discussed in greater detail in Chapter 2. I am pleased to share a quote from my great-grandfather's journal. Finding the journal was both a miracle and surprise. It included a clipping from a speech of a well-known Suffragette: "We will have what men have....It may not be much, but we mean to have it.... We refuse to be poked in the gallery much longer... but insist on being placed on the floor of the house... The drunken loafer at the back of the house says, 'Down with her petticoats' I say 'Up with the petticoats and down with the trousers then all things will be visible in their true light.'" I found the clipping to be inspiring and amusing. My great-grandfather clipped it out in the early 1900's. I found his journal while cleaning out my great aunt's apartment after she died in 1975 and the sentiments shared are a foreshadowing of what we are experiencing now; especially with the #METOO movement. It gives a whole new meaning to being transparent and women's rights. It was a testament to women's empowerment in 2018 when a historical number of 87 women were elected to the US House of Representatives and the Speaker of the House was a woman, Nancy Pelosi. The Speaker has shown herself as a woman of great faith and service. She was anchored and demonstrated true grit and courage when the Capitol was under attack on January 6, 2021. She is a historical hero for our time. My prayers are with her family given the despicable and heinous assault on her husband Paul by a man who reflects the deranged messaging on the internet. The Speaker has been a target for political pundits and members of Congress on both sides of the aisle. This mode of operation has been weaponized and throughout it all Nancy Pelosi has stood tall. This mode of operation has been weaponized and throughout it all Nancy Pelosi has been a beacon for love.

In an attempt to escape the political tug of war I had gone to visit a friend. Her kids were playing video games. Unfortunately, I witnessed the lack of respect and angry competition that is promoted in videos for young children. It was an educational experience for me to watch her kids play video games. What was most disturbing was at first glance, the site looked like a peaceful setting with colorful jewels, cuddly cartoon characters and rainbows then with a push of a button or "joy stick" the children began racking up points by having the characters destroy each other. This idyllic setting became a battle ground and at the same time the kids began to fight over the "joy stick." Are our children becoming desensitized? The military uses video games to train recruits, obviously not the playful colorful ones that I witnessed at my friends' house. Even the more graphic, which includes guns and ammo and possibly blood, is indicative of the overall impact on the families and communities affected. There are no words to describe the live video streams of terrorists beheading hostages. Technology in these situations is being used to promote fear and hate – it causes us to disconnect from humanity and desensitizes us to being interconnected as discussed earlier in this chapter.

We are witnessing a time in society when it is becoming much more challenging to be open to the possibility of peace and love. However, this is probably the most important time to be open to peace and love. Bumper stickers that read "Armed Infidel" do not help move us forward, nor do bumper stickers with the confederate flag emblazoned with "TRUMP" printed in big bold letters. Bumper stickers that read "Coexist" and "Tolerence" that include the symbols of a myriad of religious symbols are a much more positive message.

Young people disconnecting and getting lost in their iPhone has become an everyday reality in our society. At a meeting a friend said he passes a school bus stop, and the only interaction he witnesses among the youth is them staring at their iPhones. Our youth are clearly exercising their thumbs but what about other muscles? The lack of verbal skills and the habit of simply pushing the "send" button can cause difficulties in communication in the future especially in regards to personal face to face (rather than facebook) interaction. Communications can become much more challenging to comprehend given high-tech modes of operation; we as a society can easily lose the heart connection.

HEART, MIND, BODY & SOUL

Uniting our minds and hearts is essential. The disconnection of our hearts and minds can prove destructive. When focusing on the greater Truth we can begin to view unconditional love as an effective response to hate. As described in *A Course in Miracles* there are key questions that can help us to focus on the Truth: Who am I? How would you have us serve? Where would you have us go? And What would you have us say and to whom?

The joining of heart and mind can help us discern; it helps us to balance. Aristotle is quoted as stating: "A mind that is not connected to the heart is like the sun that has no warmth". Wisdom is the union of the mind and heart, and as a result we witness compassion. Intellect void of compassion is cold and can be cruel and hurtful

Elisabeth spoke about us all having four quadrants – emotional. intellectual, physical and spiritual. There is also an illustration and detailed discussion on the quadrants in regards to the Continual Flow – the Conscious Evolutionary Oneness (CEO) in chapter 5. When we are able to share unconditionally, it will allow us to experience love without judgements and we are able to be liberated from the fear of death. When we can reach deep within and understand the loving bond between the heart and mind as well as the human and Divine we can experience "heaven on earth" – a world of compassion free from hate, poverty, greed, cruelty and war. The heartfelt knowledge that the Christ's message: "The Kingdom of God is within" provides the courage and strength to sustain us during the windstorms. We can take refuge in the union of a Divine presence, as Mother Pollard shared: "God is gonna take care …." And as Saint Francis prayed: "Lord, make me an instrument of your peace." And as Bob Marley beautifully sang "One Love! One Heart! Let's get together and feel all right …As it was in the beginning – One Love! So shall it be in the end – One Heart! All right!"

BEYOND LIFE & DEATH

The difference between life and death is simply form. It's a transition that allows us to be free. Working with Elisabeth and hospice has taught me that life is to be cherished and getting beyond the fear of death is embracing our humanity as a whole. We are both temporal and eternal beings – to cling to one and at the same time deny the other causes a wrenching of the soul and suffering. We All deserve to be joyful and peaceful. To reach the state of "the peace of God, which passeth all understanding" (Phillipians 4:7 KJV) may not be achieved in the temporal form. However, we might understand once we embrace the eternal here and now. Death is inevitable, we can't escape it no matter how rich or poor we may be – no one leaves here alive. As a pastor shared "he never saw a U-Haul attached to a hearse."

To deny the existence of evil in this world is simply buying into the power of positive thought dogma. Dogma whatever its origin is dogma. Webster's dictionary defines dogma as a set of beliefs and practices that are hierarchical and accepted without question. There are people who may perpetuate evil; we can focus on the evil or simply be a witness and shine our light. When we choose to fear evil, we are strengthening the power of the evil. Fear and evil are reflections of the same destructive energy. There is a uplifting saying that: "Fear knocked at the door. Faith and love answered. There was no one there." It is acknowledging fear and at the same time acknowledging that with the strength of faith and love that fear is basically diminished and vanquished. As was shared in Chapter 1 the term "Fear Not" appears in the Bible 365 times.

We can choose to live our life in love or in fear. A true leap of faith and a testament to unconditional love is trusting that we will be in alignment with the greater good. When we lose a loved one it's difficult, however the loss occurs and the term hang on can take both a physical or spiritual perspective. We can hang on until the bitter end or surrender and trust. Peace comes after we surrender and there is a truce. And the true refuge for peace is within our own heart. The ego never is willing to let go however the compassionate heart releases and accepts that Divine will and free will are One.

In effect we can choose to celebrate a life, at every birth, birthday and passing or we can choose to mourn a death. Elisabeth strongly believed that life is a gift to be celebrated and death is simply a transition. We need to free ourselves of guilt and shame in the process. Too many people who die or their family members have "if only" haunting them. Let it go! Being at peace before we Rest in Peace (RIP) is the greatest gift we can give ourselves and ALL those we love. When it's time for our eulogy – how would we like to be remembered - reflecting peace or fear? (The topic of RIP is discussed in greater detail in Chapter 7).

Emotions at the time of someone's death can be mixed and very mercurial. Sadly, when my mother's cousin passed away the cousin's two daughters had been estranged. The cousin had written both daughters letters. However unfortunately, one of the daughters took both letters and never shared the letter her mother had written to her sister. It's no surprise that the sister who had not received the letter was feeling isolated and dealing with health issues. Emotions people witness at the time of a passing can be angry and hurtful. People are feeling guilty for whatever reason. We can't live anyone's life nor their death. We can pray for peace and trust. When someone dies and people grieve they are grieving and experiencing the pain reflected in their own lives. Those who have crossed over are no longer shackled with the burdens of the temporal life.

Death is a learning experience, as is life; loss and joy come in many forms. It's our choice to learn or literally bury our heads in the sand and hold on to the grievances. When my father passed away my uncle didn't want us to tell our grandmother because it would upset her. In hindsight, even before working with Elisabeth, I believed that death cannot be denied and that we are all entitled to grieve. I felt my uncle's request not to inform my grandmother that my father was dead was unrealistic despite his wish to shield my grandmother from the loss. I didn't want my mother to be placed in the position of lying to my grandmother If my grandmother called to speak to my father what was my mother supposed to say!? My uncle suggested that we tell her that he was playing cards or in the bathroom. This was an extreme case of denial. My grandmother would be left with the impression that my father had a gambling addiction or serious stomach problems, and worse yet, she would not get a return phone call. We agreed that my grandmother needed to be told in person and not over the phone I had gone to visit her to share the news that my father had died. However, my uncle acquiesced and had gotten the courage to tell his mother that his brother had died before I arrived and I was there to console her. Ironically when my grandmother passed, my uncle hadn't called to tell me or my sister that she had died. I had gotten this feeling that my grandmother had passed and I tried calling her but there was no answer. I then called my cousin, I knew it was a strange question but I had to ask "Did Grandma die?" Her response was "I am so glad you asked." While I am remembering this I am not sure whether to laugh or cry – I am choosing to smile. In sharing this dysfunctional experience about death in my family it is my hope to help people understand that everyone's response to death is unique. Fear, however, seems to be at the core.

When my mother's closest friend died, neither my stepfather nor stepsister wanted my mother to be told. I strongly believed that she needed to be told. I can only assume that my stepfather was trying to protect my mom. I made a deal with him that if she asked me about Rhoda I could tell her the truth. I admit it wasn't difficult to get a conversation focused on Rhoda since she and my mother were so close.

When I finally told her that Rhoda had passed away; I will never forget how she got teary eyed then looked rather mindful (to my knowledge my mother never meditated). I will never forget she was smiling and infirmed me "Guess I am the last comic standing." I smiled and nodded in agreement. She wouldn't be sending anymore birthday cards to Rhoda or expecting to receive any from her. They were friends for over sixty years – they knew each other's strengths and weaknesses and they truly loved each other. It was a love that deserved to be honored both in life and death. When my father died, Rhoda was there for my mother. When Rhoda died, I was also there for my mother and Rhoda's family.

People deal with grief differently and the best we can do is to love those who have passed and those who are still alive; and to love them unconditionally. With the work I've done with Elisabeth and volunteering for hospice; I have been humbled to witness the intense emotions shared during these dramatic family moments. Witnessing these personal experiences I realize the importance of being there, to share the light and to smile both in life and death.

Our fear of death or the possibility of rejection can cause us to shut down. In a fear driven society we are unable to extend a helping hand or in turn unable to ask for help. To sincerely share love unconditionally without regret or strings attached is acknowledging that we are ALL worthy. If we knew we were going to die tomorrow, who would we call today? What would we say? Who would we pray would be there to hold our hand, whose hand would we want to hold? What are we waiting for?

I AM WORTHY / WE ARE ALL WORTHY – "PEACE" OF A GREATER WHOLE

As was mentioned earlier in this chapter, we ALL deserve respect. Having a sense of Self-worth gives us the opportunity to share in the spirit of love. We are ALL inter-connected. Pope Francis has been an example of being open to reflecting that we are a "peace" of the greater whole. The religious and economic wars along with the environmental disasters have created havoc on the world stage and the result is millions of refugees. The Pope has been playing a key role in getting other religious leaders to sign a joint declaration calling on the international community to make the protection of human lives a priority and to extend temporary asylum to those in need. In addition, the Vatican has become an asylum for a number of Muslim refugees as a show of solidarity. The Pope also went to Myanmar to plea that the Rohinga be respected and dealt with compassionately. In fact, the Pope is quoted as stating: "I beg the Lord to grant us more politicians who are genuinely disturbed by the state of society, the people, the lives of the poor!"

We all are worthy of being a light shining the message of peace and love. In union we can become much more aware and conscious of the role each of us can play. It's not a question of waiting for a spotlight to shine on us individually; it's a question of being open to having the spotlight shining within each of us and to be willing to be "brilliant" in our own way to be of service. George Fox, the founder of the Religious Society of Friends (Quakers) had the insight to so eloquently share the belief that "Let your life speak." He is quoted as stating: "Friends, meet together and know one another in that which is eternal, which was before the world was." Having the understanding that we are ALL One from the same source gives us the strength and courage to embrace our worthiness in a manner which is both humbling and empowering.

As the Statue of Liberty holds her torch high, to be a beacon of hope, the base of the statue has the inscription of the inspirational poem "New Colossus" by Emma Lazarus. The most inspiring and memorable quote being: *"Give me your tired, your poor, Your huddled masses yearning to breathe free, The wretched refuse of your teeming shore. Send these, the homeless, tempest-tossed to me, I lift my lamp beside the golden door!" A light of hope and freedom. We are all worthy.; We are a "peace" of a greater whole. Heart to heart we recognize ourselves in All."*

I am grateful for having had the opportunity to attend a special event to celebrate the 10 year anniversary of the South Mountain Friends Fellowship (SMFF) Group at the Maryland Correctional Institution in Hagerstown, MD. This is a Quaker Meeting that is sponsored by the Patapsco Meeting. An a cappella group sang which was a pure delight. It was an honor to be a part of the group and to witness the joy and strength of the inmates participating in the celebration. A couple of the inmates brought the service dogs they were training for disabled veterans. We concluded the celebration in silent prayer and singing "This little light of Mine, I'm going to let it shine."

What the men from SMFF have taught me has been priceless. I have been in communication with four of the men and they have been phenomenal teachers. For the sake of respecting their privacy, I will not be utilizing their real names. I have been humbled by the grace that they have demonstrated in challenging situations. They are both Black and White gentlemen that have created a bond that defies institutional barriers. In 2017 SMFF had disbanded because the Maryland Correction System had closed the honor dormitories that housed at least three of the SMFF inmates and several of the men had literally been scattered to the wind to other facilities, no fault of their own. As a result, the prison denied the continuation of the Quaker Meeting. However, the men continued to keep the faith. One of the inmates I'll call Tom, an attractive African American, (mentioned in Chapter 3 pg. 42) has strong ties with his mother and is committed to make her proud. Another of the inmates, I'll call Michael, is attempting to startup another Quaker Meeting where he has been imprisoned. He's been a tutor in the prison and been instrumental in helping one of his fellow SMFF inmates who has learning challenges, who I'll call Andy. Andy considers Michael his #1 man since he keeps him out of trouble, protects him and helps him with his spelling. Andy has a smile and laugh that he generously shares as well as a heart warming "Amen to that". Michael is an avid reader, writes short stories and poetry. *The Feather* is a story he wrote about finding a feather in the prison compound. He thought it could possibly be from a seagull and then we discussed that it could possibly be from an angel – he was fascinated as well as amused. I was surprised and very touched when he sent me the feather for safe keeping. The correctional institution and judicial system can be less than fair and extremely demoralizing. Even with its hardships and dehumanizing aspects an inmate, that I'll call Jack has risen to the occasion of demonstrating grace. Jack has a life sentence, he was incarcerated at the age of 21 years old and has served 38 years. In almost four decades Jack has not received one infraction. He's been instrumental in developing "Lifer Conferences" that include victim rights advocates that emphasize the importance of reconciliation. While in prison he was blessed with finding a soulmate, Kathy, and they have been married for eighteen years. Together they have been attempting to find legal means of getting Jack's sentence modified so that he would be eligible for parole. Unfortunately, their attempts have been thwarted. Witnessing blatant inequity and the fact that justice has a blind eye to redemption is disheartening. Seeing Jack being in shackles at the court house was disconcerting. However, witnessing Kathy and Jack's faith, courage, love and grace during these challenging judicial ordeals has been inspiring.

Inspirations and Thoughts from Moments & Windstorms

- The bottomline to heal is to be conscious of the "ONENESS" and getting past the separate tribal mentality and understanding that we breathe the same air, drink the same water and that the sun shines on us ALL regardless of religion, race, creed, gender, and nationality or political affiliation. We All come from the same Source.

- Everyone wants to be respected. Fear that we may not be good enough or worthy erodes our self-respect and accepting the Christ message: "Love thy neighbor as thyself" is essential to promoting peace. Loving ourselves in the spirit of "agape" - a love which exemplifies compassion and wisdom is the foundation. We are witnessing a time in society when it is becoming much more challenging to be open to the possibility of peace and love. However, this is probably the most important time to be open to peace and love.

- Death is a learning experience, as is life – loss and joy come in many forms.

- Having the understanding that we are ALL One from the same Source is a blessing that gives us the strength and courage to embrace our worthiness in a manner which is both humbling and empowering

- Unity is a pivotal aspect of ensuring a true sense of community and peace. We are all interconnected. The more we recognize that we are a part rather than apart the more united and peaceful we will be. Words and actions have either a positive or negative impact – Being a catalyst that shines a "light" during negative times is our choice. Is there a time when you were or you witnessed someone being a "light" in times of darkness?

- Do you have a tattoo? If yes - what is the message? If no what would you include as the message?

Chapter 7

FORGIVENESS

"Without Forgiveness there Really is no future" Nobel Laureate Archbishop Desmond Tutu

"Most people need to experience a great deal of suffering before they will relinquish resistance and accept before they will forgive" Eckhart Tolle

"I am sorry. Please forgive me. I thank you and I love you." Hawaiian HONOPONO PRAYER

"It is in pardoning that we are pardoned" Francis of Assisi

After my personal experience of betrayal, isolation, inequities, abandonment and watching the programs that I had promoted for over thirty years being dismantled and imploding; writing about forgiveness is challenging. However, moving into forgiveness is a necessary step towards peace and freedom - both as a person and as society.

SOUTH AFRICAN TRUTH AND RECONCILIATION COMMISSION

The South African Truth and Reconciliation Commission was established in South Africa after apartheid was abolished and Nelson Mandela was inaugurated president. The underlying purpose of the Commission was to help South Africans heal from the atrocities and inequities that caused years of racial strife and brutal massacres. There is a heart wrenching account of a white South African policeman, Mr. Van de Broek, who had brutally murdered and tortured a black man and his son. The frail and elderly wife and mother of the victims appeared before the Commission, testifying that she was forced to witness the heinous actions on the part of the policeman who ordered the torture, killing and cremation of her family. The last words she heard her husband say before he died were: "Father, forgive them."

The strength this woman demonstrated was miraculous. When the Commission asked her how she felt justice could be served, she had three requests. First, she requested that Mr. Van de Broek go to the place where he burned the bodies of her husband and son and gather up the dust so she could give them a decent burial. Second, she told the Commission that although she lost all her family she still had a lot of love to give and that she requested that Mr. Van de Broek come to the ghetto twice a month and visit her so she could be a mother to him. Thirdly, she wanted Mr. Van de Broek to know that he was forgiven by God and that she also forgives him and that she would like to embrace him so he knows that he is truly forgiven. At that point the policeman fainted and many of the people in the hearing room, also victims of oppression began, singing "*Amazing Grace.*"

This particular story is very moving to say the least. On a personal basis, it truly touches my heart since I had agreed to stand up against apartheid and had been arrested in front of the South African Embassy. There were a number of famous celebrities who had protested in this manner and the organizers of the protest wanted to have someone witness how authorities interacted with simple citizens. The DC Democratic State Committee called and asked if I would be willing to be arrested; I told them that I would pray on the request. The next day I called and told them that I would be honored to take a stand against apartheid. A group of around ten people met downtown and we were taken to the South African Embassy to peacefully request access to the facility to present our concerns regarding the atrocities of apartheid. We were denied, access and we simply stood outside holding hands. Police came and requested that we leave the property; we were told if we didn't move that we would be arrested. We chose to be arrested and we were taken to a Police Station only five blocks from where I lived.

The Police treated us graciously and offered us coffee and also gave us playing cards. None of the protesters, black or white, male or female were put behind bars; they simply kept us all in a small room in the back. The organizers had not informed us that for purpose of obtaining bond over the phone we needed a person who could verify where we lived and where we worked, preferably a person who lived in DC Thank goodness, again my "fear not" sense of humor was present, because dealing with the Bonds officer over the phone was challenging. This was before cell phones, however I have a pretty good memory and I was able to give the phone numbers of several of my friends. I hadn't told them that I planned to get arrested and that I needed them to stay by the phone. The bonds officer got back on the phone with me and was rather rude and bluntly stated "we can't grant you bail, no one will vouch for you." My initial response was "WHAT!?" He then told me that none of my friends were home and that their husbands answered and couldn't tell him where I lived. They said they were pretty sure I lived in DC but they couldn't give the exact name of the organization I worked with, but they were pretty sure it had something to do with child care." I took a deep breath then politely and calmly explained "I don't give my friends' husbands my business card." I asked him if I could please give him the number of a Board member of the child care program that I work with even if the Board member didn't live in DC? One of the police-men saw I was having a problem. Luckily, he had seen me around the neighborhood, and he was willing to vouch that I lived in the city, so he spoke to the bonds officer and then he handed the phone back to me. There was still the issue of where I was employed; I gave him the name and telephone number of the treasurer, who luckily was home and confirmed my place of employment. The next morning, I received frantic calls from friends checking to make sure that I was home safe as well as a call from Rudy, the treasurer who was amused that I had gotten myself arrested and that he was able to get me the bond approval. In less than twenty-four hours we were all released on bail. We were treated with respect, and I truly believe that sev-eral of the policemen were sympathetic to the peaceful protest. They were simply doing their job and we were simply doing what we felt was right. The contrast to the human interaction was stark regarding the authorities in South Africa and the manner in which the DC Police Department reacted to the everyday person. Once the organizers were assured that peaceful protesters would be treated graciously and respectfully the Anti-Apartheid Marches snowballed. There was even a march with children and baby carriages on Mothers' Day – Mothers against Apartheid.

GUILT & FEAR

Dr. Elisabeth Kubler Ross is quoted by a number of grief counselors and mental health professionals regarding loss and the five stages surrounding death: anger, denial, depression, bargaining and acceptance. The irony is that while I was working with Elisabeth, she stressed that society had taken these stages too literally and that the stages were not linear. Indeed, for many, some stages would not appear and that for some stages people would go back and forth. Basically, most did not experience the stages in a straight line.

Additionally, Elisabeth felt that the greatest enemies of obtaining peace were fear and guilt. These emotions are obstacles to freedom both from the personal perspective as well as the interpersonal/ social perspective, be it the community, national, or international realms. Family feuds, school yard bullying, mass shootings and terrorist acts are precipitated from the same toxic feelings of fear and guilt – the bottom line is not feeling worthy. Elisabeth believed that guilt was a label that was insidious and has a negative impact on our lives. We can regret our actions rather than create a toxic label of guilt that is an obstacle to healing. We can choose to be open to joy and peace which will help us overcome feelings of unworthiness. Unconditional love and forgiveness are possible antidotes to guilt.

Unconditional love for ourselves is the foundation for palliative remediation and gives strength to the true meaning of the Golden Rule discussed throughout the book.

Unfortunately, the wars we are witnessing in our families, our communities and our world have undermined the foundation of peace within ourselves. The drug epidemic is a reflection of the pain, guilt and inequity that is experienced in society. Suicides in the 21st century have also increased dramatically. Feeling disconnected and isolated can be overwhelming. The guilt becomes unbearable and in order to deal with these feelings of unworthiness – drugs and/or suicide can be viewed as a way of coping with the pain. Death from the scourge of drugs just in the United States is steadily increasing. In 2017 the number of overdose deaths was estimated to be 72,000 people a 10% increase from the previous year That doesn't include the collateral damage such as the impact on children, the loss of human potential or the deaths from drug wars and violent infighting within the drug cartels. Simply reviewing the statistics on suicides among teens and within the military is staggering The Center for Disease Control estimates that suicide is the 10th leading cause of death in the United States. Suicide is the second leading cause of death in the US military. A Mayo Clinic study found that the Army suicide rate increased 80% from 2004 to 2008.

The forgiveness witnessed at the South African Truth and Reconciliation Commission is a testament to the healing process. In effect it is not only the "victim" that is hurt it is also the perpetrator who unfortunately attempts to eliminate their own fear and guilt using acts of brutality. Such atrocities are counterproductive, self-destructive and self-perpetuating. A cycle of hate and violence begets additional hate and violence unless the healing balm of forgiveness is applied generously. Forgiveness, in truth, is a form of compassion without judgment, and in effect, unconditional love. Perhaps the notion of forgiveness seems circular, as if it is all semantics. Regardless, in October 2006, The Amish Community came together exemplifying forgiveness by however one understands it or by whatever name it is called

AMISH GRACE

An Amish schoolhouse near Nickels Mine, Pennsylvania was the scene of the slaughter of innocent children. The gunman, Carl Roberts IV – a 32 year old milk truck driver, entered the schoolhouse killing five young girls, seriously wounding five others and then killing himself. School shootings have sadly become less than unexpected in our news media – despite the shocking nature of the acts. The list of such tragedies keeps growing since Columbine, several colleges, public schools, churches even child care centers have been targets, including Sandy Hook Elementary in Newtown Conn.

Given the tragic nature of the senseless act, what becomes amazing regarding the shooting in Pennsylvania is that the Amish community almost immediately forgave the killer and offered support to the killer's family, even attending his funeral. Several parents who had lost loved ones in the shooting extended an invitation to the Roberts family to attend their daughters' funerals.

In their book *Amish Grace: How Forgiveness Transcended Tragedy* the authors Donald Kraybill, Steven Holt and David Weaver-Zercher wrote: *"When forgiveness arrived at the killers home within hours of his crime, it did not appear out of nowhere. Rather forgiveness is woven into the very fabric of Amish life, its sturdy threads having been spun from faith in God, scriptural mandates, and a history of persecution."* The Amish place a special emphasis on the teachings of Jesus, especially the Sermon on the Mount, specifically with regards to the Lord's Prayer wherein Jesus says "Forgive us our debts as we forgive our debtors." Amish are conscientious objectors to military service as are the Quakers. They believe that any retaliatory act that is vengeful, including war or bringing suit against another person in court, is wrong. The Amish strongly believe in unconditional forgiveness. The aforementioned authors describe the Amish as carrying forgiveness in their hearts.

NEVER TOO LATE – RECONCILIATION ALMOST 50 YEARS LATER

Congressman John Lewis was and continues to be a stalwart and hero in the Civil Rights movement. He was active in the Student Nonviolence Coordinating Committee (SNCC) involved with the Freedom Riders, the voter registration march across the Edmund Pettus Bridge and the March on Washington. He basically put his life on the line. In May1961 he was among a group of students who had participated in an effort to protest segregation in the south utilizing the nonviolent approach demonstrated by Dr. Martin Luther King, Jr.. Lewis had been brutally beaten as he got off a bus in SC to integrate a local lunch counter when he was attacked by Klu Klux Klan members Then in February 2009 Congressman Lewis was approached by an ex-Klansman, Elwin Wilson, who stated his remorse and offered his apologies. Congressman Lewis accepted Wilson's apology along with forgiving him. It was an emotional meeting between the two men at the Congressman's office on Capitol Hill Lewis felt that Wilson was "very, very sincere" and believed that it took raw courage for Wilson to come forward, to share the need to get hate out of his heart and encourage others to do the same. Both men hoped it would lead to a great deal of healing. Even after his passing the spirit of Congressman Lewis is needed more than ever in the healing of our world. While facing my own personal pain being shuttled to a myriad of different medical facilities as well as witnessing the chaos in the world it was John Lew's book "Carry On" that gave me solace and strength to forgive.

FORGIVING IS AN ACT OF SELF PRESERVATION

When we forgive another it is not necessarily an act of absolution nor judgment. Many famous writers and activists have expressed the hardship of tyranny, deprivation and isolation however stressed the power of solidarity and our need to support each other and empathize with each other because each of us is more alike than we are unalike. Each in their own way focusing on the common good and the resilience of the human spirit to overcome.

Focusing on revenge, anger and resentment is akin to drinking poison and expecting the person who caused your pain to die. Revenge, anger and resentment are toxic to the sender and such emotions are simply an escalation of the negative energy, and sadly no healing by either party occurs whether it relates to personal grievances or international warring factions.

In accepting the important role of forgiveness in our lives we are moving forward toward wholeness. In forgiving, we open our hearts to infinite positive possibilities and create a peaceful refuge. As Eleanor Roosevelt stated: *"All human beings are born free and equal in dignity and rights."* Our own self-worth is based on our ability to look into the mirror acknowledge that we are worthy and, consequently, our brother/sister is also worthy.

Being unforgiving can create obstacles to reaching our full potential. Continuing to hold unto past grievances results in our expending energy on those transgressions which is wasting energy – draining us physically, emotionally, as well as spiritually. Such an energy drain can negatively impact on our productivity, health, and happiness.

As I look at the words forgiving and for giving I am reminded what a difference a "space" makes. The former is an act of judgement and pardon while the latter can be viewed as an act of generosity and grace. It's similar to our discussion relating to a part and apart, the former being united and the latter being separated. While typing the word "apartheid" I realized that the preface begins with the dictate of separation. Simply a little space can make a big difference.

Society often views forgiveness as a sign of weakness when, in fact, it involves a great deal of courage. Surrendering our "rightness" and accepting the "wrongness" can be difficult when viewed from a right/wrong perspective. However, when viewed from the vantage point of peace, forgiveness can truly be a beautiful experience. Archbishop Desmond Tutu has stated: *"With each act of forgiveness whether small or great we move toward wholeness.... Forgiveness is how we bring peace to ourselves and the world."*

To continue revisiting childhood traumas, racial and ethnic inequalities and personal injustices will keep us stuck in the pain and negativity enjoined by such events. I am not suggesting that we walk around with a "V" for victim tattooed to our foreheads. Indeed, we have the choice to have the "V" stand for victor. More importantly, we don't even need any tattoo – we simply can acknowledge our worthiness as well as our wHolyness and move forward. To again quote Archbishop Tutu: "Without forgiveness we remain tethered to the person who harmed us they will hold the keys to our happiness, they will be our jailers." There is another beautiful quote from Archbishop Tutu that I've paraphrased to include the "we" rather than focus on the singular individual. It's one of my favorite quotes and I believe it is a perfect lead into the section that follows: "Dear Children of God, we are loved with a love that can never be shaken; a love that loved us long before we were created, a love that will be there long after everything has disappeared. We are precious, with a preciousness that is totally quite immeasurable. And God wants us to be like God. Filled with life and goodness and laughter and joy Amen!"

CHALLENGE OF FORGIVING OURSELVES

Letting go is essential and. while doing such might not be easy; doing so can free us from fear and guilt and in turn help us achieve our heart's deepest desires. Making the choice to forgive is the first step; accepting forgiveness is the second. Often, it's the second step that presents the real challenge. That step requires us to forgive ourselves for making the mistake that put us into less than desirable circumstances; simply acknowledging that it is what it is; letting go of past circumstances; and simply focusing on the present while surrendering.

The final act involves acknowledging that our apology may go unrequited even challenged. One might view this as adding insult to injury which could simply deepen the hurt and pain. That's the time to focus on loving ourselves even more. Shining a light on the darkness is a much more compassionate state to be in than wallowing in the dark. Understanding the key role of balancing ourselves internally is much more critical than hoping for a balanced response externally. The light and joy always comes from within. Perhaps that's what Jesus meant when he advised his disciples to "turn the other cheek" and "first seek the kingdom of God...."

The path of forgiveness involves courage and understanding. While grief and loss are bitter and painful, at the end of the journey there is a sense of freedom. Some call it the light at the end of the tunnel when, in fact, the light is within us all. Freedom is the ultimate realization of Being; that we are simply a "Peace" (piece) of the "Whole" (holy Source or whatever you may call it). Accepting Being Divine and Eternal allows the Life Force to flow which, in turn, results in an understanding and unconditional love that is actualized.

Forgiving ourselves in the most compassionate manner is a positive tool to manifest the greatest good. Consequently, guilt and fear are transformed; transcending suffering and experiencing joy and contentment becomes a reality.

Forgiving ourselves without pointing fingers - simply expanding our arms and hearts to the widest possibilities gives us the opportunity to forgive the past and be open to the possibilities of all the love the universe has to share. We cannot expect to force anyone else to open their heart; the gift is to open our own heart in the process of forgiveness. Reinhold Niebuhr states that "forgiveness is the final form of love."

In remembering my mother, there is a sense of joy and contentment. While my childhood was not easy, in hindsight I am able to understand my mother's life was challenging and she had a great deal of insecurity and anger, as discussed in Chapter 5. As a result, her love was toxic; however she did the best that she could. Accepting that she did the best she could gives me the ability to forgive and let it go which then allowed me the space to be there for her during her final days and share love. Later in life, even though she was suffering from Alzheimer's and unable to speak, I had the opportunity to lay next to her "heart to heart" and the fact that I was able to witness her smile was priceless. I am also extremely grateful for the support we received from Hospice – especially with regards to the music therapist. She began singing "I love you a bushel and a peck, a bushel and a peck I do." To my amazement my mother began singing along with the music therapist and so did I. Tears of joy were streaming down both my mother's and my faces.

It was more than a cathartic moment it was truly soulful. It is a moment I will take to my grave and pray that it will be a loving memory that my mother took with her.

YOU CAN'T TAKE IT WITH YOU

In Eckhart Tolle's book *The New Earth*, he discusses a woman who is in the process of dying of cancer and she is upset because she believes the woman who is her caregiver has stolen her ring. Her distress and suffering was reflecting that she couldn't understand how anyone could be so hard hearted to do this to her – that something was happening that shouldn't have and thus an injustice – a travesty was being visited upon her. The woman was emotionally distraught and agonizing whether to confront the caregiver directly or call the police immediately. She kept insisting that the ring was much more than the monetary loss since it was a family heirloom.

Tolle asked insightful questions that helped the woman to get past her anger, go within and let go. The questions were: "Do you realize you will have to let go of the ring at some point, perhaps quite soon? …How much more time do you need before you will be ready to let it go? Will you become less when you let go of it? Has who you are become diminished by the loss?" He encouraged the woman to feel rather than think the answers. She began to smile and seemed more peaceful. She explained when she became present and felt her response that she became aware of her ultimate "I am-ness" and felt very alive.

She had simply surrendered and was simply in a state of being. She relinquished all judgments and anger while she completely accepted the loss. She began to understand the importance of letting things go. In the last few weeks of her life she began to glow and gave many of her possessions away even some to the woman she initially thought had stolen the ring.

After she passed they found the ring in the medicine cabinet in the bathroom. Had the ring been there the entire time or did the woman return it? We'll never know, however, rather than focusing on the external drama the woman chose to go within during her last days on earth and move forward on a more compassionate and loving path. The process did not involve accusations; the events unfolded from a conscious state of simply being without blame or guilt. The bible describes it as "the peace of God which passeth all understanding." In the end the woman passed peacefully and the ring was either never stolen or was returned. She was able to experience a sense of Divine Presence - a serenity and complete freedom from material possessions; a state of whatever.

While being in a state of whatever is freeing, at the same time it can be somewhat unnerving. To gain a sense of balance, in the middle of my own loss and grief, I am finding that acceptance and compassion for myself as well as for family and friends can be healing. If I were to die tomorrow, clearly those would be two emotions that would give a deeper meaning to "RIP" Rest in Peace. It's not a question of "if" it's a question of "when" because we will all die.

Many of us have a fear of death; a fear that results from the mystery as well as possible guilt, shame, anger and resentment. These emotions can make Resting In Peace more difficult and clearly makes actually living even more challenging. Whether we call it forgiveness or simply letting go, it's to our advantage to choose to release these emotions. There is nothing wrong with acknowledging a perception of negative circumstances and at the same time accepting the presence of accompanying negative emotions and then releasing them. Denial is an obstacle to a peaceful transition as well as a peaceful life. Letting go of these heavy emotions makes our load lighter. It's easier to breathe and enjoy the day. Holding onto past pain only prolongs that pain. Life is for giving and we can decide to give up the pain, giving ourselves unconditional love which makes room for peace here and now, rather than waiting for the hereafter. There is a need to embrace space that provides the healing space necessary to lift-up, surrender and be truly open.

Emotions are energy frequencies that can be toxic or loving and we have a choice of which energies we will radiate during our transition. We also have the choice to create a loving space for ourselves, regardless of the chaos we are experiencing. That would mean having a soulful response and accepting the external events as experiences that are helping us grow in this life's journey. Do we really want to wait until we're on our death bed to be peaceful and loving? Will it be too late? What's stopping us from feeling those emotions now?

As previously discussed, Dr. Elisabeth Kubler-Ross shares that when people are on their death beds there are only two things they'll remember – first, the moments which are the times we shared with someone that made us smile or made someone else smile and second, the windstorms which are the painful times when we experience grief and losses. Elisabeth believes both the moments and the windstorms are blessings. While going through the windstorms it's hard to consider them blessings; though as Elisabeth emphasized that: if there had never been windstorms we could never witness the beauty of the Grand Canyon.

VISION QUEST

In exploring different modalities to embrace forgiving totally a friend recommended a wilderness experience at the Friends' Wilderness Center which is only several miles from where I live in WV. In communicating with the leader of this adventure I learned that it is nine days of camping including three days of fasting. The fasting was not intimidating; I had never gone camping in my life. The closest I came to camping was sleeping in a cinderblock lodge near the Grand Canyon. I kept an open mind and heart and kept believing if this was meant to be and in Quaker Speak, "a way would open." A friend offered to lend me all his camping equipment and to instruct me how to pitch a tent along with all the amenities which included a head lamp. A friend asked if I was afraid of bears, in all honesty I was more afraid of bugs. Before going forward on this quest all participants were required to forward an application and attach a letter stating our intentions. The following is an excerpt from the application:

"The concept of truly going within and recognizing my own strength and courage to continue the journey as a peaceful warrior is indeed an intention.

This 9 day Medicine Walk can prove to be the healing balm that can help me through these turbulent times in my life. It can in turn help me to clarify the best manner to unite this experience with my creative talent as well as highlight the need for unconditional love. These nine days will be the catalyst in being a spring board for discerning how best to proceed.

I am in major transitions. Basically, at the age of 63 years old I am feeling that everything that I knew and trusted has been shattered. I pray I am at the point in my life where the challenges and obstacles that I have been experiencing will be simply stepping stones to share in the process of life. I feel blessed that I am still able to smile and that I continue to reach up and out to help others to understand that life is worth living and sharing regardless of the circumstances.

Being open to asking for help and support. I pray that I am at the point of a metamorphosis and ready to fly.

Learning to trust myself is a critical intention. In navigating life's ups and downs it's important to find the space where I can share my knowledge, tenacity, love and humor. Being open to surrendering and believing in the greater whole and understanding that I can be a colorful asset. Learning humility is an intention. Expressing myself even when it hurts and when I feel vulnerable is an intention. When I ask myself "who are my people?" It continues to echo in both my heart and mind we are ALL ONE and all is well. To be able to see the oneness manifest in the world would be a joy. To experience and identify with that joy is an intention. Mass shootings have become rampant in the United States. After the mass killings in the Orlando nightclub this past weekend, my desire to be a light shining attention on our critical need to be open to unconditional love is more important than ever. My overall Intention is both a personal and communal sense of being whole and compassionate.

On July 5th, 2016 I began the Vision Quest at Fiends Wilderness Center. I am glad to say I survived and experienced some moving insightful moments. I learned probably more about the two legged homo sapiens than the animals with fur. I also learned that I don't necessarily enjoy camping; more specifically I don't like "pissing" on myself, I never quite got the hang of relieving myself in the woods. Guys really have it a lot easier. I admit that I appreciate creature comforts, like restroom facilities. The sound of the animals at night and the stars were a treat. I was the oldest person on the Quest by at least twenty years; the vast majority were millennials. WOW did I get a view of these young people who seemed somewhat self-absorbed and lost. I am happy to report that I camped the entire nine days and fasted for three. The other participants kept complaining they were starving. For people who kept professing that they wanted to get back to nature, they drank an enormous amount of coffee, smoked habitually and were attached to their iPhones.

A wonderful labyrinth I found had a beautiful message "I am on thy path O God. Thou O God in my steps ." I journaled everyday focusing on the sounds, smells and sights of nature. The facilitator stressed the importance of getting in touch with our "dark side" I began to realize that the "dark side" was simply the space between the light.

Part of the schedule involved "circle ceremony" where people shared their stories. I had the feeling that the millennials were some-what intimidated by the length and depth of my story. I admitted while cloistered in the woods that the nature of unconditional love was echoing in the leaves blowing and was a core part of my being regardless of my past challenges. There were some heart wrenching stories about lost loves and family dysfunction. At one point a young man broke down crying about his brother committing suicide from a drug overdose – I looked around the group, they seemed immobile, frozen in time, shutdown. No one moved as a fellow "quester" shook uncontrollably. I slowly moved towards him and held out my hand and he grasped it (reminding me of the time the three year old at the child care center grabbed my hand pg. 74) I then moved even closer and held out my arms to hug him – our eyes met and I shared that his brother is with him that he is at peace in his heart and that he will never stop loving him. He seemed comforted by the message and we smiled and we hugged. The group was still and motionless. Had I crossed a boundary letting this young man know that someone was willing to cross a boundary to demonstrate they cared? The litmus test for me is – would I do the same thing again? The answer is YES. Would I regret not reaching out and sharing? The answer is YES.

There were several interactions that were very telling. At the end of the quest, I found out that several of the millennials had bet that I wouldn't complete the Quest. They lost that bet. On the last evening it was decided that the group would take a six mile hike up to Rattle Snake Ridge. They assumed I would refrain from this last exercise however I was committed to be present throughout the entire process. Two of the assistant facilitators came to me to express their concern, I said I would start out before the others so that I wouldn't hold them up and they could hike and pass me. It didn't matter the speed or the time it took it was more important to embrace the experience and trust. The two facilitators walked with me, I appreciate that they took the time, I also laughed and noted that there were two escorting me so if there was a problem one of them could stay with me and someone could go back to base camp for help. It was thoughtful however they underestimated me. I did walk with a wooden staff to help me keep my balance (when I moved to the mountain my stepdad had whittled several walking staffs for me, he enjoyed whittling and I enjoyed the staffs) I was able to make it up to Raddle Snake Ridge – slow and steady. When I arrived those already on the ridge clapped and I took a bow. The young man who had wept and we experienced a hug in the circle came up to me. He pointed to a cloud in the sky that looked like an angel and said: "I think that's my brother" I smiled and agreed. It's an angel cloud that I will never forget. On the way back down from the ridge while it was getting dark I kept singing Broadway show tunes. One of the guys came up to me and warned me there was a bear cave near by; I simply laughed kept singing and told him that the bear had the opportunity to enjoy the music and perhaps would dance. By the end of the quest I was tired, but I was smiling.

No camping trip is complete without some bug stories. A friend shared an old camping trick that every morning at least a week before you start camping and during the hike you drink apple cider vinegar – it was a nontoxic way to repel bugs of being a bug repellent. I also used bug spray and Avon's Skin-soSoft. Whether it was the Deet spray or the non- toxic approaches that limited the number of the bug bites is anybody's guess. Unfortunately, some of the participants were bitten mercilessly and were covered in lotion to stop the itching. I got used to ants crawling all over the tent, I explained to them that I was a vegetarian and had no interest in any of them crawling into the sleeping bag or my mouth, and I am pleased they somewhat honored my personal space. Bugs did teach me a lesson in humility. While using the outhouse I noticed a tick on my upper thy. I came to the circle pulled down my pants and asked if anyone had any tweezers and could pull out the little sucker. I am very glad that there were people who were willing to assist. When I got back to the house and took a long awaited bath I noticed another tick – I got some antiseptic and a tweezer and was able to get the tick, head and all completely removed. That sealed the deal; I really had no interest in camping again. My friend who lent me the camping equipment insisted that I get tested for lyme disease, I did and am pleased to report that it was negative.

I truly enjoyed watching the facilitator's four year old son enjoying nature and just breaking out in pure giggles that were contagious. He tickled my heart. Singing songs at the campfire was fun. My meditations and prayers included the millennials several of whom were teachers and I also included their students. I left the quest knowing that it wasn't over and that I still had a lot of work to do and that we are all still in the process of evolving - each of us is on a journey. One young woman was insisting that she wanted to go to a tattoo parlor before she drove home to North Carolina. I offered her the name of a friend's son who is a tattoo artist. In my heart I could hear a loving WHATEVER! Response.

"FEAR NOT" BEING OPEN TO UNCONDITIONAL LOVE

As previously noted in Chapter 1, "Fear Not" appears in the Bible 365 times The famous quote from the book and movie *Love Story* by Erich Segal:, "Love means never having to say you're sorry" sounds good on the big screen; however, in real life it's not always that simple. The fact that we are alive means we will experience joy as well as sorrow Taking responsibility for our actions resulting from the sorrows and hurts we cause exhibits our willingness to be open and to stand in our truth and state: "I am sorry" – especially to the ones we love, as well as for ourselves.

Everyone has their own truth and often may view themselves as innocent. Apologizing takes strength as well as courage to recognize the consequences of our actions, whether wantonly negative or not. It takes even more courage to accept that there may never be an apology forthcoming or that any apology we might offer could be rebuked or rejected. It is at that critical moment that we open ourselves to unconditional love that helps us to move forward. Being mired in a fear of not being forgiven traps us and those we are not forgiving in an emotional quagmire of guilt, shame, anger and resentment. The resulting pain can be overwhelming.

There is a story shared to promote healing: when a Hindu man came to Mahatma Gandhi for guidance in order to help alleviate his pain of losing his child who was killed in a religious war, The man was also burdened with guilt since he had killed children in the war Gandhi suggested that the man adopt a Muslim orphan, but that the Hindu man raise the child in the Muslim faith. In war children are lost and parents are killed and Gandhi's suggestion demonstrates the need to view both sides with compassion – again requiring the strength and courage to overcome the quagmire resulting from fear and hatred. Whether we are involved with religious wars, political battles or family feuds; are we willing to let go of the pain regardless of who is right or wrong? Is there a right or wrong? Reaching reconciliation allows us to experience peace and freedom without judgment or blame. It's an act of selflessness and accepting the oneness of us all.

Well documented Near Death Experiences (NDEs) and Life After Life Awareness help us to reach an understanding of the universal essence of us all Being Alive. Both anger and resistance cloud our view and ability to recognize that the Golden Rule of loving our neighbor as ourselves is the cornerstone of every major religious tradition. When we begin to love ourselves and accept our own Divinity in a corporal form, we will begin to accept the Divine spark within all beings. Unconditional love becomes an empowering and inspirational message when reviewing the stories illustrated by Gandhi's suggestion to the Hindu man and the young Jewish girl's sharing her memories about the death camp at Majdanek with Elisabeth. Those who have experienced NDEs and After Life Awareness seem to universally share the transformational experience of unconditional love. The messages shared by Dr. Eben Alexander, author of *Proof of Heaven*, summarizes the existence of heaven on earth and within; simply put: "First, that you are loved and cherished, dearly forever. Second, that you have nothing to fear. Third, there is nothing you can do wrong."

When we take these loving messages of Gandhi, Elisabeth and Eben Alexander to heart, we can truly be open to the moments and windstorms that Elisabeth witnessed during people's transitions. I feel blessed that she gave me the opportunity to see that her life work was about living and not fearing death.

Life is a progression of stops and starts. We are continually faced with the alpha and the omega. As Elisabeth so beautifully describes we are caterpillars destined to become butterflies. The anger and resentment we experience constitutes an obstacle to being free and flying. Her wisdom is with me always and I am grateful that she shared her commitment of unconditional love with me as well as the passion she had for overcoming fear.

The resulting play *TORCH,* about Elisabeth, is a labor of love and is dedicated to the Divine Life Force within us all. We will all die, and the manner in which we die is reflective of the manner in which we live. We can consciously choose acceptance or denial. In grappling with personal windstorms, it's my experience that acceptance and letting go with compassion can be a blessing. Forgiving ourselves is opening ourselves to unconditional love for ourselves and our neighbors in the broadest possible sense and for the greatest good. *TORCH* is designed to share the brilliance of the Divine and shine a light within that will be a beacon for understanding, peace and joy. The journey we all travel goes b*eyond life and death.* We ALL have the opportunity to shine on this journey. Being open to the glow of unconditional love is experiencing the AHAA (A Heavenly Awareness) of life here and here after.

Personal loss is clearly an in your face teacher. I want to strongly thank Mitch Albom and Morrie Schwartz in helping to shed a light on their own struggles with forgiveness in the #1 New York Times best selling book, *Tuesdays with Morrie.* Mitch's candor in sharing the painful estrangement with his brother, Peter, as well as Morrie describing the estrangement of a close friend truly touched my heart. The fact that Mitch dedicated his book to his brother is a testament to the power of healing and the need to navigate "F"ing relationships. My prayer is that we all can find a "Coach" like Morrie and embrace the courage to move forward building bridges and exit laughing. Life is too precious to die with regrets.

Inspirations and Thoughts from Moments & Windstorms

- True forgiveness is a selfless act that requires courage and a sense of unconditional love for ourselves and the person who is being forgiven; it is a heartfelt act.
- A judgmental state of mind can result in being self-righteous which is not necessarily an act of forgiveness.
- Forgiving ourselves can be extremely challenging and at the same time extremely rewarding and liberating. It is critical that we get past the guilt, pain, fear and shame in order to truly experience the greatest good possible and live our lives to the fullest.
- Letting go of the past is key to forgiving ourselves and others.
- We are continually faced with the alpha and the omega. We are caterpillars destined to become butterflies. Letting go of resentment and anger allows our soul to soar and fly beyond our dreams of life and death.
- Near death experiences as well a death bed experiences bring to light the importance of forgiveness. Living life being aware of the liberation of simply forgiving is truly a Divine gift we give ourselves. Both tears and laughter are a blessing.
- Are there people and circumstances you need to forgive? Carrying losses and resentments weigh us down. LET IT GO!
- Do you have any interesting camping stories you'd like to share?
- Do you love yourself unconditionally? Why or why not?
- We are ALL WORTHY of Unconditional Love. *

Chapter 8

FULL CIRCLE

"Humankind has not woven the web of life. We are but one thread within it. Whatever we do to the web, we do to ourselves. All things are bound together. All things connect." Chief Seattle,

"May this circle be unbroken......." Ada R. Habershon

"The care of the Earth is our most ancient and most worthy, and after all our most pleasing responsibility. To cherish what remains of it and to foster its renewal is our only hope.... The earth is what we all have in common." Wendell Berry

"No one is born hating another person because of the color of his or her skin, background or religion. People must learn to hate, and if they can learn to hate they can be taught to love for love comes more naturally to the human heart than its opposite." Nelson Mandela

"Love Thy neighbor (no exceptions)" Bible, Leviticus 19:18; Matthew 23:39 and Mark 12:29-31 plus (No Exceptions) added by Friends National Committee on Legislation

There have been many artists and activists who have spoken truth to power. Many have paid dearly – be it with their life, their freedom and or their loss of community. I believe that at this critical point the threads that Chief Seattle describe begin to shine and there is a thin line between life and death, peace on earth is more than a holiday greeting. We become one with the Divine, overcoming the "F"ing Relationships", uniting with the "Flow of Life" and finding refuge in "Forgiveness". We are grateful for each breath and accepting our individual as well as communal responsibility for ensuring that we reflect Life, Love, Light, Laughter and Limitless possibilities. We are ALL stewards of the greater good. It takes courage and chances are that we will have to navigate windstorms in the process. As we embrace and are embraced by the full circle we are both simply humble and evolutionarily transformative. Being human isn't easy being Divine is sublime. Balancing these two powerful essences requires patience and faith

Moving from the District of Columbia to West Virginia was simply witnessing a state of colonization to a state of marginalization; both of which are toxic. Getting past the toxicity is challenging: the only way is to accept and surrender that our goal is to be open to the Full Circle and recognize we are all one. This process can be the most humbling and exhilarating.

Writing this book during this unprecedented time in history can be viewed as both a moment and a windstorm: both from the view of the mountain and the political bowels of our nation's center of power as well as the medical malaise that continues to threaten us. The impeachment of Richard Nixon was discussed in chapter 1; and it was noted that President Gerald Ford granted Nixon a pardon. Will Donald John Trump be acquitted, receive a pardon or will complete havoc ensue? I can honestly say I do not know. I do know I will continue to pray and testify to promote clean air, water and soil. With faith we come full circle be it from the perspective of Chief Seattle, Wendell Berry, Nelson Mandella, or Ada R. Habershon.

It is essential that we overcome the lemming mentality. Democracy and independence can never be taken for granted. Freedom is an individual choice that is not necessarily easy. When faced with daunting challenges courage is needed. We can choose to be the monkey trapped in the organgrinders cage tethered to the disheartening and demoralizing requiem. Embracing our own SELF-WORTH we can awaken our loving spirit, our oneness and our desire for Peace on Earth reflecting the beauty of being alive.

WALKING THE TALK

On Wednesday, September 18, 2019 Tracy Danzey had a news conference in front of the Jefferson County, WV Courthouse. She is a woman of conviction and determination. Spirit Spoke – I heard a loving message 'Walk with her. Help raise consciousness. We can no longer be silent.' Voices come in many shapes and sizes. Be it walking across Denmark to protest the environmental injustice of the construction of a Danish factory in West Virginia that would generate the toxic emissions banned in Europe. The toxins would go beyond the West Virginia borders polluting the air, soil. and water of surrounding areas. As Tracy walked through Denmark there was a group of us that walked 60 miles along the Chesapeake & Ohio (C&O) Canal, from Harpers Ferry through Maryland, Virginia to DC.

During Tracy's news conference a still small voice came to me "Walk in Solidarity along the C&O Canal." The still small voice did not include a GPS nor any other instructions. While faithfully moving forward I got clarity that the C&O was the Chesapeake & Ohio Canal hiking trail that is a National Park.

Tracy Danzey a coal miners great grand-daughter and resident of Jefferson County, West Virginia (WV) began, her courageous journey to walk throughout Denmark to bear witness that a Danish Company is in the process of building a highly polluting factory across the road from an elementary school. In solidarity a group of concerned citizens from the Eastern Panhandle of WV began walking the C&O Canal from Harpers Ferry, WV to Washington, DC to also reflect our concerns for the need for equity. The Danish people and government are the world's leaders in environmental protection and innovative environmental solutions. All children and citizens in West Virginia and the surrounding geographic area deserve the same equitable environmental protections that are valued in Denmark.

Tracy is a survivor of cancer due to the polluted waters in WV that she swam in as a child and as a result her legs were amputated and half of her pelvis removed. Her story is inspiring, the fact that she walked 70 miles, shore to shore, across Denmark's Zealand island, Kalendborg to Copenhagen, is daunting in itself – walking through Denmark with no legs is a testament to her concern and love for her family and her community.

Her community in turn echoed that concern. People who were unable to fly to Denmark could come together on the C&O because they were concerned about the environment and our children's future and felt the need to take a careful and thoughtful review of the horrific polluting policies in West Virginia (WV) which knows no boundaries. Rockwool's toxic production will impact rural as well as metropolitan locations throughout the DC area, covering 60 to 70 miles or 100 kilometers. This is a powerful story and we were committed to embark on a non-violent protest focusing on a local as well as an international perspective. Our intent with each step was to raise consciousness regarding the blatant disregard the state of West Virginia has demonstrated in protecting our environment and our children's future and the threat to our national parks, our agricultural industry and the health of our residents.

Scientists have sounded the alarm nationally and internationally regarding the climate crisis our world is facing. We in Jefferson County, WV are dealing with it locally. However, the toxins that this factory will produce knows no boundaries and the tri-state area along with our US Capitol will be victims of both air. soil and water pollution. Th factory proposes to burn on a daily basis over 90 tons of coal and using 1.5 million cubic feet of fracked gas on a karst landscape. The fossil fuel that will be utilized will continue to poison our environment. Given the environmental protections enforced in Denmark, the company is prohibited to build the type of facility they are building in West Virginia The Danish people pride themselves on being environmentally responsible and green. Tracy's walk and the fact that we are marching along the C&O Canal is demonstrating our commitment to encourage national and international leaders to focus attention on our children's future. We are urging those in Copenhagen and Washington, DC to take action to prevent environmental inequity.

The Chesapeake and Ohio (C & O) Canal is a historical park that is a beautiful national treasure. The watershed along the Canal, part of the Chesapeake ecosystem, is potentially threatened by the Facility operated by the Danish company. It's critical to note that the Danish government would not approve the facility as designed in WV to be built in their country because its design threatens the environment.

This environmental dangers and injustices of building this highly polluting plant is being addressed on a number of levels. The community is providing a creative approach to challenge Rockwool on legal, scientific and moral grounds. We the people are coming together step by step in our commitment to focus on the need to overcome corrupt and inappropriate behavior that jeopardizes a vulnerable and marginalized population especially children, the elderly, people in low income neighborhoods and those with compromised health issues.

One of the most WOW experiences was witnessing a woman who was committed to walk all 60 miles with a walker. Her determination was amazing. The support she received from a neighbor and her husband still brings tears to my eyes. The trek that Tracy was committed to walk in Denmark was brought close to home. Throughout the walk the smiles shared were priceless. Solidarity had an ALL for ONE and ONE for ALL presence we were focused on the quality of life. Getting beyond personal baggage and sharing the greater good. The walk became greater than ourselves again understanding "we are our brother/sisiter's keeper." Keep smiling being grateful – stop bitching. While walking realizing we were on a civil rights march; a march, at least for me, that focused on civility, safety, the greater good, justice and especially our children. Intimidation is unacceptable and it is time for the local school system to take courageous action to protect the students, families, teachers, staff and the community as a whole. In testimony presented to the Board of Education shared the vision of David standing up to a Danish Goliath.

Praying that corporations would come to appreciate the Divine spark we share and get beyond toxic behavior before they kill us, themselves and the planet. Science is not the enemy, the lack of respect for science and it running a muck brings us to a point where we truly need to "Love thy Neighbor" here before we reach the hereafter. When we get beyond the rhetoric and greed; science can be our friend in protecting the environment. Getting beyond a tribal mentality and realizing that we are ALL mortal heading towards immortality. We are all worthy of respect. Until WE can state "We are worthy" we are short changing ourselves and the world. Watching the water flow in all directions and watching the awe of the children experiencing the majesty and roar of the forceful presence was truly a gift. Feeling the mist was a baptism I shall never forget and grateful that a Friend captured that moment even though I kept insisting that I didn't want my picture taken since the solidarity walk was more than me it was us all coming together. I continue to pray we will ALL recognize the importance of coming together, be it baptized by the mist or a smile that lights up our hearts.

Simply coordinating the two walks became an awkward dance. Reaching out to the media was a challenge and it was frustrating. I was encouraged by friends to create a facebook page as well as utilize the internet and link with Tracy's facebook. I watched with joy as key information was shared and was horrified that there were persons who took advantage that advertised points of view that were contrary to our message. I was also shocked and somewhat amused that if you're not listed as a FB member your name can't be listed with the pictures posted. Personally, I felt hacked and betrayed - we deserve better our world deserves better.

After completing the walk a couple of us went to see the movie Dark Waters. The movie focused on the legal battle with the Dupont Company, located in Parkersburg, West Virginia, regarding the chemical pollutants that adversely effected the people working in its factory as well as the community and the live stock living in the vicinity of the factory. I found it extremely disconcerting when a Dupont executive read a document that referred to those who were impacted as "receptors" and the lawyer representing the plaintiffs then showed the executive a picture of a baby that had suffered birth defects and asked "Is this one of your receptors?". That child was innocent!

The walk ended on November 7, 2019 however my resolve is stronger than ever. What form will that take? I can honestly say I don't know. I continue to pray and meditate. The quote by George Bernard Shaw "Life is no brief candle to me but a splendid torch I have gotten hold of for the moment and I want to make it burn as brightly as possible before handing it over to future generations" is poignant and continues to ring true for me along with the hymn Full Circle.

To lean more about the C&O Solidarity Walk there is a link https://facebook.com/solidarityCOWalk

DAVID & GOLIATH

During this process we were aware that it is difficult to raise this issue while our country and the world continue to promoted angry political messages on cyberspace platforms exponentially that intimidate our local school board, Praying they are able to recognize that this is the time for courageous action and to overcome toxic behavior. In testimony shared the vision - of David standing up to a Danish Goliath. Children were drawing colorful pictures to show how much they love nature and deserve clean air, water and soil they also want to have fun playing outside! The kids helped to touch folks' hearts and do the right thing David delivered the pictures and prayers and Goliath was moved to modify the facility with a much safer design They began practicing the GOLDEN RULE committing to a much safer faciilityy to keep the children safe witnessing that the drawings and prayers can override the corporate lawyers' brief, and toxic agreements. The innocence of the children's colorful pictures along with the slingshot that David was carrying illustrates that miracles are possible given faith. Positive dialogue can begin and corrective action taken. By being open to compassionate listening, continuing to care and share. We can reach higher ground coming to a peaceful resolution, Nature is a mirror of our well-being. Returning to "Love Thy Neighbor" is a reunion of Heaven on Earth. While walking the C&O if one listens carefuly we can hear the water and trees calling for HELP! Their beauty is inspiring. At the same time, while humans were pushing and pulling lacking solidarity and creating personal and organizational barriers there are still difficulties needing to be overcome. Pleased that, when we opened our hearts to be touched by witnessing a unity of peaceful understanding it becomes a sublime experience that resulted in superseding greed and promoting an eco-centric approach to interaction.

SOLIDARITY

The war in Uktraine is truly a challenging event on the world stage. Politicians threaten to cut funding while others threaten to utilize tactical nuclear weapons. Hubris on either side is counterproductive.

I am fortunate to be able to witness a group of Quakers throughout the world focusing on Peacebuildjng Perspectives; believing that "way will open" on a local, national and international level, We understand it takes patience and resilience.

On a personal, creative manner I approached the Washington, DC government as follows: Please rename Tunlaw Road to Peaceful Way and hang yellow and blue flags with peace signs on them along with hanging DC flags. Like many people in DC and the world we view the actions taken by the Russian government as horrific; and we are hoping for a peaceful resolution.

I have lived on Tunlaw Road for over five decades. I am humbled that I had the opportunity to work for the first elected Council of the District of Columbia. I have also been involved in promoting quality early childhood education and Head Start.

I have watched the city grow and recognize the key role DC elected officials play in the local, national and global arena. As, you may know, the Russian Consulate in DC faces onto Tunlaw Road. The Permanent Mission of the Russian Federation to the United Nations Office in Geneva is on Avenue de la Paix, which means "Avenue of Peace". I wrote the DC government to help champion an initiative to rename Tunlaw Road, NW to "Peaceful Way"

The message cannot be overemphasized that we need to respect our neighbors and highlight the need to be positive role models for our children. It's still an inequity that the entire DC funding and judicial codes are subject to congressional oversight and as we are witnessing chaos. "Tax Without Representation" is much more than a tag line appearing on the city's license plates. The communication stressed the importance of sovereignty and freedom for both Ukraine and DC. We have the power given our location to make powerful statements; changing the name of Tunlaw Road, NW starting at Calvert Street to 39th Street where Victory Gardens exist that began during WWII and continue to this day is symbolically appropriate. It's a strong silent deafening siren to help raise consciousness in keeping families honored, safe, respected and free - issues that resonate with DC residents as well as the Ukrainian people.

IT'S A BEAUTIFUL DAY IN THE NEIGHBORHOOD

After the solidarity walk I saw two movies that provided interesting juxtapositions regarding their neighborhoods. Throughout this process I kept remembering "Love Thy Neighbor."

I went to see the movie, *It's a Beautiful Day in the Neighborhood* going to friends for Thanksgiving. I felt I deserved a treat. It was indeed a treat and we had fun talking about the loving message. The movie was loosely based on an Esquire Magazine cover story written by journalist Tom Junod. It was much more focused on the friendship that developed between Junod and Mister Rogers. People left the movie theatre feeling uplifted.

A Beautiful Day in the Neighborhood was clearly a 180 degree turn from Dark Walters which is discussed earlier in this chapter and was also a true story based on the New York Times Magazine article on the pollution in Parkersburg, WV and the lawyer, Rob Bilott who the NY Time's article stated was "Dupont's worst nightmare". However both Mister Rogers and Rob Bilott were clearly passionate and committed to the greater good.

Reviewing the life stories of these two men helped me to understand that David taking on Goliath is more than a biblical story. Mister Rogers was open to push the envelope and share his heart felt message: *"I love you just the way you are"* He was portrayed as dorky by late night comedians however he kept the faith and focused on the children when they were facing challenging life circumstances. His caring and gentle nature was a safe space for children during turbulent times. His program resonated with the children. Junod shared that Fred Rogers identified with the number "143" because he believed that the number reflected the number of letters in the following message: I=1, Love=4 and You=3. Rob Bilott loved his grandmother and it was that love and connection that was the catalyst that facilitated his decades long battle against a corporate giant. Fred and Rob were heroes in their own right; exemplifying perseverance and a love greater than themselves. A love greater than we can imagine that overcomes inequities and in turn promotes our greatest potential. I am not sure whether either man started out seeing themselves as heroes however they responded to their better angels and the world benefitted. In their own ways they were miracle workers.

As a footnote, the West Virginia State legislature took two totally different approaches to the release of the movie Dark Waters. One group wrote a letter of protest condemning the Hollywood portrayal of the events that happened in Parkersburg, WV. Another group of Delegates took action introducing legislation to address pollution in drinking water from the chemicals depicted in the recently released feature film "Dark Waters." Delegate Evan Hansen (D-Monongalia) and colleagues in the House of Delegates sponsored a bill to protect West Virginians from this pollution, in order to avoid future human health impacts and costly lawsuits. The legislation is SB 485 PFAS which highlights the danger of forever poisonous toxic chemicals. The bill requires the identification of sources of these chemicals so that contamination of rivers and streams used as drinking water sources can be stopped. It also requires the development of science-based clean drinking water standards that public water systems will need to meet to keep their customers safe. I applaud the efforts of the group of. WV legislators who were willing to support legislative action that promotes the fundamental right of the people to have clean air, pure water, and the preservation of the natural, scenic, historic, and aesthetic values of the environment. Unfortunately, the legislation didn't pass possibly because an executive of Rockwool is in the WV Senate.

As was expressed throughout this book the Golden Rule is a spiritual corner stone of a number of major religions. I will surrender and humbly pray and meditate without ceasing. I will continue to LOVE Thy Neighbor as Thyself. When faced with daunting challenges courage is needed. We can choose to be the monkey trapped in the organ grinders cage tethered to the disheartening and demoralizing requiem. Embracing our own SELF-WORTH we can awaken our loving spirit, our oneness and our desire for Peace on Earth reflecting the beauty of being alive.

Inspirations and Thoughts from Moments & Windstorms

- Full Circle experiences are anchored in our beings, Are there reasons that you might feel comfortable or uncomfortable discussing unconditional love and forgiveness?
- How would you describe your thread in the web of life that Chief Seattle describes?
- What is your relationship with nature? Are there steps you are committed to take to bring you closer to nature?
- What resonates within you when exploring the concept of walking the talk? Was there ever a time you felt marginalized or bullied? How did you respond? Was there ever a time you marginalized or bullied another person? Have you since reconciled?
- Are there medical challenges that you, a friend or family member experienced that youcould share?
- If you have seen the movies *Dark Waters and/or It's a beautiful Day in the Neighborhood* how would you review them? Would you like to see them? Are there movies you've seen or books you read that you'd recommend?
- Are there other questions regarding this chapter and book that could prove helpful"

Acknowledgements

Giving thanks to the Divine Life Force and the Loving Presence which is the Creative Source for ALL. Grateful for the faith in the lessons and miracles that have given birth to the word in helping us to evolve.

Grateful for family and friends who demonstrated the need for support. They did the best they could and helped me to witness the importance of forgiveness and understanding. Sue I am impressed with your loving approach caring for rescue dogs. Your help with numerous issues is fabulous and enjoy laughing together. Thankful for the friends who understood the importance of simply being there for better or worse and were open to love; Connie, Anne and Linda you have been amazing. The hospitality of friends in DC including Sandy, Judy and Rochelle when visiting the city was much appreciated. Acknowledging the friends on the mountain who reached out along with their families. Our laughing together, talks, walks, advocacy and especially our Chi Gong exercises were uplifting.

I am grateful to the authors, activists, advocates and artists who came before and were committed to shine a light on love. Their ability to write from the heart is inspiring. Grateful for those who still dream and share the love. Special thanks to Kasmira, her commitment and youthful enthusiasm to publish her book encouraged me to publish. We are never too young or old to inspire.

Many thanks for those in Washington, DC and in West Virginia who touched my life. Especially grateful to the early childhood community who helped me to learn and grow. The interaction with the

Playwrights' Forum expanded the possibilities and nurtured the talents of many of us in the theatre community. The friendship shared with Elaine and Ernie is a gift. To the Buddha Buddies and the buddies from the South Mountain Friends Fellowship you all highlighted the need to share and the importance of friendship. Felllow advocates in WV committed to promoting the clean air water and environment we all deserve, The folks at Quaker Earthcare Witness sharing our story needing environmental protection. The persons at Hospice of the Panhandle many thanks. The opportunity to witness both living and giving during individual transitions is inspirational. The caring staff at Bolivar Harpers Ferry Family Medicine. The messages from persons at the Miracle Distribution Center were joyful and loving. The list continues to grow and I am forever grateful. Special thanks for those involved with the Shepherd University Life Long Learning program, particularly Karen Rice.

The librarians at Bolivar-Harpers Ferry, Charles Town and Shepherdstown were extremely helpful with their patience and guidance. They enabled my book addiction with a caring understanding.

This book would not have been possible without the help of Quaker Friends and programs. The support of Goose Creek Friends Meeting has been immeasurable. The encouragement from Friends at Shepherdstown Meeting particularly Carole and Bill have been fruitful. Kris your continued commitment to peace and networking is phenomenal. Debbi volunteering with you on the Anti Racist Committee has been a learning experience and a blessing. Your patience is a joy. Patricia it's been special both dramatically and comically. Remembering several near death experiences, negotiating with the medical bureaucracy and walking the C&O Canal as well as enjoying treats at local ice cream stores.

I have experienced an up-lifting and hopeful interaction with the International Quaker World Peace Meeting via zoom. The persons participating in Quaker Peacebuilding Perspectives continue to energize me. Persons who participated in the Friends Committee on National Legislation (FCNL) were truly teachers as well as messengers for "Love thy Neighbors – No exceptions"

The insight of Friends who shared their educational expertise and technological talents helped this project become a reality. Sincerely appreciate Perry's support. Gratitude goes to Sean and Ed who assisted me to overcome tech challenges.

Daily interaction with Pendle Hill zoom is a blessing. The furry four legged animals are loving companions. The opportunity to participate with the Sacred Listening practice is a bonus.

Thanks to the numerous community organizations committed to protect the environment in Jefferson County, WV. The volunteer enthusiasm has been creative and heartwarming. A special SHOUTOUT to Mary Reed - you are truly a beautiful spirit. The tree the Sierrea Club planted in your honor in front of North Jefferson Elementary School is well deserved. A wide range of expertise has been instrumental in drafting papers that highlight critical talking points included in government submissions. A number of these reports were submitted to the Jefferson County School (JCS) Board of Education and are included in the JCS archives.

The folks at Brilliant Books were open and supportive The publishing process was dealt with professionally. I was humbled and appreciative in the manner they approached the content and message of Soulful Courage + Torch. It was a definite plus that Sofia shared her caring and love for the project.

A very soulful thanks to my mentor Helen Taylor who continues to be an inspiration. She encouraged my passion to advocate for children and the need for us to work together to ensure that every child reach his or her fullest potential regardless of race, gender, religion, ethnic, social or economic background. Helen has since passed over however her spirit is still very much alive in my heart.

Special thanks to Elisabeth who taught me to embrace the "moments" and the "windstorms" of life including Swiss chocolates. How sweet it is!

Appendix

TORCH:
A Glorious Celestial Light Show and Dramatic Interactive Theatre

NOTICE:

IMPORTANT NOTE: Beginning this book with the message that "there is a reason for everything in the world" and the final closing point emphasizing that "We are ALL WORTHY of Unconditional Love. " is simply paying homage to Elisabeth and the Divine Light within us ALL. I am praying that we can ALL Love Life and RIP here now as well as the hereafter.

TORCH

A Play
By Bobbi Blok
A Glorious Celestial Light Show
and Dramatic Interactive Theatre

B. Blok
(304) 725-2488
wvahaa@aol.com

DEDICATION

Dedicated to unconditional love
and the life force within us all.

With Love,

BHB
12/2005

CHARACTERS

DR. ELISABETH KUBLER-ROSS

ELISABETH is petite yet is a giant in word and action. During specific scenes of the play it is obvious that she has become physically frail due to the numerous strokes she has suffered. She speaks with a Swiss-German accent.

KARLA

KARLA is a playwright as well as an advocate for young children. She is in her thirties. She embraces life to the fullest. She is passionate and has a wonderful sense of humor.

GUY

GUY is Elisabeth's personal assistant aka secretary. He's in his late twenties has a good sense of humor and he is a very attractive gay actor who plays a number of characters in the play.

STAGE

The backdrop is a breathtaking view of the mountains of Elisabeth's childhood in Switzerland which captures the majesty of all fourseasons.
Lighting is essential in setting the place and time.

SPECIAL STAGING NOTES (option): This play can be designed for actors to read from the script and include creative lighting as indicated in the play. The actor playing Guy can enter and exit with costume changes; while the actresses playing Elisabeth and Karla could have limited blocking and at the same time be on book (similar to the VAGINA MONOLOGUES) The only set design is an archway in front of the curtain that is draped with a sky blue fabric with billowing clouds giving it a heavenly aura

ACT I

Before House lights totally dim:

GUY (V.O.)
Please remember to turn off your cell phones and we would like to remind the audience that the taking of pictures and recordings is prohibited in the theater. However we would like to encourage you all to imagine that the theatre is aglow with colorful rainbows and butterflies – awash in forgiveness and transformation. As Elisabeth would say (begins speaking in Swiss-German accent) Once we shine and are bathed in the light; we become little children marinated in unconditional love and we can ALL heal. ENJOY!

(BLACKOUT)

SCENE 1

SETTING: Farm House in Headwater, VA. The stage is designed to allow the lighting to provide the freedom to indicate a variety of scenes and locations. Center stage is a comfortable chair, an end table with a telephone and pizza on it. There is southwest clutter and various types of knick-knacks (Dream-catchers, woven baskets, lamps, antiques, unopened mail, wind chimes, plants and pinecones); upstage right is a free standing wall with a Medicine Wheel and a painting of a butterfly; there is a covered mattress lying on the floor, a desk cluttered with mail and an easel; stage left is a kitchen table with benches and a vase of beautiful flowers; an oven; there are ashes scattered all around the stage, and there are Christmas decorations everywhere, outside the window you can see the desert rocks and the US Capitol.

AT RISE: The entire stage is engulfed in flames. There is a blackout. Then there is a spotlight on Karla, sitting at the desk with a notebook computer.

KARLA
Writing a play is like peeling an onion.
And if life is a stage ...

(Points to audience)
We're all characters in this play - take your pick protagonist or
antagonist, heroine or villain. Yet life is never quite that simple -
we're all dancing along though we're never quite sure of the next
step. Who's to lead and who's to follow?

Keeping one's balance isn't easy especially when perspectives
change and roles become unclear. Keeping focused is critical.
When all else fails make them laugh.
How many of you are afraid of death? Don't worry this play is not
about death. It's about living life straight from the gut.
Taking action - no holds bar. "LIVING & GIVING" or"ET2"
how's that for possible titles?

(Laughs)

I met Elisabeth in October 1991.
(Walks over to the kitchen table)
I wonder what Elisabeth would have to say about all the polarization and chaos in the world? Religious "wars" are raging.
Preachers threaten to burn the Koran, there are demonstrations
against Moslems and there are shootings at mosques, synagogues
and churches. Terrorists are ruthless and extreme. Bullying comes
in all shapes and sizes. While I was a substitute at a local elementary school one of the young boys was teasing a sweet young girl
that she was going to go to hell because she didn't go to church.
Needless to say, I comforted the young girl and asked the young
boy what church he attended. I told him the Jesus I knew would
not tease someone about the church they went to in fact he taught
us to love thy neighbor. Now the last time I checked there were
no exclusions, in effect only love thy neighbor if they go to your
church. I am pleased to report that I gave the boy the opportunity

to apologize to the little girl. She didn't believe he was really sorry so I asked him if it came from his heart. He looked at me as if I was nuts then smiled and said yes. I pray he really was sincere.

(Begins speaking with a Swiss-German accent)
Please make yourself comfortable. I have to apologize for being dressed informally though I have a good excuse; my plane just arrived. I'm constantly flying all over the world. But honestly, I'd be dressed this way even if I arrived three hours earlier, but I thought it was a good excuse. There are hundreds of people who want to meet with me. I only agreed to speak privately with two people from the workshop. This young mother dying from breast cancer and this other pushy woman from DC - an advocate for young children who's a playwright.
(Stops speaking with the accent) Her Swiss-German accent is embedded in my brain

[Lights begin to change a kaleidoscope of rainbow colors
to symbolize a state of mind and turn past into present]

As is my journey with Elisabeth with an "s" not a "z"

Elisabeth wants to start a hospice for AIDS babies, I am an advocate for young children as well as a playwright in DC.
Perfect - we talk about children and politics.

I wonder where Elisabeth is? When we set up this interview for developing a play, she insisted that I meet her at her farm house rather than her office. We had discussed several ideas. We agreed that there needs to be more compassion in the world, the need for people to open their hearts.. We decided to focus on our love for children. Shining a bright light - a TORCH, taking action to help children reach for the stars [Backdrop the – Milky way- picture of "Children are Stars"]

While we talk, Elisabeth insists that we bake cookies. I never made cookies before.

(Begins speaking in Swiss-German accent)
It is about time you learned. (Puts the flour in the bowl and stops speaking with accent). I had no idea how much flour.

(Starts speaking again with Swiss-German accent)
You'll know when there's enough flour and then you'll add the eggs Good. I need to go to my house to get the sprinkles to decorate the Christmas cookies.

(Stops talking with accent)
She insisted that I use my hands to mix the dough.

(Mixing the dough clumsily) I have never done this before. I just want to interview Dr. Elisabeth Kubler-Ross. The author of *Death and Dying*; TIME Magazine listed her as one of the unsong heroes of the last millenium.
I know her as a woman who loves baking Christmas cookies and cakes. All the different shapes: bells, Santas, trees, wreaths, my favorite being butterflies. Okay, butterflies may not be "Christmasy" but they are very pretty. She makes thousands of cookies and sends them to friends all over the world.

GUY ENTERS

GUY
(directed to audience)
I know Elisabeth as one tough cookie. She talks about "Wants" and "Needs." All I know is that I want to be a lead actor and I am here playing bit parts because my need is to pay the rent.

Now this is where it can get confusing. We are floating between time and space. The time is between 1991 and 2016; the place between Head Waters, VA, Scottsdale, AZ and West

Virginia. We ask your indulgence and encourage you to open your heart and utilize your imagination. Now to return to 1991

EXITS

ELISABETH ENTERS

ELISABETH

My favorite Swiss recipe is for a type of cookie that is like a very hard sugar cookie called Mailanderli. If the cookies aren't hard enough they turn into crumbs by the time they arrive in Switzerland. The exact recipe and measurements is in my cookbook but I never bother measuring ingredients, I don't have the patience, I bake from the gut.

I started to teach my daughter Barbara how to bake cookies before she was in kindergarten. I still can remember my mother teaching my sisters and me how to bake when we were very young. In fact it's amazing the things you can remember when you are little.
(Tastes the dough)
Needs a little more lemon juice.

KARLA

I think it might need a little more than that

ELISABETH

Well when you've finished mixing everything together just put it into the oven. (Turns on the oven)

KARLA

For how long?

ELISABETH

You'll know.

KARLA

Right.

ELISABETH

Good.

KARLA

When will I get a chance to interview you?

ELISABETH

You already are. (Hands Karla a cookie sheet then exits)

KARLA

Right (Begins mixing dough)

I wonder if Lillian Helman, Shaw or Shakespeare ever baked cookies? I just hope I don't have to eat these.
This is not what I was expecting. Friends who knew Elisabeth and knew me said we needed to get together. What were they thinking?!

True, we both feel passionately about children. Young people being bombarded with the horror of violence on the streets on television.

(Looks down at herself covered in flour)
Why did I wear black pants?!

(Still struggling with the cookie dough, talking to herself)
Okay, am I supposed to roll the dough or simply plop it on the cookie sheet?

(Then looks at the audience and waits for some sugestions)
Roll or plop?

(Pause) Plop sounds good.
(Begins putting dough on cookie sheet
and places them in the oven)

Oh look - bunny rabbit and butterfly cookie cutters. I thought we were making Christmas cookies.

Spotlight on Karla playing with cookie cutters.

I have to admit that Elisabeth's workshop moved me as did she. I had read her book DEATH & DYING after a close friend of mine passed away in 1983. I stumbled across her biography several years later. I never imagined meeting her. Sitting in the conference center watching her lecture I knew I was truly watching a character.

[Spotlight on Elisabeth stage left].

ELISABETH

(Walks over to chair with a cup of coffee and lights up a cigarette) I must have a cigarette before going in front of a large audience. I hate being nagged about my smoking. I tried acupuncture to stop smoking, they put something in my ear, but it caused me to smoke twice as much. I don't have the patience for this healthy "new age" stuff. I still can't stand tofu and
I still love a cup of coffee.

(Takes a sip of coffee)

Once while I was making a house call to an eight year old child with cancer there was another little boy in the adjacent room; no one included him or spoke to him nor did the parents even bother to introduce him to me.
I asked him "Who are you?" and ...

GUY enters acting as little boy.

LITTLE BOY

His brother.

ELISABETH

I need you to walk me to my car.

LITTLE BOY
ME!?

ELISABETH
Yes you and you alone.

(To audience, giving them the eagle eye)
Then I give the mother the eagle eye, that means you stay right where you are and you're not going to come out and start snooping; mothers are very good at snooping but I didn't want her to hear what we are talking about.

LITTLE BOY
I presume you know I have asthma.

ELISABETH
Really?

LITTLE BOY
(Looking very sad)
I guess having asthma isn't good enough. My parents buy my brother all kinds of wonderful toys like an electric train set. I told my father that I needed a football but he said "NO!" When I asked, "Why not?" he got very angry and exploded "Would you rather have cancer?"

ELISABETH
(Smiles)
Don't worry. If you NEED a football - you'll get a football.
(To audience)
I realized that I needed to go back to speak to his parents.
(To Little Boy)
Don't worry you'll get that football.

LITTLE BOY
(Smiles)

Gee THANKS!

EXITS

ELISABETH

Many siblings of dying children are ignored or worse yet taken for granted. It is critical that we reach out to the siblings so they don't feel nonexistent.

As a triplet I knew what it was like to feel like you were invisible, a nonperson. I never had my own private space. We didn't even have our own initials. My father was so thrifty that he gave everybody the same initials so that you only had to embroider one initial. My father's name was Ernst, my mother's name was Emma, my older brother was named after my father, and the firstborn triplet was me; the second born was Erika and the last was christened Emma but we call her Eva.

Now where was I - oh right, I never had my own space. When I grew up I didn't know a pair of shoes, a blouse, or a ribbon or even a grade card because nobody ever knew who was who. Our teachers never bothered telling us apart, we deserved "A"s and "F"s but it was easier to give us straight "C"s. And in the old days they dressed twins and triplets totally identical.

People didn't know us by names they called us the triplets. So I never had anything that was mine, it was a nightmare, like being a cloned object. I hope genetics never comes to the point where we can clone people, it would be horrible. My sister was forever on my mother's lap, my other sister was forever on my father's lap - there was no third lap left. And at that time I had no idea that my parents didn't know that they always had the same child. A child's interpretation is that my parents don't love me, I'm not lovable, I'm not touchable. I could have literally dropped dead and nobody would have known which one. I'm not even sure that I'm not my sister - you understand? So as a very little child I learned that grownups don't care. They don't care. I heard a lot about my birth, especially since I was a triplet, and it is imprinted in my mind. My parents wanted a girl, and as my mother got bigger and bigger the expectation was naturally that they were going to have a big gorgeous beautiful baby daughter. And you can imagine my father's disappointment when I was born - I was the ugliest two pound shrink, then 55 minutes later my other sister was born and she was an identical scrawny baby and was also given little chance to survive. And my mother kept saying there was more to come. And the doctor and my father told her she had problems - which people always say when they don't want to face reality. But my mother kept insisting that there is more to come, they tried to talk her out of it, and then she gave birth to a six and half pound baby. Naturally, they then had to drop their denial.

[Stage lights up - smoke is coming out of the oven]

KARLA

Oh my God.

ELISABETH

(ENTERS)
What are you doing?!

KARLA

I am not sure - I guess that means they're done.

ELISABETH

Right - well done. Try again.

KARLA

Okay.
        (Begins putting dough on cookie sheet)

ELISABETH

What are you doing?!

KARLA

I am not sure.

ELISABETH

You need to roll the dough.

KARLA

Okay - roll the dough.
(To audience)
Not plop.
(Begins to roll the dough)

[Oven timer starts to buzz]

KARLA
(Goes over to the stove and burns herself)
Ouch!

ELISABETH

Burning yourself is a sign of a good baker.

KARLA

Right.

ELISABETH

Keep rolling.

KARLA
(To audience)
I am rolling.
(Continues to roll out the dough)

ELISABETH

I remember my mother rolling the dough - not too thin, not too thick, just right. My mother's greatest fear was to become a vegetable, and her greatest fear came true. She wanted me to promise that if she became a vegetable I would give her an overdose. I got so angry and made it clear that I was totally opposed to mercy killing. The only thing I would promise my mother is that I would help her to live until she died. I hope you understand what I'm saying, euthanasia is a NONO. No doctor has the right to "play God," whether it is to prolong a life through unnatural means or to end a life unnaturally. Life is a precious gift of God.

KARLA

What about Dr. Kevorkian?

ELISABETH

That man needs to be stopped.

[Guy enters as Kevorkian walks up to shake Karla's hand]

KEVORKIAN

Pleasure to meet you.

KARLA

Thank you. I am not sure who you are

KEVORKIAN

Just call me Jack. Heard you were contemplating suicide. Just thought I might be able to help.

ELISABETH

Your help is not needed.

KEVORKIAN

I have a "death machine" that I would be more than happy to lend to Karla.

ELISABETH

Happy is hardly the word I would use. More like egomaniacal

KARLA

You said we always had choices.

ELISABETH

Yes, but

KEVORKIAN

There are no buts – if the young woman has decided that life is not
worth living it's her life and she can dispose of it. Licikity split no
more hassles no more pain.

ELISABETH

Life is not that simple.

KARLA

No more pain sounds good.

ELISABETH

Suicide simply deals with the physical pain. The spiritual plain
becomes even more tormented.

KEVORKIAN

How do you know?

ELISABETH

I know doctors should not play God.

KARLA

Why does God cause such pain?

ELISABETH

There are lessons we need to learn.

KEVORKIAN

There are those who believe that God has abandoned us. And there
are those who don't believe in God.

KARLA

I believe in God.

ELISABETH

Then believe that your life is a present from God. And you need to
live it to the fullest in the now.

KARLA

But the pain from the past is killing me

ELISABETH

Let it go.

KEVORKIAN

Easier said then done. I have invented a machine and all you have
to do is push a button.

ELISABETH

You know where you can stick your button? We live in a quick
push button microwave society. Life is not necessarily easy.

KARLA

But does it have to be so hard?

ELISABETH

The key is finding peace of mind. Love can help us find that peace.

KEVORKIAN

Love is temporal. Death is finite.

ELISABETH

Such Nonsense! Divine love is ever lasting. Death is simply a transition.

KARLA

I feel like my life is imploding, the chaos in the world is unsettling to say the least. There is hate and toxics that are invading

our lives, it's becoming devastating – personally, environmentally, politically, socially, locally, globally …

ELISABETH

ENOUGH! Life has its challenges. Sometimes people lie. The world can be toxic, we need to overcome the past. We need to get past the pain and anxiety. Fear and anger are toxic energies. We need to be able to forgive each other including ourselves. Holding onto the anger simply makes us toxic and increases the pain.

KARLA

How do I know you are not lying?

KEVORKIAN

You don't.

ELISABETH

At some point you need to trust your heart and let go of the past.In the present we can experience love (notices Karla has taken out a note pad) What are you doing?

KARLA

Taking notes.

ELISABETH

You don't need to do that.

KARLA

But I need to know what to write.

ELISABETH

You'll know. You'll learn.

KEVORKIAN

Don't forget to mention me.

ELISABETH

Such nonsense. Take your pushbutton "easy fix" death machine and leave.

KEVORKIAN

I'll be back.

ELISABETH

Naturally, I remember another terminator who made the same threat. We need teachers not terminators.

[KEVORKIAN EXITS]

There are so many lessons we still need to learn. The Number 1 Lesson – is Unconditional Love

KARLA

I want to be a good student and learn. Life lessons can be overwhelming.

ELISABETH

Just watch and listen. Before 1969 I was a mother, a wife, a doctor - living in a beautiful house in Chicago. Then LIFE Magazine does a story about me and my work with dying patients. The press made it sound like I discovered death. Death was here before I came and it will be here after I leave and in between, God willing, I'm going to live and teach unconditional love.
I don't like people being nosy and poking around. I became famous and all of a sudden my privacy is invaded. I regret having done that piece in Playboy, I didn't pose but I definitely felt exposed and violated.

KARLA
(To audience)
I ordered a copy of the article from Playboy - the solicitations I now get in the mail are unbelievable - I am not even sure they're legal.

ELIZABETH

When you're famous people may try to use you. I've learned from experience it's best to avoid phoney baloneys. Yet I thank God, (kisses pointer finger and lifts it towards heaven) You need to remember to thank God every chance you get for the special people in your life. Here let me show you. (Takes the rolling pin and begins rolling the dough more vigorously. [Bowl falls off the table and breaks] Some things are not meant to be long in this world - like the AIDS babies.

(Looks at the mess on the floor)
I know you can't bake. Can you clean?

KARLA

Can you use the magic word?
PLEASE?

ELISABETH

Please.

KARLA

Thank you. (starts cleaning up the mess)

A portion of the profits from this play will be donated to AIDS programs for children.

ELISABETH

First write the play.

KARLA

Right.

ELISABETH

Children who are dying are like old wise souls and they will practically tell you everything and anything. Children are not afraid of opening their hearts and they are wonderful teachers.

The most honest people I know are psychotics, children and dying patients. You know a number of our AIDS babies once they are marinated in love have tested negative and will live to a ripe old age. I want to help AIDS babies. But the world is full of small minded people who are frightened and filled with hate. It's one thing to lecture about unconditional love yet the people in Headwater, Virginia just didn't understand.

KARLA

Driving to the farm house I saw a number of confederate flags on the bumpers of pick-up trucks and flying in the front yards.

ELISABETH

You'd be surprised at the number of Born Again Christians who don't know the first thing about being Christian.

My dream is that my farmhouse will be filled with babies, fifteen to twenty infants and toddlers with AIDS.

[There is a knock at the door, off stage]

ELISABETH

EXITS and ENTERS (comes back with a torn bedsheet sewn into a sack) The parcel simply has the address: Dr. Elisabeth Kubler-Ross, Virginia, USA.)

KARLA

Who was there?

ELISABETH

One of my staff. Look at this?! Dr. Elisabeth Kubler-Ross, Virginia, USA.

(She begins to open it. In the process she sticks herself with the needle that is still attached to the thread holding the sack together) Ouch! There's still a needle attached to this sack.

(She becomes even more curious and continues to open the package. There are five doll babies, beautifully dressed in homemade clothes and a note. Elisabeth is impressed with the knitting and detail of the doll clothes. She begins reading the note out loud)

I'm a 79 year old woman from British Columbia, I saw you talking about your work with AIDS babies. God Bless. Before seeing you on TV I simply sat alone in my apartment doing nothing. I figure if you can fight for those babies the least I can do is make them lovely dolls to play with and cuddle. I went to the local flea market to buy the dolls, I don't have much money, but I was able to pay fifty cents for each doll. In the morning I shop and in the afternoon and evening I knit and sew. Such joy. Please accept this gift of love and special thank you.

(Elisabeth stops reading the letter and admires the dolls) These are the best-dressed dolls I've ever seen, these will be a treat for the children. The fact that these dolls got to me is a miracle. And I'm in need of a miracle. The Highland County community is in an uproar about my wanting to establish an AIDS hospice for infants and toddlers.

Politics, money and fear are apparently starting to contaminate the picture, and I feel as if I'm putting my hand into a wasp's nest once again - the story of my life!

Yet how can I turn my back. I receive thousands of notes each year and one of the most heartbreaking was scribbled on a small piece of paper.

(Pulls out a piece of paper from her pocket and hands it to Karla)

KARLA
"Dear Dr. Ross, I have a three-year-old son who has AIDS. I can no longer take care of him. He eats very little and drinks very little. How much would you charge to take care of him?"

ELISABETH

With all my work with death and dying patients I have never charged a penny for my services. I'm deeply moved by the plight of these babies with AIDS. Finding a way is not always easy.

When I first began working with death and dying patients my fellow doctors thought I was a vulture. When I started to push for a hospice movement in the United States people thought I was crazy. There had been hospice programs in Europe for centuries. It took us three years to establish the first hospice in America over twenty years ago. Now, there are hospices all over the country. A lot has happened since that struggle. I always wanted to be a doctor or a farmer. And given the fact that I have to deal with ridiculous celebrity nonsense I need a retreat. I have to admit the lack of privacy is a pain. There are times when I'm in an airport and someone comes up to me and asks me if I'm Dr. Elisabeth Kubler-Ross.

Guy ENTERS (carrying a suitcase dressed like a tourist)

GUY
(Runs up to Elisabeth)
Wait don't tell me....it's on the tip of my tongue... Dr. Dr. Dr. Ruth .... No, No, No. Aren't you Dr. Elisabeth Kubler Ross?

ELISABETH

No my name is Jane Doe, it's the most wonderful name in the world. Don't you think?

GUY

NAH ... You're Dr. Kubler Ross, the author of Death and Dying. Don't you remember me I took one of your workshops in 1990?

ELISABETH

I'm sorry but I had a stroke I can't recall your name. I have a miserable short term memory.

GUY

That's cool.

(To Audience)

I thought she was already dead.

EXITS

ELISABETH

(To audience)I can't even go to the bathroom without someone asking me to autograph their book. You know what it's like to be in a stall and having people shove a book underneath for you to sign?

KARLA

No - I try to avoid using public rest rooms.

ELISABETH

It's time to start decorating the cookies. There is some frosting and some food coloring in the pantry.

KARLA

(Walks off stage comes back with the frosting) You've got enough food to feed an army. I couldn't find the food coloring.

ELISABETH

I know I've got some. You need to look harder.

KARLA

There are cartons everywhere - the shelves are stacked.

ELISABETH

Keep looking.

KARLA

Okay it could take a while, sorting through all the boxes of supplies.

EXITS

ELISABETH
Try the top shelf next to the window.
My farmhouse in Virginia is always filled with guests. I always
wanted to live on a farm but my husband would always find reasons why it wasn't the right time or place. Though after 20+ years
of marriage Manny left me. My husband married another woman
and they had a lovely baby. Manny has since died but we were
close till the end. I blame the press and the
unbelievable demands on my time for ending our marriage.

GUY ENTERS
GUY He told you on Mother's Day he wanted a divorce

ELISABETH
I don't want to talk about it. He might have divorced me but I
never divorced him.

GUY
(to audience)
She always referred to Manny as her husband never as her "X"

EXITS

KARLA
ENTERS
(Comes back into kitchen with food coloring)
I found it!

ELISABETH
Good. I'm very self-sufficient here on my beautiful 250 acres of
farmland. I don't need anything, I have more than I need. We eat
all our own vegetables, and beef, and make our own breads. We
can make a rainbow of colors to decorate the cookies.
(Begins to color the frosting)

KARLA
(Takes cookies out of the oven)
These don't look so bad.

ELISABETH
They'll look better once we decorate them.

KARLA
Don't we need a knife to ice the cookies.

ELISABETH
No - we can use our fingers.

KARLA
Like finger painting.

ELISABETH
Exactly.
(They start frosting the cookies with their fingers)

ELISABETH
When I first saw the place it was totally dilapidated but I'm not one to shun hard work. I restored the original farmhouse and barn, built a greenhouse, a beautiful cedar home - I call my tepee, a log cabin for my sister Eva when she comes to visit, and a conference center for my workshops. The idea of building a facility for these babies excites me.
I have wonderful animals. I love animals. I know the toddlers will love petting the animals too. My dream is to have Noah's Ark with two of each animal, but they are multiplying and I can't keep up with all the cattle and sixty sheep. Would you like any wool?

KARLA
No thanks - I don't knit.

ELISABETH
I do - I can't sit still I have ants in my pants.

KARLA
(Laughs)

ELISABETH
My St. Bernards, Ganuf and Higa will slobber all over you with
kisses. I have llamas, ducks, chickens, burros, cats and of course
beautiful bunnies. They are all my babies.

My farm is called Healing Waters. My office is located several
miles away, it's called Shanti Nilaya which in Sanskrit means
the Final Home of Peace. During a research project with a group
of scientists I was induced to have an out-of-body experience and
the only memory I had when I returned to my physical body was
the word Shanti Nilaya. At that time I had no idea about the meaning or the significance of this word.
These cookies are starting to look pretty good.

KARLA
I always enjoyed finger painting in school.

ELISABETH
Here's some sprinkles.

KARLA
Thanks.

ELISABETH
Would you like to taste one?

KARLA
No that's okay - I am not really hungry.

ELISABETH

Did I tell you about my trip to Hawaii?

KARLA

I don't think so ...

ELISABETH

Well, it turned out to be a real personal learning experience for me. Hawaii is gorgeous. And when this woman called me and told me she found the perfect site for me to conduct my workshop on unconditional love in Hawaii, I was thrilled and sent her a deposit for $2,000. I'm not a detail person, so I didn't bother to ask "What island?" and "When?" I figured she'd send me the necessary information when the time came.

A month before the workshop she sent me a letter telling me the date and location. I looked at the calendar and I had a total temper tantrum. You have never seen, especially a person who preaches unconditional love have such a rage. I was really mad - those crooks, those idiots, I used very nasty language; they gave me Easter week. My Easter week is terrible, I have two kids at home, who at least during Christmas and Easter, Mommy is home, they count on that, I was always home on holidays. I ranted about my poor kids, I'm gone all the time now I won't even be here on the holidays. Then I calmed down a bit, and said it can't be that I'm having such a temper tantrum about Easter because we can always paint the eggs the weekend before or the weekend afterward that can't be what's getting me so upset. Then my next line of defense was that Easter is a miserable week for workshops because you don't get any Catholics, and it's terrible. You also don't get any decent Jews because the Jewish holiday is about the same time as the Catholic and my biggest fear is to have a workshop with only good Protestants. No, God forbid, I could not do that. I could not survive that. So I was furious, I was mad, I looked for all kinds of excuses.

I went to Hawaii a total sourpuss; I mean so "icky", "nasty", "yuck" anybody who could have looked at me I would have spit in their face. And I have to talk about unconditional love and show them how they can get to that place.

Guy ENTERS acting as a Protestant minister

MINISTER
Oh, Dr. Ross – welcome to Hawaii; it's such an honor to meet you. We are having wonderful weather – we ordered it just for you. Let me take your bags, it won't take us long to get to the workshop site. It's a residential school for girls on the other side of the island.

ELISABETH
Are the students still there?

MINISTER
(Laughs) Oh no, the girls went home to be with their families for Easter.
Elisabeth (shoots him a dirty look).

MINISTER
Here we are. This room has the prettiest view. Make yourself at home.

ELIZABETH
Home …. Home – who was he kidding;! I was ready to scream as soon as I saw the room I was actually close to killing him. What I really resented was that it was obvious that he had not told the teenagers that somebody else was going to move into their rooms during the Easter vacation. It was like entering a sacred place, where I had no business. And you know what teenagers allow to lie around, I mean, it was shocking, I could not enter that room, it was stepping into a sacred private place.
When this guy showed me the room, there was no place else I could go because the workshop was full, but I was up to here (hands over head) with hate and resentment beyond anything I can describe to you.

MINISTER

Elisabeth...

ELISABETH

Call me Dr. Ross ...

MINISTER

Dr. Ross your group is eating too much. It's costing us too much money.

EXITS

ELISABETH

Really; I was afraid to let him know what I thought of him because when you're so full of hate you're afraid of letting the lid off and possibly killing 'em. You know what I did? I went to every person and said "Wouldn't you like to finish the spaghetti? There is one more meatball - let's finish it." All week long, those who ate like pigs I loved them four times more than those that ate a little bit. What do you call that?

That's revenge. I watched myself becoming nastier, nastier and nastier; but not in a nice open way and I always prided myself on being so straightforward and honest. By Wednesday, to make a long story short, I was ready to put him through a meat slicer, by Thursday I would have put iodine on every slice; by the last day, I cannot remember what it was, but it was very ugly, I totally ignored this guy and I looked at everybody else. If I had looked at this man I would be in prison today and he would be DEAD. I know I would have killed him.

On my flight back from Hawaii, I had a stop over in San Diego and then home to Chicago to be with my family. During the plane trip my psychiatrist came up in me: "How am I going to get in touch with what buttons this man pushed in me?" And just before landing in California I got the message, "You just learned that you're allergic to cheap men." I did not know what that meant. It was purely an intellectual message from my brain - I'm allergic to cheap men. I had no idea what it was.

So I get off the plane and my friends pick me up. Friends I had trained in assisting people to deal with unfinished business - and I really trained them well.

GUY ENTERS acting as old friend.

OLD FRIEND
How was the workshop?

ELISABETH
Fine.
>   (To audience)
I thought I would get away with it. In a second they knew it must have been a nightmare for me. You never ask anybody more than three times and then...

OLD FRIEND
How was your workshop?

ELISABETH
I said fine.

OLD FRIEND
Are you sure?

>   (Goes over and starts petting Elisabeth's head)
Why don't you tell me all about the Easter Bunnies?

ELISABETH
(Explodes)

"EASTER BUNNIES!" I'm a physician, I'm fifty years old, I'm a psychiatrist, no less, I don't believe in Easter Bunnies anymore. If you want to talk to your clients like that, you know, be my guest, that's your choice. But don't you ever, ever, ever talk to me about Easter Bunnies.

(Begins sobbing)

OLD FRIEND

Elisabeth went through more agony in those eight hours than her entire life. She just poured it all out. It's like a dam broke.

ELISABETH

I'm absolutely convinced that you can be raised by animals. We had a few bunnies at home and my father delegated the bunnies as my job. I had to clean up their stall and I had to feed them. And the bunnies were the only living creatures who knew me. Can you imagine what that means to a child - that they come to the gate when I come and they don't come when my sisters come? And I loved them more than anything I could describe to you. Whenever I needed a hug I went to my bunnies. They were always warm, always cuddly, always wonderful, always sweet. When I needed to cry I soaked their fur with my tears - they were my mattress work, my externalization, my love objects, everything. And I would have survived easily with my bunnies except my father's greatest weakness was that he was a thrifty Swiss, and the Swiss are mostly thrifty, they're not cheap but they're terribly thrifty. And so every six months this very well-to-do man had the desire for rabbit roast and he ordered me to take one of my rabbits to the butcher (pause) and I had to pick one of my love objects. And I talked all the way to my rabbit - walked half an hour down to the village. Delivered him to the butcher, I always waited outside, I couldn't stand the smell of that butcher shop. Then he would come out and bring me a bag with warm meat in it and I had to carry it up the mountain, deliver it to my mother's kitchen and like a good well-behaved Swiss girl I had to sit at the table and see my family eat (PAUSE)To me cannibals; my beloved love object. Because I had the illusion, and I stress ILLUSION, that I'm not lovable and they don't love me I turned it around and said I don't love you, I don't need your love, and I denied my needs except with my bunnies. And I never shed a tear. By the time I recuperated six months later the drama repeated itself and the next bunny and the next bunny and the next bunny.

When I was six and a half I sat stoically alone in a room and I only had Blacky left. And my father said you have to bring your rabbit to the butcher. I could not say no to him, it is impossible. So I begged Blacky to run away. "Run away, get your freedom, I will find you somewhere, I will bring you some food somewhere in a hidden place." But the bunny didn't budge because he loved me so much he trusted me. I eventually had to bring this rabbit to the butcher and I remember like it was yesterday and it was decades since then, the butcher brought out the paper bag with the warm meat and he said "Damn shame you had to bring this rabbit in, a day or two she would have had little bunnies."
Do you understand for a little girl it was the most devastating thing that could have happened to me? But you can't cry, you don't show them how vulnerable you are. It's going to kill you if you show them all the rage. And the unfairness, the grief and the pain that you have inside of you. So I walked home like a zombie, like a robot and kept everything bottled up.

Fifty years of putting the lid on and on and on and on; in the mean time I went to medical school, I went through psychiatric residency, I went through child psychiatry, I even went through a classical Freudian analysis but they never talked about
Easter Bunnies. Every time I saw a cheap man, you know what I mean by cheap man (pause) penny ... penny ....something, (pause) penny pinching, and you see lots of them in Switzerland, every time I saw a cheap man I had to put the lid on tighter and tighter

and tighter. So this pain was never touched upon. Until I was able to get to the bottom of my soul. Now I can see a cheap man - and it's his problem, not mine. I can even eat rabbit roast if necessary. Do you understand what I'm trying to say? How many of you have had your buttons pushed? Have gotten angry? Have wanted to kill? That's good because it's a way of getting in touch with your unfinished business. I'm not suggesting you kill anyone.

I'm simply telling you that you need to be honest with yourself and deal with the pain you've bottled up.
Encourage your children to share their pain. Encourage them to cry, encourage them to show their anger. And if anything, anything, touches you negatively always know that this is your unfinished business. I say go through the pain, go through the rage, become a maniac if necessary, it will free you up to become whole again.

KARLA
What's your unfinished business?

ELISABETH
I have some chocolate coconut patties from Hawaii at the house. I'll get them for you - they're delicious.

EXITS

KARLA
I didn't have the heart to tell Elisabeth I didn't like coconut. I still have the box of chocolates she gave me.

EXITS

(BLACKOUT)

SCENE 2

SETTING: several months later
[Lights up]
AT RISE: Karla showing Elisabeth the play; they are in a heated discussion

ELISABETH

I do not want to be bothered with reading the play in bits and pieces. Have you spoken to my lawyer?

KARLA

Yes - Mort's very nice, a real gentleman. The only problem is he says you won't return his calls.

ELISABETH

You know how lawyers are?!

KARLA

You're getting to be a real pain in the ....

ELISABETH

I don't want any swearing in the play.

KARLA

What about hand gestures?

ELISABETH

Only thanking God (kisses finger and points to heaven) but don't over do it.

KARLA
(Is ready to flash Elisabeth the finger)
At least read the first act I've written.

ELISABETH

How many acts are there?

KARLA

Two.

ELISABETH

Good - then you only have one more act to write before I read it.
I've baked you an apple pie FOR YOU to take home.

KARLA

Whoever said practicing unconditional love was easy - lied.

ELISABETH

Remember it's the tough things in our lives that will be our blessings. And I've had more of my share of blessings. I need you to
help clean Eva's cabin.

KARLA

I came here to work on the play.

ELISABETH

Patience.

KARLA

EXITS then ENTERS out of breath as if running

GUY ENTERS as the Handyman

ELISABETH
(Looking at GUY)

What are you doing here?

HANDYMAN
(In a thick southern WV accent)
Your secretary, Angela called said you were tired needed a ride back to your house.

ELISABETH
Nonsense, they don't know what they are doing in that office. We're working here.

KARLA
(Still out of breath)
There are dead wasps in that cabin.

ELISABETH
If they're dead; they can't sting you.

KARLA
My Dad was highly allergic to wasps. I have no interest in finding out if I am also allergic.

ELISABETH
In life we have two choices, we can choose love or fear

KARLA
Right now, I'll choose the latter.

ELISABETH
Did you love your father?

KARLA
Yes. We were very close. I remember when I was thinking about going to college my Dad told me I needed to study teaching or nursing otherwise I'd end up being someone's secretary and I was too smart for that job. I still don't think he totally understood my work as an advocate for young children and he never considered working in the theatre as a real job.

ELISABETH

My father wanted me to be his secretary. Ugh.. I'd be anything else but be his secretary. His conviction to make me his secretary gave me the motivation to move out and focus on what I really needed to do… what I really loved. I wanted to be a doctor and I found jobs in laboratories.

HANDYMAN

Well, do you need me to drive you back to the house?

KARLA

I can drive her up to her house.

HANDYMAN

You can forget that – it's a disaster area. She won't want you to see the mess.

KARLA

She should only see my apartment.

ELISABETH

Does it have dead wasps(giggling)?

KARLA

That's not funny.

ELISABETH

When you've worked with dying patients as long as I have you realize there are only two things we will look back on when we are on our death bed. One of them is the windstorms of our lives; it is the times in our lives when we wish we wouldn't live anymore, when all our dreams are shattered, when your house burns down, when you get divorced, when you are ridiculed by your peers and when you have a stroke. It is all the tough testings, all the horrible things when we are at the crossroads when we have to make a decision. Because it is the windstorms of our lives that direct us in the direction we should be going if we only took the time to care, and had the nerve, the tenacity, and the courage to stick our necks out. And we will remember that. Should we shield the canyons from the windstorms, we would never see the beauty of their carvings. After we review the windstorms, we will recall the moments, and the moments are when we have experienced total unconditional love. The windstorms of our lives are the lessons to be learned that will make us stronger.

During those crossroads we feel isolated and alone – we are lost. It's crucial – the need for being there; that's the reason uncon- ditional is essential. No disrespect to anyone, people who lose someone through divorse realize that death is not the ultimate loss. Being unable to share can be devastating Feeling worthless, rejected and unloved, our trust is shattered. The key is persever- ance and patience.

                          KARLA

BULLSHIT!

                        ELISABETH

I said no swearing

                          KARLA

You can talk about unconditional love all you want - at this moment I am pissed!

                                                  EXITS

[Spotlight on Elisabeth]

ELISABETH
(Reading Letter)

Dear Elisabeth - I have to admit last week when I was at Head Water you gave me what you would call a "positive" kick in the pants. We all have our own destiny. Driving home I not only decided to finish the play but wanted to finish it for your birthday. I worked day and night to complete it. I know birthdays are special so I am also sending you authentic florentines from a Swiss pastry shop. Have a Happy Birthday and enjoy the chocolates while you're enjoying reading the play.

[Spotlight on Karla]

KARLA
(Reading letter downstage left)

Thank you for your birthday card, for the manuscript which is excellent and naturally for the chocolates and the delicious florentines which I love. I also love the idea that you actually received my positive kick in the pants and decided to finish the play! HA! HA! Until we meet in person again, love and blessings - Elisabeth

She ended the letter with HA! HA!
If it was only that simple. I called her house - there was no answer. Then I called the office. Elisabeth's home had been burnt down.

[The entire stage is engulfed in flames]

(BLACKOUT)

END OF ACT ONE

ACT II

SCENE 1

> AT RISE: The curtain is down. With the use of lighting the stage and theatre is in a blaze of fire and smoke. THEN there is a Spotlight on Karla holding a mobile phone.

KARLA

The Highland County police said the fire was an accident. I don't believe it - neither does Elisabeth. Thank God (kisses finger and points to heaven) she was out of town.

(Dials phone.)
[Spotlight on both Karla and Elisabeth on telephone.]

ELISABETH

Hello.

KARLA

I just called your office. Are you okay?

ELISABETH

Someone shot and killed my llama. This was no accident. It's a miracle that my Totem Pole and Teepee didn't burn down. Everything in my home is ashes - all my books.

Over 4,000 books were burnt, many of them autographed by many famous people, even President Nehru from India. So many things that cannot be replaced.

My beautiful home is simply ashes. They still haven't found the persons, I don't think they will; honestly I don't think the people in Highland County really care; who knows they probably threw a party for the bums that finally got Dr. Elisabeth Kubler-Ross to move out. It was only things, though I'm upset that they shot one of my llamas. Thank God I was out of town, or I'd be dead too. I was in Pennsylvania receiving a life time achievement award in healthcare.

Everything is ashes - I don't even have a clean pair of underwear.

KARLA
I'll send you some new underwear.

ELISABETH
And some chocolates too.

(BLACKOUT)

SCENE 2

> SETTING: Curtain- up. The stage is designed to allow the lighting to provide the freedom to indicate a variety of scenes and locations.
> Elisabeth's new home in Scottsdale, AZ.
> Furnished in southwestern style very open space; there is the same clutter listed in ACT I in addition there is also a hospital bed center stage which is in the living room/dining room area right off the kitchen. The overstuffed chair is now upstage right near a front of a large flatscreen TV angled in order for it to be seen from the chair and the bed. There is also yellow Police tape hanging from the chairs and draped on the kitchen table. There is a nightstand with a portable phone on it.
> AT RISE: Karla is standing far down stage at the edge with spotlight on her.

KARLA
Elisabeth's son Kenneth came to Virginia, and helped her pack-up what furniture she had left in the Conference Center. He was obviously and justifiably concerned for his mother's safety. He took Elisabeth out to dinner and then off they flew to Arizona.

Elisabeth swore he kidnapped her. I know she feels safer living near him. I also don't know how she would have survived the fire without his help.

(Points to a cup full of feathers)

Before she left she went to the chicken coop and collected these feathers. Elisabeth truly misses her animals. The coyotes and birds in the desert have become her best friends.

Elisabeth is definitely one tough cookie.

EXITS

[Stage lights up]

ELISABETH

(Center stage sitting on the chair)

Kenneth is a very special soul, and I'm not just saying that because I'm his mother.

(Walks over to photo albums and holds them)

I was so afraid that my family's photo albums had burned, my children's baby pictures. Thank God, they were saved. Kenneth reminded me that I had given him the pictures prior to the fire to put together in a photo collection.

(Telephone begins to ring and Elisabeth answers it)

I hate telephones. Yes, what is it?

(Pause)

No I don't need my roof leak proofed.

(Hangs up)

Ever since I moved into my new house every water purification company, roofer and vacuum cleaner salesman in Scottsdale has been calling. Who'd believe I live in adobe house with a hottub. These sales people keep calling and calling and promise these fabulous prizes if you only let them come out and let them show you their wonderful product. Such nonsense. But I have to admit I bought a new vacuum cleaner, it even massages your feet and scalp, for what I paid for it it should clean my house by itself.

(Telephone begins to ring again)

I hate telephones. Yes? I told you I wasn't interested, I don't care how super duper you say it is.

(Hangs up)

KARLA

(ENTERS carrying a pizza)

ELISABETH

Thank you for bringing the pizza. Since I've moved to Arizona I don't have many visitors. It's close to impossible to get a pizza delivered living in the middle of a desert - turn right at the dirt road, turn left at the oversized cactus than go a couple of miles - look for the broken fence post then turn left. Would you like a piece of pizza?

KARLA

No thanks.

GUY ENTERS

GUY

I thought I heard someone come in.

ELISABETH

It's only Karla, I told you about her, she's the one working on the play. She brought pizza - you want a piece?

GUY

No thanks. (Turns to Karla)Hi, my name's Guy; we'll be sharing the guest room; don't worry I am gay.

KARLA

Fine - I snore

ELISABETH

Stop chit chatting I am hungry and the pizza is getting cold.

KARLA

Would you like me to heat it in the microwave?

ELISABETH

I'll burn my tongue. Just get me a plate and napkin and I'll eat it now before it's too cold. I am starving.

KARLA

Would you like me to go food shopping for you?

ELISABETH

There's plenty of food in the kitchen.

GUY

She sends me to the grocery every morning.

KARLA

I know Elisabeth always has enough to feed an army.

ELISABETH
(Smiles)

I left home when I was sixteen years old. One of the toughest choices I ever made was to leave home yet it was the biggest blessing. It led me to do relief work in postwar Europe. I tapped into an inner strength - I learned compassion, I learned what it's like to be hungry.
Are you sure you're not hungry?

KARLA

I am sure.

ELISABETH

Did I ever tell you about the war?

KARLA

You were the "best delouser in the world."

ELISABETH
(Laughs)

You know I had an apprenticeship in a hospital laboratory. It was 1941 and thousands of French refugees began arriving in Zurich; hundreds and hundreds of children were sent on foot by their parents in order to save their lives. Suddenly the whole hospital needed volunteers to help bathe and delouse the children. The hospital basement began to be called the bathhouse and I gave baths to hundreds of children. I loved it.

Switzerland was not prepared for the onslaught of refugees.

There was no food for the children. My friend Baldwin and I made arrangements to borrow rations from the hospital kitchen. The children were fed. But the hospital administrator did not approve of our rationing the food to the children; and he gave us twenty four hours to replace the food or provide food coupons, or we would lose our jobs. My boss, Dr. Abraham Weitz, a Polish-born Jew, heard of my possible dismissal, and went to the synagogue in Zurich and the Jewish Community - God knows where he went - but he saved my life and I was able to replenish the hospital kitchen. I promised right then and there that I would go to Poland and help his people.

The day after World War II ended, I joined the International Voluntary Service for Peace and helped rebuild war torn Europe. While I was in Poland, I went to the concentration camp at Maidanek. I wanted a deeper understanding of what the victims of the Holocaust suffered and of our capacity for hatred and cruelty.

The gates of Maidanek were sprawled open as if they had been rammed by a tank. I walked through the barbed wire fence. The smells of the gas chambers, the crematoriums and the concentration camp were overpowering. I saw train loads of baby shoes of 960,000 innocent children who were murdered by adults who had children at home - mothers and fathers.

I stopped at another railroad car and looked inside. It took me a moment to realize that the tangled material on the floor was human hair, hair shaved from women on their way to the gas chamber and used to make coats for Germans. I was sick. Then I noticed a beautiful young girl, with eyes full of sorrow, staring at me. I went up to her and introduced myself. Her name was Golda. She was German-born and Jewish. We sat on a patch of grass and shared memories. She told me that her father had been taken away in the middle of the night by the Gestapo and was never heard from again. In 1944 her mother, older brother and sister had been deported to Maidanek and herded into a gas chamber, but because she had been pushed to the end of the line by a Capo, they were unable to squash her in and the steel door was slammed in her face. She was the sole survivor. Golda pointed to the crematorium chimney and whispered, "The ashes of my mother, brother and sister floated up there." I asked Golda what she was doing now. She hesitated as if I wouldn't understand. But then she told me that when she was first liberated from the concentration camp, all she wanted was revenge. Yet in order to purge her bitterness she deliberately chose to help German children who were victims of the war, many of whom were paraplegics. Golda was struck by the fact that if she got revenge she would be no better than Hitler himself. She told me that she had come back to Maidanek, and she would stay at Maidanek until she had completely forgiven Hitler.

I sat there silently trying to fathom how within the human mind and heart there lay the potential for such cruelty and hatred as a Maidanek, and such forgiveness and love as was epitomized by Golda. I was stunned. I began to think. If I had grown up in Nazi Germany, could I have been tempted by Hitler's Aryan dream of grandiosity? If I had been mistreated like Hitler had been as a child how would I have turned out?

I will never forget the barracks where the prisoners had carved their initials in the wood and the messages of the dying - yet there were also figures of butterflies. Carvings of butterflies were every-where. The messages of these men, women and children were not of despair, but of freedom and hope. The images of the butterflies will stay with me forever.

Golda was committed to touch one human life and turn it from hate to love; then there would be purpose as to why she was saved. And she touched my life more than anyone else in the world. Golda taught me the lesson of unconditional love - love with no expectations, no "ifs", no strings attached. She also taught me that there is this potential Hitler in all of us. Golda inspired me to go back home to study medicine and human behavior.

I will never forget asking Golda how it was possible for men and women to kill millions of innocent people and at the same time to have families they loved. She looked at me very seriously and simply said, "You could do it too."

KARLA

Could you?

ELISABETH

Could I what?

KARLA

Do it too?

ELISABETH

I will always remember Golda and the "blessed Polish soil."

GUY

Well Elisabeth we're waiting.

ELISABETH

For what?

GUY

Your answer. Could you do it?

ELISABETH

In every one of us there is a Hitler and a Mother Theresa... and I could tell you a few things about Mother Theresa. Now don't bother me I am eating my pizza.

GUY

You could answer the question between bites.

ELISABETH

(Ignores Guy and turns on the TV)

GUY

(To audience)

Elisabeth is stubborn and if she wants to ignore you – baby, she will ignore you.

KARLA

I don't remember you telling me about the Polish soil.

ELISABETH

(Turns off the TV)

I was working in a worksite organized by the Quakers to rebuild the village of Lucinia, Poland. We set up a makeshift medical clinic. I slept outdoors in my blanket and one midnight I was awakened by a baby crying. I thought it was a dream and tried to go back to sleep but the whimpering continued. Then by the light of the moon I saw this woman holding her three year old child who had all the signs of typhoid. I couldn't cure typhoid - I had no medicine. The mother pleaded with me to help her son; he was the last of her thirteen children, the others had been murdered in the concentration camp; she brought him out of the camp determined that he would not die.

So in the middle of the night, I made two cups of tea. The mother had absolute faith that I could save her only remaining child. I realized our only hope was to take the child to the hospital in Lublin, twenty miles away. We took turns throughout the remainder of the night carrying the boy. It was nearly noon by the time we reached the gray stone walls of the Lublin Hospital.

When we finally arrived the hospital already had too many patients and they refused to admit a dying child. I was furious. The doctor simply turned us away. I went running after him and grabbed his arm. I told him some Poles were no better than the Nazis! I promised him that if he did not help this child I would go back to Switzerland and tell them how a Polish doctor would not save the life of one child who had miraculously survived the camps. The child was admitted. Yet the mother and I were instructed to leave the child in the doctor's care for three weeks and in that time he would either be buried or well.

We both returned to the clinic. During the day the woman helped with cleaning out the clinic, fetching water from the river, boiling syringes and rolling bandages. At night the woman shared my blanket under the stars. Then one morning, three weeks later, I woke up to find that the woman had left. About a week later I found a handkerchief filled with dirt by my blanket and a penciled note written in Polish that read "From Mrs. W., whose last of 13 you have saved, a gift of blessed Polish soil." It was the finest present I had ever been given. (PAUSE) It was lost in the fire.

(BLACKOUT)

KARLA

(Sitting on the mattress with a yellow pages and rubber hose)
You're probably wondering why I am sitting here with a yellow pages and rubber hose. It was one of the key components of Elisabeth's workshop - it enables us to externalize our angers and fears. (Pause) To vent our emotions and let it out (Kneels down holding rubber hose and begins hitting yellow pages) I want to understand ... I need to understand - Bombings that murder innocent people and CHILDREN - ethnic cleansing - countless shooting at schools – surrounded by toxins both in the environment and social media - hate crimes - racism - children killing other children ...

EXITS

[Spotlight on Elizabeth]

ELISABETH

(Walks onto stage as if in a lecture hall)
I know from personal experience that we are constantly being tested and constantly learning. Human beings consist of four quadrant the physical, emotional, intellectual and spiritual. And if those four quadrants are in harmony you will have no fears and no anxieties.

GUY

"E" Are your quadrants in harmony?

ELISABETH

(TURNS on TV and ignores Guy)

GUY

Fine ignore me. It beats being disowned because your family finds out you're gay. No more hiding in the closet. Now I am hiding in the dessert after attending her workshops. It blew my mind.

ELISABETH

We have five day workshops all over the world where people can finish their unfinished business. That means to get rid of all the negativity within themselves. Fear and guilt are literally the only enemies of man. The youngest person who attended the workshop was an eleven year old girl and the oldest was a ninety-two year old lady.

GUY

All I wanted was a hug. My dad called me an abomination. Karla goes over and hugs Guy. Her cell phone rings she answers it begins to cry then exits.

GUY

I want a Hug from Elisabeth.

ELISABETH

Such nonsense- I need to focus on my workshop. During the workshops we aim at an emotional healing of old, unresolved wounds involving grief, guilt, unfairness, injustice, and so forth. It is critical that the participants externalize their pain. Without touching or harming anyone, they are encouraged to beat out their frustrations with sections of a rubber hose, shred phone books, scream or sob - "whatever it takes for them to bring their pain to the surface." About one third who attend have a terminal illness or have had a tragedy in their family be it a death, accident, divorce, abuse or murder; about one third are physicians, clergy, social workers, psychologists, and nurses; and about one third are just average people like lawyers, housewives and plumbers. During intensive sessions the days and nights are filled with piercing screams and uncontrollable crying, as well as explosive pent-up hate.

You know, over 25% of the people attending my workshops were abused when they were children.

When you allow someone to vent anger and pain caused by abuse, they will make a horrible sound that you will never forget. Yet at the same time it is a beautiful sound because once such rage has been acknowledged and released that person will never hurt a fly.

51

GUY

Then do you hug them?

ELISABETH

Again with the hugging (shakes her head)
My workshop is preventive criminology

The highlight of my career was a workshop I held at a prison in
Edinburgh, Scotland. I stayed in the prison for a week working
with inmates and prison staff. I insisted that we live under the
same conditions as the inmates. The beds were hard as rocks and
there was no hot water but it was 1000 percent better than my
wildest dreams. The authorities at Saughton should be applauded
for being the first in the world to have the courage to try such a
radical approach. It gives me hope that this can be duplicated in
other prison systems in other parts of the world.
I must have shredded 25 telephone books into a million pieces
when I began dealing with the repressed inner pain from the childhood experience with my precious bunnies. I sobbed for eight hours
straight. It changed my entire life. When I began to reach out to
my patients, there were doctors who were frightened of my work,
jealous of the attention I was getting, they made me feel unwelcome, isolated. But I had to move on to allow my patients to share.
I resented colleagues who were critical of my work calling me a
vulture. I simply want us to live until we have to say good-bye. No
denial I remember in my workshops twenty years ago there were,
excuse the expression, "flakey Californians", who would immediately go into a trance when someone began screaming in real gen-
uine authentic pain. It gave me the greatest pleasure to walk up to
these people while they were in a trance and stick them with a little
sewing needle to try to make them conscious and aware.
Are any of you from California? Last time I lectured in California,
there were a number of people sitting in the audience with pyramids on their heads. Do you know how ridiculous it is to look
out and see people meditating wearing these metal things on their
heads? I am glad I don't see anyone wearing any pyramids on their

heads today. It's a new fad in becoming spiritual, but it's a bunch of phony baloney. We are all spiritual beings.

EXITS

KARLA
ENTERS

(walks over and sits on mattress starts
beating a yellow pages to shreds)
All she wanted to do was to establish a hospice for AIDS babies. Things got out of hand and people were obviously misinformed and writing nasty letters in the newspaper.

(Starts reading one of the Letters to the Editor)
It has been said that helping Kubler-Ross care for AIDS victims is the Christian, caring thing to do - rubbish. This county does not have the facilities to provide for these children adequately. Highland County is a beautiful and safe rural environment. We have a Maple Festival every year. There is no AIDS here - keep AIDS where it belongs in the big cities.
A man who had earlier worked on the construction of Elisabeth's log cabin, and had been fired for just cause, took this opportunity for "sweet revenge." He went up and down the county collecting signatures on a petition to forbid the building of the hospice for the AIDS babies. He was telling everyone that the hospice was a means of importing AIDS into the county. When people wouldn't sign his petition he threatened them; he told one man if he didn't sign that he'd never find another construction job in the county.
Elisabeth organized a community meeting.

GUY
A bull in a china shop could have been more organized and accommodating.

ELISABETH
(ENTERS)

Please make yourselves comfortable, just ignore the TV cameras and microphones. I have brought six medical experts tonight to help me to answer community concerns.

KARLA

(Still beating the yellow pages with the rubber hose) The people were downright mean and asked the stupidest questions. Ten years she lived in Virginia. She was always getting threats that her farm would be burnt down, she got bullets through her bedroom window and even had cross burnings on her property.

[VOICES of people asking questions are heard coming
from the auditorium. The voices are on a tape]

ANGRY MAN

(Tape) Why did you pick Highland County?

ANGRY WOMAN

(Tape) Yeah, you should have stayed in California! (Applause and cheers on Tape)

ELISABETH
(Calmly)

Because I live in Highland County and this is where I work. These children need sunshine and a garden and playmates, and they have to be allowed to see and touch a flower and watch a butterfly in flight.

MAN

(Tape) What about our schools? And what about our taxes?

ELISABETH

The children will be between the ages of six months and two-and a halfyears old. They will not use the schools. They will stay on my farm. They do not pose a health hazard to the community.
Highland County will not pay a penny.

MAN

(Tape) But we don't need facilities for such a dread disease as AIDS.

ELISABETH

Yes it is a dread disease. As Jesus taught two thousand years ago working with the lepers ...

WOMAN

(Tape) Who do you think you are, Jesus?! You should be ashamed.

ELISABETH

No, I'm not Jesus; I'm simply trying to follow his teachings and love our fellow man and help them. I will not be ashamed of helping needy children.

WOMAN

(Tape) Dr. Ross, how would you compare leprosy with AIDS?

ELISABETH

Leprosy is much more contagious than AIDS.

WOMAN

(Tape) Are you sure? Is it a proven fact?

ELISABETH

Yes, an absolute fact.

MAN
(Tape) Highland County has the opportunity to be a good Samaritan.

(Jeers from the crowd, some booing some applause on Tape)

WOMAN
(Tape) What do you intend to do with those children?

ELISABETH
To marinate them in love. To give them toys and lots of hugs and kisses. To give them twenty-four hour medical attention. To help them live until they die.

MAN
(Tape) What is this live until they die stuff? Do you teach them to die in the name of Jesus Christ? Are you bringing a cult into the area?

ELISABETH
I'm a Christian, and I'm not bringing a cult into this area.

[The crowd becomes disorderly again]

MINISTER
(Tape) Let us remember one thing: this is the House of God.

ELISABETH
Yes you in the back ...

WOMAN
(Tape) The Bible says "Suffer the little children to come unto me." In God's name I am willing to help you in anyway possible.

[The crowd begins to boo]

KARLA
(In an emotional frenzy shredding yellow pages with rubber hose)
STOP IT! They should have been applauding not booing.

ELISABETH
They were scared.

KARLA
It's unbelievable. (PAUSE) How many of us have been touched by the AIDS epidemic or drug crisis?

GUY
(Raises his hand)

KARLA
Everyone should be raising their hands. I am still up-set that Elisabeth's request for a hospice permit was denied. I can't believe the amount of hatred that was stirred up by the thought of creating a safe and loving place for these tiny dying babies. The fate of the infants who are born with AIDS is heartbreaking.

ELISABETH
I need a secretary.

GUY
I thought I was your secretary.

ELISABETH
In your dreams.

GUY
More like a sleep walking nightmare.

KARLA

You do have a tendency to crush them.

ELISABETH

I've always said that when life puts us through a tumbler it's our choice whether we come out crushed or polished. I need someone I can trust.

KARLA

Thanks but no thanks.

ELISABETH

You enjoy baking cookies.

KARLA

Forget it.

ELISABETH

Just for a little while.

KARLA

Let's change the subject - last night you talked about a loving soul - a very special person, Momami Dali, yet I don't remember hearing about his teachings. Has he written any books?

ELISABETH

Who?

KARLA

"Momami Dali"

ELISABETH

Who are you talking about?

KARLA

The man you were talking about last night and the fabulous meeting you had with him.

ELISABETH

You mean - Mohammad Ali.

GUY

Even with Parkinsons Disease that man is gorgeous - the muscles on him. Sweetie let me tell you....

ELISABETH

Behave.

KARLA

Of course - Mohammad Ali.
(To audience)
She never mentioned he was a boxer, let alone a heavy weight champion of the world ...

GUY

Who could dance like a butterfly and sting like a bee.

ELISABETH
(An impish smile)
You get to sleep with him tonight.

KARLA

Separate beds?

GUY

Of course.

EXITS

ELISABETH

Our teachers show up in the most unexpected shapes and forms. Remember to always thank God for the special people in your life. The best teacher I had in all my life was a black cleaning woman, I initially would never have picked her as one of my teachers, but that was a long time ago when I was working at the University of Chicago. I was persona non grata because they hated this foreigner who talks about death and dying instead of making us famous for all the cancer patients we cure. And I felt very alone and I began to notice that every time this cleaning woman was in a room with one of my patients something enormous happened in that room and I couldn't pinpoint and define what happened.

[GUY ENTERS acting as cleaning woman]

ELISABETH

And one day I saw her and it took all my courage and I probably asked her in a very stupid way "What in the world are you doing with my patients?"

CLEANING WOMAN

I'm not doing anything, I'm only cleaning the floor.
[They begin snooping around each other]

ELISABETH

I tried to stay close to her to see what it was about this woman and she tried to do the same thing with me. She finally had the nerve to grab me by my white doctor coat, pull me back into the nursing station and share a horribly sad story with me.

CLEANING WOMAN

I live in the ghetto and the stench of urine in the stairwells is over-powering. I had six beautiful children. Because of segregation one of my poor babies died in my lap of pneumonia sitting in a hospital emergency room. I was unable to get appropriate medical care for my child because of racist policies.

Death is not a stranger to me anymore, he's like an old acquaintance. You understand I'm not afraid of death anymore, and sometimes I walk into the room of your patients and they look so scared, I can't help but to walk over to them and touch them and tell them that it's not so horrible.

ELISABETH
(To audience)
Do you understand that I promoted this woman to my first assistant, much to the dismay of my colleagues. And I share this with you to stress that you have to be open to all possible teachers. If you ask you will always get a helper that will show up, it is 100% true that you always get what you need, though you may not get what you want, but you have to learn honesty and humility.

KARLA
Last night I had two dreams and you were in them.

ELISABETH
Really?

KARLA
Really. We were in a Native American setting, we were in a circle and there was a very powerful Medicine Man - White Oak who was holding each of our hands. There was a real sense of peace and understanding.

ELISABETH
(Points to the Indian Medicine Wheel)
That's an Indian Medicine Wheel. Our society has a lot to learn from the native cultures, we have lost touch with mother earth and it is the old ways that we should again embrace to save our planet. I have always felt a bond with American Indians. Before coming to America I had a dream and saw myself in Indian dress, riding a horse across a desert land toward a pueblo village. While driving through Colorado with Manny and my mother-in-law I

had again experienced that vision and I had never known such a feeling of harmony transcending time and space yet I could not find the words to describe it at the time.

KARLA

There was this other dream ...

ELISABETH

Also about Native Americans?

KARLA

No, it was more like an "I LOVE LUCY" rerun - and we're playing Lucy and Ethel, they/we get a job at a chocolate factory and the conveyer belt breaks and we have to start shoving all the chocolates in our mouths.

ELISABETH

Sounds like a fun job.

(Lights dim We hear a television in the background - the TV show In the Heat of the Night is playing.)
My favorite television show is In the Heat of the Night. I like the sheriff and his deputy. If only we had someone like that in Head Water. I sometimes watch Highway to Heaven. I never had time to watch television before. I get tired easily.
My favorite movie is ET. But I always have trouble with the VCR. I couldn't figure it out before this last stroke and I sure can't figure it out now. I now give ET hugs and kisses.

(Kisses pointer finger and reaches out to audience)
My bones are so brittle, it hurts when someone tries to hug me. I'm getting very tired. (lays down on the bed) Retirement is a blessing. No more Dr. Elisabeth Kubler-Ross.

(Falls asleep —wakes-up yelling)
I want to die, I want to die

GUY

Here we go again. That's become her favorite mantra. Her main focus is facing death.

KARLA

Yet when we've talked it's about living and giving.

GUY

And boy can she "Give it"

ELISABETH
(Screaming)
I want to die, I want to die.

GUY

There's a hammer right next to your bed – knock yourself out.

ELISABETH
(Laughs)
I am going to sleep – hopefully I won't wake up.

GUY

Only the good die young.

ELISABETH

If that's the case, you'll live forever.

KARLA

What about unconditional love and embracing life?

GUY

Wait right here I'll get you the 800 # and website for HALLMARK

[EXITS]

KARLA

Wait a second …

GUY ENTERS as JACK KEVORKIAN

KEVORKIAN

Did somebody call for me? (Does a comical bow) Dr. Kevorkian at your service.

ELISABETH

I am not interested in dealing with Dr. Death.

KARLA

What are you interested in?

ELISABETH

Living until we die. It's the living that's important. Dying is simply a transition.

KARLA

It's the in-between that's the killer. Facing the loss of a job, losing health insurance, medical challenges, friends and family dying, foreclosure, being betrayed by loved ones

ELISABETH

Exactly! – that's when we are tested. There are lessons we need to learn and sometimes we are the student and sometimes we are the teacher. The fun part is to exit laughing – we need to be patient and open.

KEVORKIAN

Exactly! – that's why I am here to open the door.

ELISABETH

The door to death. Doctors have no right to prolong life or facilitate suicide. The dying are our greatest teachers. As students we learn that when we are willing to be patient the glory and peace of eternity is ours.

KARLA

I remember your book Death and Dying had five stages. The movie Groundhog Day was based on those five stages.

ELISABETH

Life is not that simple. There is both physical and emotional pain. Remember the four quadrants – emotional, spiritual, intellectual and physical?

KARLA

True and I feel like I am going in circles (starts spinning around)

ELISABETH

Stop!

KARLA

Now what?

ELISABETH
(Points to KEVORKIAN)
Kick him out. (struggles getting out of bed) I need help.

KEVORKIAN

I am here to help.

ELIZABETH

That's definitely a matter of opinion. Assisted suicide denies our spirit the opportunity to grow.

KEVORKIAN

Yet when the body is in pain and terminal....

ELISABETH

That's your problem you focus on the terminal. We need to focus on the eternal and spiritual ….

KARLA

Peace on Earth!

ELISABETH

Exactly!

KEVORKIAN

I can see I am wasting my time here

[EXITS]

KARLA

What just happened?

ELISABETH

He doesn't understand – he's bitter.

KARLA

What about you?

ELISABETH

I am tired (curls up and goes back to sleep).

GUY ENTERS

GUY

When you care to give the very best
          (hand Karla a piece of paper).

KARLA

(Hands him back the piece of paper after a quick glance)
No thanks, I am not interested in an 800 app website quick fix.

GUY

Oohh I think someone is in denial.

KARLA

More like acceptance.

GUY

Exactly! She needs to be dead before she can become immortal.

KARLA

That's true for all of us.

GUY

Some more than others.

KARLA

Elisabeth has had a number of strokes. As a result she's become very depressed. She remains a world renowned doctor and at the same time an extremely challenging patient.

[Spotlight on Elisabeth]

ELISABETH

I truly hope that every doctor should have the experience of getting sick and feel what it's like to be a patient. Prior to my first stroke, the last time I was in a hospital was when I gave birth to my daughter, Barbara, and the treatment I received then was also horrible, I couldn't leave the hospital fast enough and returned in my white doctor's coat to sign Barbara out as well so I could give her the care only I could give my new baby at home. I'm really very proud of my son Kenneth and daughter Barbara. Kenneth was the prettiest baby I had ever seen, he's now a photographer.
Barbara was premature and was a real fighter, she had only been given a 50% chance of surviving, yet she made it - she now has her PH.D. in psychology.

Now what was I starting to talk about ... oh, right my first stroke. Being in the emergency waiting room was a nightmare.

(nods back to sleep)

KARLA

She was paralyzed on the right side and that's terrible for a smoker especially when she can only smoke with her right hand.

She couldn't talk anymore. Yet it was very upsetting when people kept asking her questions - it was very frustrating. Elisabeth and her friend had to drive all the way over the mountain to get to the hospital. Once they got there, Elisabeth needed three things - 1) To go to the bathroom, 2) To have a cup of tea or coffee (none of that decaf stuff), and 3) To smoke a cigarette. The hospital staff kept her waiting for three hours before they allowed her to go to the bathroom. She wanted to go home. It took them 5 hours to admit her at this very well known university hospital; they had to sort through her insurance.

Elisabeth is not a detail person. They finally verified that she was really well insured and that they didn't have to worry about her paying her bill since she was on the medical faculty of the university.

ELISABETH

There was a big icky doctor, that I didn't like at all. He was a big "schnook." In a very loud voice, so everyone could hear he said "Dr. Elisabeth Kubler-Ross," (I hate that when people do that) "you naturally will stop smoking" and I was able to say no. He told me he wouldn't admit me unless I promised to stop smoking. I sat there in the emergency room hoping for a decent doctor and then this nice young doctor came in explaining that they had a problem because the Dean's wife wanted a smoking room and there was only a double room available. It was no problem. The Dean's wife and I became roommates. She was a delightful woman and we became good friends. Every time I heard that arrogant "schnook" coming, I'd give her a signal and we would sit-up in bed and start smoking. I never enjoyed smoking as much as I did during those three days in the hospital.

The hospital care was depressing. The nurse was a total sourpuss. She kept sticking a flashlight in my eyes every hour around the clock to check on me - it was so obnoxious.

At least if she had to wake me up at least a little music would be nice. I asked her if she could bring in a Swiss music box. She said "I can't do that." I asked if she could whistle? She said "NO." Now I believe that it is very important to have your patients tell you their favorite music and whenever possible to play it for them. Just for your information Hank Williams, Sr. is my favorite singer. Is anyone old enough to remember him? Needless to say, there was no Hank Williams songs being played or whistled in the hospital. I could only stand staying in there for three days and then I knew I would never get well in that place and I had to return to my farm where I could eat all my fresh vegetables and sit on my porch and enjoy my animals and mountain. I climbed my mountain everyday, first on all fours then on twos and then I was finally able to really make it and then I got well.

(She falls asleep)

KARLA

After her farm was burnt down and after moving to Arizonia, Elisabeth suffered a massive stroke on Mother's Day. She was in severe physical pain and experiencing a state of deep depression. She simply wanted to die.

All her books and videos had been lost in the fire; including the Hank Williams Sr., video I bought her for her birthday the year before.

I thought buying her ET might cheer her up - yet buying it prior to its rerelease was not easy. Yet when I explained the situation to the woman at Amblin Entertainment she was very helpful even though I never mentioned Elisabeth's last name. You see her house had burnt down when she was a child and she could identify with Elisabeth.

(Walks over to Elisabeth carrying an ET video)

ELISABETH
(Wakes up)

Oh good - my favorite, ET. There are times when I simply want to drift away like a purple balloon. When I die - I want hundreds and hundreds of balloons at my funeral - and we've already gotten Steven Spielberg's okay allowing a picture of ET to be on each balloon. Do you know who ET is? I can't wait to go home. It's a wonderful movie. It's my favorite - I already told you that didn't I? Everyone should watch it at least once, ET is a nice extra-ter-restrial. I had a dream that there where hundreds of ET centers - we weren't invaded - I was simply dreaming of Elder/Toddler Centers. It would be a place where older people could marinate young children in love and the children could play connect the dots with age spots. Children love old people - the more wrinkles the better. We need more love and understanding in the world. I've already picked out my coffin.

KARLA

Have you picked a date?

ELISABETH

Soon.
(Pulls out a caterpillar/butterfly doll)

You think we're pretty now, but we're really pretty ugly. The time will come when we leave our physical body ...

(Turns cocoon inside out and it becomes a butterfly) and the real us will be a butterfly. I've come to the point where I'm ready to spread my wings and fly like a butterfly. It's been almost thirty years since I wrote ON DEATH & DYING.

Grief work is being done all over the world and hospices have popped up in the U.S. like fast food restaurants. I wrote that there were five stages of dying: denial, anger, bargaining, depression and acceptance. People have taken the concept of the five stages too literally, so now I don't talk stages. Life is not linear.
(Falls back asleep)

KARLA

That was almost four years ago and Elisabeth is still alive and kicking as best she can. Her house is overflowing with ET dolls and posters. She even has an ET mask which she wore during a charity race - and a friend pushed her in her wheel chair. Both she and ET are definitely characters. I remember in the early eighties going to see Steven Speilberg's movie "ET". It was a real treat for me to take the five year old daughter of a woman I worked with to the movie. Both she and I were excited about seeing the movie. While I was parking the car I noticed she was staring at me and she had a troubled look on her face. I asked her what was wrong. She informed me that her father had told her that she shouldn't trust white people and that white people hated Black people. I stopped the car leaned over and hugged her and told her I loved her. I also told her that there were people who didn't know any better and judged people based on the color of their skin but there were also smart people like her and me who knew better. We held hands while watching "ET" and we both cried when ET was able to finally go home. On the drive back to her house she was very quiet. I asked if anything was bothering her. She said she was thinking. She then made the profound statement "Elliot loved ET even though he was different." I agreed. She than proudly announced that she also loved ET and I confirmed my love for him too. We were both smiling the rest of the way home.

BLACKOUT

SCENE 3

SETTING: Guest bedroom. There are two twin beds in the room.

AT RISE: Karla and Guy are getting ready for bed.

GUY

I usually sleep in the nude but for you I am wearing my silk jammies.

KARLA

Thanks. I am sorry I only brought my torn flannel night gown. I didn't realize I'd have a roommate.

GUY

No sweat.

ELISABETH
(Off Stage)

BE QUIET!

GUY

Go to sleep and you won't hear us.

KARLA

How did you and Elisabeth meet?

GUY

Her psychic recommended I come out and meet her. I just showed up at one of her workshops and I never left. She's had me running around feeding birds and taking her shopping at Burlington Coat Factory.

KARLA

How long have you been here?

GUY

Obviously too long.

ELISABETH
(Off stage)

SHUT the door!

GUY

Then you won't be able to hear what's going on.

ELISABETH
[Turns on TV]

GUY
Don't worry you're definitely not my type especially with the torn
flannel night gown... I can hardly wait to hear you snore.

KARLA
[Laughs]

ELISABETH
[Turns off TV]
Stop fooling around!

GUY
Elisabeth told me you worked with children after 9/11

KARLA
A friend of mine was the principal at one of the elementary schools
in DC and I went to help because one of their teachers and several of
their students were on the airplane that flew into the Pentagon. I was
on the floor working with the four and five year olds drawing pictures.

GUY
Elisabeth would have been right there on the floor with you.

KARLA
[Smiles]
The kids were adorable and really loving.

[Lighing begins to change, designating another space
and time. Spotlight on GUY as Danny, a little boy &
KARLA, as a little girl, Kisha, sitting on the floor]

DANNY
[Holds up a picture made with crayons]
I made a picture of a potato blowing up. When the potato blew up it was all messy.

KISHA
Did it blow up in the plane?

DANNY
No - my mom left it in the microwave and it went KABOOM

KISHA
WOW!

DANNY
Did you see Miss Smith crying?

KISHA
Yeah - I guess she's really sad. I think I'll draw her a picture.

DANNY
Me too. I wonder why all the teachers are wearing red hearts and ribbons.

KISHA
I know why.

DANNY
Why?

KISHA
Because ...

DANNY
Because why?

KISHA

Because one of the teachers and the little boy were in the plane that crashed and they're not coming back.

DANNY

Where did they go?

KISHA

My mom said they went to heaven.
                [Holds up a picture with hearts]
This is for Miss Smith. I hope it makes her happy.

DANNY

Where's heaven?

KISHA
                [Points up to the sky]
Up there.

DANNY

Can you get there flying a plane?

KISHA

I'm not going on any plane.

DANNY

If I were on that plane - I'd kick those bad guys and I'd tell their mommies; that they were being mean and they'd get a time out and then everything would be okay.

KISHA

You're just being silly.

DANNY

[Holds up a picture of a plane - flying towards the
sun along with balloons. And an American flag]
I bet the little boy's brothers and sisters would like to play with
him in heaven.

KISHA

I bet it's fun in heaven.

DANNY

How do you know?

KISHA

They talk about it a lot in church.

DANNY

Yeah. My Grandma's in the choir.

KISHA

I like singing.

DANNY

Me too.

KISHA

I like to sing when I am scared
[starts humming *Twinkle Twinkle Little Star*].

DANNY

You scared?

KISHA

Sometimes - but then my Mom and Daddy hug me and I feel better.

DANNY

That's good. I wonder if the little boy's brothers and sisters need a hug.

KISHA

I wonder if Miss Smith needs a hug.

DANNY

We could hug.

KISHA

Yeah but not now I'm drawing. I need the blue crayon please.

DANNY

Sure

[Hands her the crayon]

What are you drawing?

KISHA

Something special.

DANNY

Well so am I. I am drawing a TV.

KISHA

But the planes keep crashing over and over again.

DANNY

I don't like news.

KISHA

Me neither. So what you drawing?

DANNY

Superman, Big Bird and Pokemon fixing the building.

KISHA

[Looks over to the picture]

That's good.

DANNY

Let me see yours.

KISHA

I'm not finished yet ... could you please hand me the yellow crayon?

DANNY

Sure. When will you be finished?

KISHA

Soon.

DANNY

You always say that.

KISHA

Yeah - because I will
                [BEAT - Holds up her picture of a butterfly on
                one side and a heart on the other with the message
                by the heart "Rodney we miss you"]

DANNY

I wonder if butterflies can fly to heaven

KISHA

I hope so.

DANNY

Me too.

[Begins to draw again]
I'm drawing another TV.

KISHA

Why?

DANNY

I miss my cartoons.

KISHA

Me too.

[They hug]

[Lights begin to change scene to the present]

KARLA

Every child wants to feel safe.

GUY

As well as happy and healthy.

KARLA

Happy and healthy are good.

ELISABETH
(Off stage)

Be quiet. I am trying to sleep.

KARLA

I think we'd better go to bed.

GUY

Sure. I won't be here when you wake up tomorrow morning.

KARLA

Where are you going?

GUY

As far as my jalopy will take me.

KARLA

But she needs you.

GUY

She'll survive and find another punching bag aka secretary.

KARLA

Don't look at me.

GUY

It was nice meeting you. Keep a stiff upper lip.

KARLA

Thanks Good luck and Take care.

GUY

Back at you.

(BLACKOUT)

SCENE 4

> SETTING: Main living space, kitchen, Elisabeth's sleeping area with a hospital bed.
> AT RISE: The whistle on the tea kettle sounds and Elisabeth wakes up.

ELISABETH

Where's Guy?

KARLA

He left.

ELISABETH

Good riddance.
(Picks-up her "special" cup)
I only drink caffeine tea, none of this herbal nonsense.
(Looks at cup - decorated with butterflies with the
inscription: "Lord Help Me Hang In there; It's Worth It").
This is the only cup left from the farm ...
(Reads inscription)
Lord help me hang in there; it's worth it.
Just because I've had several strokes and I'm partially paralyzed
doesn't mean my taste buds are paralyzed. I'd like one decent last
supper before I die. I used to love canning fruits and vegetables.
Though obnoxious vegetarians drive me crazy.
Being a normal vegetarian is fine, but no butter, no milk, no eggs.
These crazy macrobiotic diets, feh! All these health nuts I'm sur-
prised they allow themselves to breath.
I was told I should become a vegetarian - I'm trying but ...
I need you to go shopping for me.

KARLA

Sure. What would you like?

ELISABETH

Baloney, salami and knockwurst.

KARLA

That's not vegetarian.

ELISABETH

I know, I'm not stupid.

KARLA

I know you're not stupid, you're simply a carnivorous vegetarian.
(Starts to exit)

ELISABETH

Don't run over the Totem Pole in the driveway.

KARLA

Don't worry.

ELISABETH

On your way out could you put some seeds in the bird feeders.

KARLA

Sure.
(To the audience)
Elisabeth is constantly refilling the bird feeder. The road runners around her house can hardly walk they are so stuffed.

(EXITS)

ELISABETH
(to audience)
The Totem Pole and tepee in front of my house is very special. An Indian friend of mine in the west wanted me to have it when he died. It was huge and it seemed almost impossible a task to bring it east. Yet a truck driver drove through the reservation, heard about the Totem Pole, and since he had an empty load offered to drive it to my farm. Yet once he got it to the farm it seemed again impossible that they would be able to get the Totem Pole up the mountain where I live. We dug a hole but people were still skeptical. They managed to drag it up and place it in the hole. The next day it poured - the heavens opened up. If the truck had come two days later it would never had been able to get up the dirt road to the mountain. And miracle of miracles the rain wedged the Totem Pole securely into the ground. Now it's back on the west coast. Now do you understand why I believe in miracles?

(Kisses finger and points to heaven)
Every child is a miracle.
We can learn a great deal from children.
I was in North Carolina doing a workshop and I was drawn to this young couple in the front row and I wanted to go up to them and ask them why they didn't bring their child. They told me that their son, Dougy, wanted to come but he had chemotherapy that morning. I told them it was very important that the son be present, and they were very open and the father left and brought this bald beautiful wide-eyed nine year old boy back with him and he sits in the front row. The father gives him a box of crayola and a piece of paper, he thought to keep him quiet, to me it was Divine manipulation, not coincidence.

GUY ENTERS as Dougy

DOUGY
(Begins drewing this picture and brings it to Elisabeth)

ELISABETH
(Looks at his picture)
Should we tell them?

DOUGY
(Looks over at his parents)
Yeah, I think so.

ELISABETH
Everything?

DOUGY
Yeah, I think they can take it.

ELISABETH
(To audience)

I then went over to the mother and asked her what was her biggest fear? And she broke down and started to cry and said that she had been told that Dougy had only three more months to live. Looking at his picture again I said that is not possible, three years that is possible, three months is utter nonsense. She hugged me, kissed me and thanked me. I told her it was not necessary to thank me. Dougy and I became very fast friends. I explained that I lived in California and I didn't make house calls on the east coast very often but if he ever needed to get in touch with me I gave him instructions how to connect with me any time of the day or night. I went back, three months passed and I didn't hear from him and I began to worry. What if the doctors were right? What if he had died and I gave his parents false hope? I was becoming very negative and I convinced myself that there was no need to drive myself crazy; my intuition is very accurate. I told myself to forget it and the day I let go of my worries the next day I got the most beautiful letter addressed in crayon from Dougy. It was only two lines:

DOUGY

Dear Dr. Ross: What is life? What is death? And why do young children have to die? Love, Dougy.

ELISABETH

I was so touched that there was no way I would dictate a letter to a secretary. I borrowed my daughter's colored felt pens and printed him a little letter in a simple language with illustrations. If I say so myself, it was very pretty, it was like a little booklet with rainbow colors. Then I had one problem - I liked it so much I really wanted to keep it. The more excuses my head gave me to keep it the more I realized I had better get it to the post office fast. And I totally let go of it. His response was not only very positive, but needless to say, he was a very proud young man to have a special little picture book from me. He shared it not only with his parents but also with the parents of other dying children.
Then ...

DOUGY

It's my birthday and I need to send you a present because you were the only one who had faith that I would make it to another birthday. The only thing that comes to me is the message over and over again that I should send you back your letter so I can make it available to other dying children.

[EXITS]

ELISABETH

Thank you.
                (kisses finger and points it to heaven)

(To audience)
The printing of the Dougy letter has reached over 10,000 young children. I met Dougy in 1977 and he died four years later. He was a marvelous teacher.

KARLA

Working with dying children is easy in comparison to working with parents of dying children. The parents are much more difficult and in pain and denial.

ELISABETH

Many times after a lecture a lot of people come up and they want to share their problems; those who run up are not the ones who need you. But the ones who are in so much pain that they can't move are in need of help. I was giving a lecture in Switzerland and I looked in the audience and I saw this man who was a total picture of pain and agony.

GUY [ENTERS] as Swiss Father in Pain

FATHER (with a thick Swiss accent)

Elisabeth walked over to me and said, "Do you need to talk?" And I said "Here?" And then she made the mistake and said, "No, but we can go in the bushes."

ELISABETH

Do you understand that it sounded like I was propositioning this man - and the way I said it in Swiss it sounded even worse.

And he had a smile on his face and I knew then that there was hope, because where there is still humor there is still hope. However he was obviously guilt ridden

FATHER

I believe God is punishing me because I had left my wife, was living with another woman and now my only son, who is fifteen years old, is dying of a sarcoma of the leg. I am convinced that God is trying to teach me a lesson.

Elisabeth told me she did not know such a revengeful God, she only knew a God of love, total unconditional love, so she couldn't help me with such a nasty God, but that she could help me with my son. I told her that she can't help us because the doctor has told us not to tell our boy that he has cancer; he told him in our presence that it was only a virus." She told me don't worry what doctors say – that she'd handle it. She told me to bring my son to her hotel room the next morning.

I brought my son as she had requested. She asked my son to draw her a picture - with absolutely no prompting. He drew an absolutely huge tree but it was totally dead, nothing, no life in it at all, there was one leaf hanging that looked like a tear drop. Here on the left side of the trunk there was a big hole with the ugliest cockroach eating at the tree from the inside. She showed it to me, I looked at it and began to cry. Elisabeth then asked my son to draw another picture after the treatment. And do you understand she couldn't say after amputation, after chemotherapy which most people know has to do with cancer?

All she said to my son - draw me one more picture after your treatment. And my beautiful fifteen year old boy draws a gorgeous tree full of thousands and thousands of green leaves like a spring after the rain; and where the one tear drop leaf had been hanging there was now the biggest, fattest bird singing its lungs out. So she asked him, "What was the bird doing on the branch?" He looked at her and said, "Silly, he just ate that bug." Where the hole in the tree was located was the most gorgeous mending you have ever seen in your life - a patch that was sewn perfectly. My son is well today.

ELISABETH

Believe in what your soul knows.
(Pause)
Oh, I am getting tired.

(BLACKOUT)

SCENE 5

Spotlight on Karla sitting on the edge of the stage.

KARLA

Miracles do happen.
Elisabeth believes there is a reason for everything. I believe that too.
My meeting Elisabeth and working with her was no accident.

There had been a shooting outside one of the child care centers I worked with. Police and news reporters were everywhere. Thank God none of the children were hurt.

All of a sudden a firecracker went off - the kids hit the ground. When I was a kid and a firecracker went off - kids giggled. We were now living in a war zone - a drug war and our children were being victimized and robbed of their childhood. Violence on television just watching the news. I felt I needed to do something.

I decided to fast; a cleansing - a spiritual healing. Our children deserved a brighter future.

I went to Friends Meeting House to pray. While meditating a book in the library caught my eye - QUEST. I had written a musical play called THE QUEST based on the writings of George Bernard Shaw. As I walked towards the book it literally fell into my hands, QUEST: The Life of Elisabeth Kubler Ross.

Do you believe in angels or guides? Elisabeth calls them spooks. Her belief in spirit guides have raised more than a few eyebrows in the medical community. There is no question that Elisabeth has pushed the envelop and is an unsung hero.

One of her favorite song was "I'll be Loving You Always"

The fact is we all have guides, guardian angels - whatever, and they're here to help us if we only take the time to listen.

Two years after my fast I found myself sitting at a conference sponsored by Dr. Elisabeth Kubler Ross in
Headwater, Virginia.

Working with Elisabeth has definitely had its moments and windstorms.

ELISABETH
(from hospital bed)
Can you check the temperature in the pool?

KARLA
I tried, the thermometer fell to the bottom of the pool.

ELISABETH
No it didn't.

KARLA
You're in bed - the pool is in the back.

ELISABETH

Check the thermometer.

KARLA

Fine.

(To audience)

I went back to the pool. The thermometer was still at the bottom of the pool. Right then and there I decided to go skinny dipping. I dived in and retrieved the thermometer - 52 degrees. My lips began turning blue and my teeth couldn't stop chattering. I got dressed very quickly and dried my hair.

ELISABETH

Did you check the pool thermometer?

KARLA

Yes - 52 degrees.

ELISABETH

That's cold.

KARLA

Yes, I know.

(PAUSE)

There's something I need to tell you.

ELISABETH

Then tell me.

KARLA

(walks over to Elisabeth)

Mort passed away, I just wasn't sure how to tell you - you probably already knew.

ELISABETH

Just say it - your lawyer's dead. Why are people so afraid of death?!

KARLA

When my father died my uncle was afraid to tell my grandmother.

ELISABETH

Such nonsense.

KARLA

It's not nonsense
(begins to cry)
My mother is very frail and despondent; her best friend died last week, they were like sisters; she was like an aunt to me. My step-father doesn't want my mother to be told that Rhoda died.

ELISABETH

That's nonsense.

KARLA

It's reality. (Getting control of her emotions) Rhoda gave me a bowl that had a quote from Eleanor Roosevelt.

ELISABETH

She was a special lady.

KARLA

They both were special. The quote read "Women are like teabags they don't know how strong they are until they find themselves in hot water."

ELISABETH

Exactly! Your mother needs to be given the opportunity to grieve.

KARLA

My stepfather definitely disagrees.

ELISABETH

Who cares?

KARLA

ME!

ELISABETH

He's afraid of losing your mother.

KARLA

I know they love each other very much. She'd be dead if it weren't
for his love and support.

ELISABETH

Denial is not supportive. It's simple, Rhoda died – your Mom can
take it.

KARLA

You don't even know my mother.

ELISABETH

I know you. I am a doctor who knows death and grieving.

KARLA

Did you know Mort died?

ELISABETH

No.

KARLA

I really liked Mort. He had a fabulous sense of humor.
He could never understand why the play had to be a one woman
show. Do you even care?

ELISABETH

I've been around death all my life - now all I want to do is die.
Mort's the lucky one, he's home. I'm still waiting.

KARLA

We're all waiting one way or another.

ELISABETH

Within each of us there is both a Mother Theresa and Hitler.
It is up to us to decide which we will be.

KARLA

You're still angry you're alive.

ELISABETH

And you're angry that your play hasn't been produced.

KARLA

No - not angry just tired. It's very hard to sell a one woman show.

ELISABETH

Then just forget it.

KARLA

I can't. You taught me too well -
I am not about to curl up and die.
I could write a play about writing a one woman play dealing with
the producers, the agents, the actresses, the directors, Guy.

ELISABETH

Ugh that show-off.

KARLA

One actress started writing script changes on a tablecloth – And
me walking out of the restaurant with the tablecloth in my brief-
case. I am not sorry. I am not bitter. I still believe in miracles.

ELISABETH

And I believe in chocolates. Swiss chocolates.

KARLA

Good. I'll send you some for your birthday.

ELISABETH

Hopefully I won't see another birthday.

KARLA

Then the coyotes and birds can eat it.

(Goes over and starts to cuddle one of the doll babies
that was sent in the sack puts the doll down)
(Directed to the audience)
George Bernard Shaw wrote - Life is no brief candle to me but a
splendid torch I have gotten hold of for the moment and I want
to make it burn as brightly as possible before handing it over to
future generations.

GUY ENTERS walks on the stage carrying a torch and hands it
to Karla

KARLA

Thanks. The world could use this to shine a light to encourage
unconditional love.

GUY

I am back! Happy to serve.

ELISABETH

I can see
(PAUSE)
I am not blind. You're glowing from within.

[There are Celestial Lights flooding the stage]

GUY

We are ALL ONE

[Kisses his pointer finger points it to heaven then goes over
to Elisabeth and Karla they give each other ET kisses].

WOW! Together we can be the foundation of the living temple
of Divine Love. Our essence sparkles and glows and is everlasting. The shadow of darkness may rob us of material fortune but
never of our spirit or will. God's Will, which is ours as well, is
never lost it is a heavenly love that cannot be denied. It's eternal. The power of unconditional love shall overcome. The truth
shall reign. A world in which we are ALL encouraged to shine and
peace offers its light to everyone. Embrace Love! Sing praise to
God Allmighty. One God, all in all, goes by many names, loves
us all. We are all sisters and brothers regardless of race, religion,
sex, nationality, creed, culture, or whatever. We are all simply vessels for Divine Spirit. Windstorms may cause cracks in the vessel,
it's temporary. Fear not, let freedom ring. Believe in the glory of
Divine Love and its healing power. We are ALL ONE

[He runs into the audience and starts handing out ribbons
that say "You are a Winner" gets help from ushers]

It's not how fast you run – it takes PERSEVERANCE Just be
willing to run and show compassion. We are "WON!" All is well;
therefore we are all "winners"[Reads Ribbon out loud] You are a
WINNER!; and You are a WINNER! And You are a WINNER!
Keep passing it on. You are a WINNER! [starts "You are a
WINNER" chant – runs back on stage.

ELISABETH
(She struggles to walk over to Guy and hugs him].

GUY
[He begins to laugh and cry] We hugged!

ELISABETH

I am glad you are back
[Elisabeth kisses her finger and lifts it to Heaven.
Guy then helps Elisabeth walk to the telescope]

It's like when you look in the sky at night and it's pitch black and
then the first star shines then another star shines. And I believe we
are living in a time where one star after the other is going to shine.
In a very short time we will see a whole Milky Way and all of us
are a part of the shining stars.

[Elisabeth looks at the torch Karla is holding and smiles]
Karla is still holding the Torch and both Elisabeth
and Guy help hold the Torch; they then "shine")

KARLA

We're Shining!
[She smiles and gives Elisabeth and Guy an ET Kiss]

ELISABETH
(Directed to the audience)
Give the person sitting next to you an ET Kiss and Smile. We can
all shine! There needs to be more compassion in the world, the
need for people to open their hearts.... Shining a bright light – to
be a torch taking action to help children reach for the stars

Lights begin to fade

[Lighting begins to change – slowly becomes a sky
filled with stars – the Milky Way. The stage and
the entire theatre are aglow in the Milkyway]

[GUY and ELISABETH EXIT
together holding the torch]

[Spotlight on KARLA sitting center
stage on the edge of the stage]

KARLA

How do you end a play? We all want to keep playing but the time comes when we have to say goodbye even though it has been a long time coming. Sometimes it's longer than expected sometimes shorter. Since July 8th 1992 I have sent Elisabeth a Birthday present which always included chocolates.

I trust they have chocolates in heaven. On August 24th 2004 Elisabeth died. I trust they have Swiss chocolates in Heaven and if they don't she'll make sure they do.

[Off stage we can hear ELISABETH and GUY laughing]

GUY ENTERS [Spotlight]

GUY
(Down-Stage Left – holding sign "Love
Thy Neighbor - No Exceptions)
Promoting Love and light, heavenly joy [Spotlight becomes a rainbow bubble surrounding GUY] Peace reigns now and forever – all trees of the field shall clap their hands (places the sign on stage, starts clapping) There will be a time when all the hate and wars and the polarization will stop! (to audience) I love that line.

KARLA
Me too. PEACE ON EARTH!

ELISABETH
(off stage)
Can you hear me?

GUY
(Nods his head in the affirmative)

KARLA

Yes!

ELISABETH
(off stage)
Good! I am swimming in Swiss chocolate
(laughs)

ELISABETH ENTERS stage right (wearing an ethereal dress with butterfly wings) We are ALL ONE (Looks at audience, Guy and Karla) I am sending you All chocolate covered ET kisses (gives them ALL an ET finger)

(Starts singing "I'll be Loving You Always" then walks over to the cloth sack and holds the doll baby that Karla had cuddled, she continues singing)

KARLA and GUY also begin singing "I'll be Loving You Always"

ELISABETH
I'll be Loving You Always (walks over enters the rainbow bubble and hugs GUY there is a joyful embrace including the doll baby)

GUY EXITS smiling via the audience

ELISABETH
(Continues singing remains in the rainbow bubble
spotlight, she is still holding the doll walks
over to KARLA and hands her the doll)

EXITS

KARLA
(still singing, smiles – begins cuddling the doll and continues to sing "I'll be Loving You Always")

(BLACKOUT)

[Milkyway Lights are off on stage however
they ae still glowing in the audience]

THE END

Printed in the USA
CPSIA information can be obtained
at www.ICGtesting.com
LVHW051028281223
767515LV00026B/62